America,
You Sexy Bitch

America, You Sexy Bitch

A Love Letter to Freedom

Meghan McCain and
Michael Ian Black

Da Capo Press
A Member of the Perseus Books Group

Published by Da Capo Press
A member of the Perseus Books Group
www.dacapopress.com

Library of Congress Cataloging-in-Publication Data is available for this book.

ISBN 978-0-306-82100-4 (hardcover)
ISBN 978-0-306-82108-0 (eBook)

Da Capo Press books are available at special discounts for bulk purchases in the U.S. by corporations, institutions, and other organizations. For more information, please contact the Special Markets Department at the Perseus Books Group, 2300 Chestnut Street, Suite 200, Philadelphia, PA 19103, or call (800) 810-4145, ext. 5000, or e-mail special.markets@perseusbooks.com.

Editorial production by *Marra*thon Production Services. www.marrathon.net

BOOK DESIGN BY JANE RAESE
Set in 12-point Apollo

First Da Capo Press edition 2012

10 9 8 7 6 5 4 3 2 1

For my beautiful family,
thank you for your never-ending love and support.
——MEGHAN

For my dad,
Robert Michael Schwartz
——MICHAEL

Contents

Buy the Ticket,
Take the Ride

Michael: This is stupid. I'm in an airplane flying across the country to go spend a month driving *back* across the country in an RV with Meghan McCain, a woman I barely know, with the vague purpose of "talking to people." About what? Politics, their lives, how they want the government to function, all of it with the idea that we will somehow gather enough material to write a book together and save the country. I mean, that is just pure stupid.

The thing is, I don't *like* talking to people. I barely talk to my wife and two kids. Why am I leaving them for a month to do this? I was perfectly happy to complain about America from my home in Connecticut. That's what I'd been doing, and it seemed to be working fine. Why did I agree to take my bitching and moaning on the road with this bubbly twenty-seven-year-old blond-haired, rich Republican chick I've only met twice? How did this even happen?

The answer: Twitter and Ambien.

During Obama's first presidential campaign, I got invited to appear on MSNBC to make jokes. You've seen these segments on cable news where a comedian comes on and makes a few lame jokes about whatever's in the headlines that day, and the host pretends to laugh while viewers think to themselves, *That guy's not funny*. My job that evening was to be the guy who wasn't funny.

I don't remember the context, but Meghan McCain's name somehow came up during the broadcast. She'd done or said something that flew in the face of Republican orthodoxy, as she often does, and I said to Lawrence O'Donnell that Meghan was my favorite Republican.

A couple of years later, I was doing a talk show pilot for E! and I needed a guest. Meghan agreed to do the show via satellite as a favor to her agent, whose good friend is *my* agent. Meghan was vivacious, charming, and she sported a new "less Republican" haircut; afterwards my extremely liberal friend Joe asked if it would be all right with me if he married her. I gave my blessing. I figured Republicans are into arranged marriages, so it would probably be fine.

Meghan: The entire project, from idea to execution, happened in only a little over a month. Michael and I sold the book before we actually met in person. I know it may seem a little impulsive and extreme to agree to write a book with essentially a perfect stranger, but I have a tendency to be impulsive and make extreme decisions. I also believe in seizing the day and making the most of every single opportunity that ever crosses my path. One of the mantras I live by is Hunter S. Thompson's "Buy the ticket, take the ride." I am a Hunter S. Thompson groupie, and if this particular scenario didn't encompass seizing the day, then I don't know what does. Besides, it sounded like a lot of fun, and I love combining anything that includes politics and having fun.

Michael: Right after E! decided they didn't need my talk show hosting services, I was up late one night nursing the onset of an existential crisis. Swirling in my brain were the facts that I would be turning forty in a few months, I didn't have a steady income, I didn't know what I was doing with my life, and I had a family to support, with no immediate prospects for employment. When I am feeling like this, I have one friend I turn to for support: Ambien.

The purpose of Ambien is to ease restless souls like mine into a deep and dreamless sleep. But Ambien is also great fun if you just want to get on the Internet and mess around for a few hours, which was my main intention. This is, of course, a mistake, the electronic equivalent of drinking and driving. Ambien relaxes the mind in such a way that you may find yourself saying or doing surprising things under its influence. For me, this normally involves writing nonsensical postings on my Twitter account while eating junk food. As a soon-to-be-forty married father of two, this is what passes for a "crazy night."

Half an hour after taking the Ambien, I am elbow deep into a bag of Tostitos and cruising my Twitter account (1.7 million followers. Not bragging. Just saying. Okay, bragging. Follow me: @michaelianblack) when I notice that Meghan McCain has just posted something. I respond to her. She responds to me. Then the Ambien seizes my fingers and types the following: "We should write a book together."

After a few moments, she writes back: "Sure!"

The exclamation mark makes me think she isn't serious because exclamation marks are rarely the sign of a serious thought. I write back: "I'm serious."

Around dawn, I wake up on the couch, covered in Tostitos crumbs, and stumble upstairs to join my wife, Martha, in bed. Something is troubling me, though, something I had perhaps done under the influence of a powerful sleeping agent. Just before falling back to sleep, I realize what it is: I think I have just proposed writing a book with a woman—a *Republican* woman—I have never actually met, based on the dubious facts that I once said something nice about her on TV, she seems cool, and my friend Joe liked her new haircut. The woman in question is also the daughter of the other guy in the last presidential election. Moreover, I'm pretty sure she said, "Sure!"

Shit.

Meghan: When Michael first popped the question on Twitter, I thought that this project could be a significant endeavor—to try and showcase two entirely different perspectives and backgrounds in a civil and funny manner, while attempting to tackle the bigger-picture problems and issues currently facing this country. All of it was right up my alley and it was an easy decision to make. Attempting to fuse two different perspectives and worlds is pretty much what I spend my life attempting to do, so that's why I said yes so quickly.

I loved the notion of teaming up with someone I barely knew and probably would not have gotten a chance to work with or really know in any significant way if we had not elected to embark on this project. We wanted to use ourselves as guinea pigs in order to look at what is going on in America—politically and culturally. Our country is going through unbelievably difficult and tenuous times, and it sometimes feels like we are becoming more polarized and angry at each other than ever before. There had to be a way to make a connection between divergent points of view, and to then take that unity out on the road as a way to hear Americans through fresh ears.

More than anything, I was enticed by the spontaneity of this plan. Ever since the election, I have had a jones to be back out on the road, so the chance to "go where no one has gone before" while using our fledgling relationship as an experiment in bipartisan mixology was a golden and bizarre opportunity to try something new and unique. I needed no convincing. It really was as simple as, "Sure!"

Michael: So here I am, about a month later, crammed into a coach seat somewhere above the checkerboard squares of the American heartland. From up here, the country looks vast and peaceful. I cannot see any foreclosure notices, no methamphetamine labs. There aren't any televisions on this plane, so I can't watch Left screaming at Right on cable news. No Internet. No Drudge, no *HuffPo*. Just a plane full of passengers heading to the same destination. It's a decent, albeit shallow, metaphor for the way I'd like my country to be. The people on this plane probably have no more in common than anybody else. Or, I guess the more optimistic way to say it is that they have just as much in common as people everywhere: We're probably all American, or at least mostly American. We probably all love our families. We are probably all glad we're not still at LaGuardia, one of our nation's worst airports. Beyond that, I know that we share at least one important goal: first and foremost, we'd like the plane not to crash.

All this common ground below us. It's hard to get a sense of America's size from the air. It's only on the ground, driving across, that you really get a feel for the enormity of our country. It's a big place. BIG. The first time I became aware of this fact was when I was nineteen years old and traveling the country as a Teenage Mutant Ninja Turtle.

In fact, my love of country came as a direct result of that first road trip. Until then, I hadn't really thought much about America one way or another. I hadn't done much traveling, except for a few lousy family vacations to Colonial Williamsburg and the Plymouth Rock, both super-boring. Once we went to Gettysburg when I was eleven. All I saw was a field.

I'd grown up in New Jersey, a state that has earned all the jokes ever made about it. I didn't bond with my hometown, didn't do a tour in the Boy Scouts, didn't put my hand over my heart when we sang "The Star Spangled Banner" at Little League games. This was in the eighties, when Americans were still recovering from the psychic shock of the Vietnam War, and patriotism was often seen as a suspect emotion, something Richard Nixon wanted everybody to feel, mostly so they didn't start asking too many questions about Richard Nixon.

Sure, I recited the Pledge of Allegiance, but I did it in that same droning monotone that children all over the country do, not even understanding the words, except for "under God," which I hated saying even at a young age. I used to just clamp my mouth during that part and thought I was a pretty bitching rebel for doing so.

As a whole, the nation seemed like a big and puzzling abstraction, not much more than something we could all cheer for every four years when McDonald's celebrated the Olympics with scratch-off game tickets. America was fine, sure, but a free small fries was even better.

Meghan: As much as I consider myself a Republican and feel in almost every way intellectually and culturally tied to both the Republican Party as an organization and its many shadings of conservative theory, on paper I am in many ways "culturally liberal." I was born into a wealthy, famous family. I went to an Ivy League school and majored in art history, which means I know a lot about pretentious artists and art critics. I'm a writer and television commentator employed by "the liberal network" MSNBC. I am a huge supporter of and fighter for gay marriage and LGBT rights. I'm unmarried and not completely convinced that the idea of marriage isn't outdated. I am almost twenty-eight and I do not have children, and I think abstinence-only education is delusional and dangerous. I live in the heart of the West Village in New York City. I consider myself a God-fearing Christian, but I'm also a big believer in karma and sometimes get a feeling like I may have had past lives. All of that being said, Jesus and I came to an understanding of each other a long time ago and my relationship with him is one of acceptance. My God isn't Rick Santorum's God, and my God loves everyone for exactly who they are. My God does not make mistakes. This list can go on and on . . . which is why I have always hated labels and stereotypes about people, especially when it comes to Americans and what exactly it means to be a "real American" or come from "real America." Because if I were to adhere to all the stereotypical terms that make someone a "real American," I might find that, in many ways, I am falling desperately short.

Michael: My feelings of detachment from America changed when I dropped out of school to become Raphael, the silent and brooding Teenage Mutant Ninja Turtle. In the early nineties, the Ninja Turtles were the shit. Kids loved them, there were a couple movies out, and some enterprising capitalists thought the time was ripe for a touring stage show, kind of like *Turtles on Ice* without the ice.

For four months, I crisscrossed the country with my friend Ben in a smelly dark-blue Chevy Astro minivan crowded with luggage and two large coffin cases containing Ninja Turtle costumes. And it was then—on the road, staying at cheap motels, attempting (and failing) to seduce MILFs, and eating more Pizza Hut than a human body should—that I fell in love with America.

Some highlights from that trip: I remember standing on the lip of the Grand Canyon and thinking about how the word "grand" didn't do it justice: A better word would be "fabulous." The Fabulous Canyon! I remember being on the Mexican border, dressed as Raphael, standing on top of an ice cream shop performing in front of thousands of kids on the ground below; walking the parade route at the Macy's Thanksgiving Day parade, tears streaming down my eyes, because the entire weight of the head was resting on the bridge of my nose. I remember standing on top of our van in the middle of the woods somewhere with our hands over our hearts singing "The Star Spangled Banner" and meaning it. But mostly I remember all the people we met: all the good-hearted Americans across the country. Everywhere we stopped, the people were kind and gracious and welcoming. On that trip, pretending to be a turtle granted superpowers due to radioactive sewage, I discovered what it means to love my country.

Meghan: I have had a love affair with the Republican Party and its doctrines that began the first day I stepped foot on my father's presidential campaign. The majority of my twenties, and I expect the rest of my life, will be spent fighting for the soul of the Republican Party to be more accepting and big-tent oriented. I believe my life's purpose is to change things within the Republican Party, so that at some point it is not considered so controversial to live the kind of life I live and believe in smaller government at the same time. I have been handed a front-row seat to Republican politics, and as I have grown into the person that I am today, I have always felt a great responsibility to pass on my knowledge about politics, share my experiences, and try to bring a fresh perspective on a political party that, unfortunately, has not always been so warm and welcoming to new ideas. Republican politics is my entire life, and I love it. It is the blood that pumps through my veins. My mother was pregnant with me at the 1984 Reagan convention. Politics is quite literally the only world I have ever known and the only world I ever want to know. It is what gets me up in the morning and motivates what I do every single day. I continue to be exhilarated by the process and find joy attempting to help inspire a new way of thinking within Republican Party politics.

I love America on a visceral level that is complicated to explain. I have a great passion for America and what it means to be an American. I love every single thing about being an American, the good and the bad, and I would fight until my last breath to defend all the ideals this country stands for. I even love everything about our crazy political process and the people it produces. And yet, one of the more exhausting parts of my political ideology is that because I have never completely toed the Republican party line, many hardcore conservatives accuse me of not being a *real* Republican and have referred to me as a RINO: Republican In Name Only. Somehow this name is given to anyone who thinks gay people should have the right to marry, or diverge on social issues from the extreme right wing of the party. In the subtle subtext of conservative talk radio and right-wing extremists, apparently this makes me less of a "real" American and not "pure enough" to be considered a legitimate member of the Republican Party. As a direct result of my personal experiences with this kind of name calling, I have never been a big fan of labeling people so linearly. Yes, Michael is an East Coast liberal-pacifist-socialist-elitist snob-comedian who has never shot a gun, wants to give away health care, open up the borders, and *loves* Obama—but that doesn't make him any less of an American than I am. Or at least that's what I'm hoping I find out during our trip.

Michael: When Republicans make fun of liberal "elitism," they are absolutely right to do so. Liberals really *do* think they know better than everybody else. But the reverse is true, too, which is to say, Republicans have developed a kind of winking anti-intellectualism. You know, it's that whole "good ol' boy, just me, my dog, and my truck" that scoffs at fancy book learnin', and relies instead upon the common-sense homilies of country music singers and Joe the Plumber. It's just as phony and contrived as Democratic arugula-munching snobbery.

Both political parties are as guilty of perpetuating the stereotypes about themselves as the other guys. But those stereotypes can't be the whole story, can they? The people we see shouting at each other on television aren't representative of normal Americans, are they? Are people in real life as mad as the people on TV?

If cable news is to be believed, then our entire country is engaged in a national pissing contest. It's just one dopey pundit trying to out-pee the next one. Is that really who we are? I hope not. That being said, I'm pretty sure I can pee farther than Meghan. Before the turtle trip, I didn't really pay too much attention to politics.

I was only nineteen and had not yet voted in a presidential election. I thought of myself as a Democrat because that's the way I was brought up. People are generally born into their political persuasions, just like their religions. Similar to my Judaism, however, my Democratic leanings were always on the agnostic side. I thought I believed in Democratic principles but wasn't certain. Honestly, I wasn't even really sure what they were.

Twenty years later, and after much contemplation, I still don't have much of an idea. Yet I identify with the Democratic Party. Why? Because I'm pretty sure I understand what the Republicans stand for, and I'm not down with them.

To quote the patron saint of the modern Republican Party, Ronald Reagan: "Government is not the solution to our problems. Government *is* the problem." To wit: government should stay out of people's lives except when a woman accidentally gets pregnant. Or when banks or oil companies need money. Republicans believe in free speech unless the language being spoken is Spanish. Also, I think they want to give guns to fetuses. If my understanding of the Republican Party is incomplete, then so be it. But that's exactly why I'm doing this road trip; my job, as I see it, is to confirm all the worst stereotypes about Republicans I hold so dear.

Meghan: The Republican Party has a long history of being for the "little guy"; it's just in the fast pace of the modern news cycle, hungry for red meat, that the message has been twisted and exaggerated to the point where the most extreme voices get the most attention. A lot of negative repercussions have occurred as a result of the twenty-four-hour news cycle. I think the biggest problem is that for anyone to get any real attention it feels like the message has to be an extreme one. The choice has come down to Glenn Beck or Keith Olbermann. If in any way you are seen as compromising on either side, automatically the echo chamber considers you a turncoat and not "pure" enough of a liberal or a conservative. The news cycle makes people afraid to compromise, lest they be crucified for finding a middle ground. It's a really scary and dangerous political climate that the media and politicians have produced for the American public, and more often than not I myself have been caught in the crosshairs. Unfortunately, if you want to get any message across, it must be done in talking points and sound bites.

That being said, the American public seems to have an insatiable appetite for extreme talking heads. Part of the problem, in my opinion, is that Republicans feel belittled and stereotyped by many members of the "liberal media elite." As a result, it makes Republicans automatically overly defensive and extreme in their reactions to criticism from liberals. I mean, at times I have felt belittled and stereotyped in the media and I'm clearly not the most extreme conservative in the news cycle. Anyone who does not think that the majority of the media is in the bag with Obama and the Democratic Party has no experience dealing with the media. As a result, you get more radical conservative opinions that serve as a pushback, with the pendulum of opinions swinging severely from one side to another. Listen, I am part of that news cycle and a member of the media; I am an employee of a news network. I am not saying there are not good people who are trying to change things in the media but, for whatever reason, they never seem to get as much attention as the more radical voices. It's this horrific, vicious cycle that just seems to be getting more and more polarized with each passing year.

What scares me more than anything is the idea that the world of politics will stop evolving. What if there really can't be such a thing as a more socially moderate Republican? I believe that if this party doesn't evolve it will die, and I don't want to watch it die, because Democrats are damaging this country and we should stop letting them. We have to start showcasing different kinds of opinions within the larger Republican tent. There cannot be just extreme voices being heard because all it does is make a lot of people tuned out and turned off from the world of politics. I believe all Americans need to start taking more responsibility for the kind of extreme rhetoric that is permeating our political culture; otherwise, quite frankly, as a country we're screwed.

Michael: Democrats are *supposed* to be the party of the little guy. They're supposed to be interested in workers' rights, minorities, helping those with less achieve more. Pro-union, pro-choice, anti–machine gun. But over the last thirty years or so, it has started to feel more like the party of small, special interests. It feels old and faded and kind of crusty, like a pair of Walter Mondale's boxers. All the great causes feel played out. There just doesn't seem like anything for us Democrats to rally around. Honestly, who's going to burn their bra over the Glass-Steagall Act?

As much as I want to be a committed Democrat, I can't quite justify it to myself. I don't know what I'm fighting for except opposing what Republicans are fighting for, which more or less boils down to Jesus and putting more money in the pockets of rich white guys.

Yes, I understand these are all stereotypes, but stereotypes are fun because they allow me to feel intellectually superior. Liberals love nothing more than to feel intellectually superior. It's what we do best. We sit around and say pretentious things while listening to pretentious bands like Radiohead and feeling smug about everything. It's a great way to be, if only because we get to eat so much imported cheese. Liberals love imported cheese. In fact, it's pretty much all we eat. Well, that and quinoa, which is a grain whose main appeal is that it's difficult to pronounce, thus making us feel even *more* intellectually superior when we get the name right. We read books we hate and watch artsy movies we loathe. We get off on it. A typical dinner table lib conversation:

"Have you read the latest Franzen?"

"I *looooved* it."

"I thought it was pedantic."

"Well of *course* it was pedantic. *That's* what I loved about it."

Meghan: Republican stereotypes sometimes hit the nail square on. We love to read, as long as it is either the Bible or a nonfiction account of a prominent party favorite, especially if it is a book about President Reagan (*especially* if it's about President and Mrs. Reagan). Over a dinner of perfectly grilled steak from a cow we knew by name and shot ourselves, and a potato that has been baked in the skin that God gave it, we love to dissect the latest entry to the Republican canon:

"Have you read Bill O'Reilly's recent book on Lincoln?"

"I loved it. Read it in three days. Hands down the best book ever written about President Lincoln."

"Bill O'Reilly is a man who truly loves America."

"O'Reilly loves Lincoln because he is a true God-fearing American in a world gone to hell."

How's that for stereotypes about Republicans?

The sound of tireless voices
is the price we pay for the
right to hear the music
of our own opinions.

—ADLAI STEVENSON

Prelude:
San Diego, California

A Hot Mess

Michael: My own view heading into this trip is that America is at a particularly crappy time in its history. We feel like a nation adrift. To use the worst kind of corporate lingo, it seems like we have lost sight of our "mission statement." What is it we do now? Who are we? What is our purpose? The answers feel foggy these days. Something about freedom, I guess, and democracy, whatever that is, and helping people, I suppose, unless it's too expensive, in which case we all have to tighten our belts a little, unless we're rich, in which case we actually need to pay less taxes, and something about the huddled masses, except for *Mexicans*. Underneath it all there's this thing called the American Dream, and I'm not sure I know what that is either.

Growing up, I guess I believed the American Dream had something to do with having the opportunity to be anything you wanted to be, to get ahead in this country despite the circumstances of your birth, to be rewarded for your brains and skill, not your parentage. The American Dream felt tangible and achievable. It felt fair. In fact, I am a product of that dream. My own upbringing was humble. I attended public schools, got decent grades, went to a good college, and began pursuing my life as a comedian. What a ridiculous, useless career, and yet this country allowed me to follow a vision I had for myself without encumbrance. That's pretty amazing. Of the 196 countries in the world today, how many of them allow their citizens to devote their lives to telling fart jokes on basic cable television? Probably not that many. But America does. And for that I (and my fart jokes) am grateful.

But does that American Dream still exist? Will my kids have the same broad opportunities I had? I like to think they will. I like to believe that America is still a place where dreams, even stupid ones, are achievable, not just for the lucky few, but for anybody willing to put in the necessary hard work and take a chance. The problem is, I'm not sure I believe it. And I have a sense a lot of people out there don't believe it either. So that's also part of my journey with Meghan.

Meghan and I are meeting in San Diego, California, where my mom and her lesbian partner, Sandy, are staying for the month. Sandy is *not* my mother's wife, at least in the legal sense, because although they have been together almost twenty years, they cannot legally marry in Florida, the state in which they reside most of the year. I probably don't need to point out that twenty years is a lot longer than many straight marriages last.

Sandy has seen my mother through some terrible health issues. Nursed her through cancer, radiation, and dozens of operations. She's been there for my mom in a way that my brother and I have not. Except for some financial aid from my brother and me, Sandy has been my mother's sole support for all these years, the person who has given her everything she's needed to survive. Sandy is, in every sense of the word except the government-sanctioned one, my mother's spouse, and that the government has the ability to deny their relationship is beyond wrong. It's immoral. Marriage is not about which partner has which genitalia, it's about upholding all those vows politicians are so fond of breaking. Why would Republicans, the party of individual liberty, have a problem with two people marrying who are committed to each other? Why would anybody?

Meghan is driving down from Los Angeles to meet me at Mom and Sandy's rental, and I am a little nervous. It's weird bringing a new woman to meet your mother when you are already married. Especially when you are going to be travelling in an RV with said woman for a month. It's also weird trying to explain it to your wife.

Martha was surprisingly cool about the idea right from the get-go. It didn't really occur to me to think that she wouldn't be, but if the situation were reversed, and she were hitting the road with some cute, younger guy for a month, I might not have been so accommodating.

Part of me wonders whether I should be insulted that Martha is so relaxed about all this. I mean, why isn't she worried that something might happen between Meghan and me? Yes, I'm getting a little pudgy, yes, my hair is thinning, yes, I have bad feet. But any single woman in her twenties would be lucky to have me. Why? Because I have panache. And Crocs.

The Crocs were a last-minute purchase made right before I left. My kids, ten and eight years old, are into Crocs and they wanted me to get a pair too. And because I am the world's best father, I agreed, selecting a green-and-black pair. If you are unfamiliar with Crocs, they are rubbery sandals that all self-respecting adults tend to avoid because they look stupid. But I figured they would be a good footwear choice for the trip since they are comfortable, durable, and do not require socks. Socks are a traveler's bane because they create lots of dirty laundry. Any footwear that saves on the number of socks I have to pack is good footwear. Plus, they look cute on me. So cute, in fact, that I think Meghan will probably have an even harder time keeping her hands off me when she sees me in them.

Which means Martha should be doubly concerned about me going on this road trip. I introduced her to Meghan a week or so before we left. Meghan was in New York for meetings, so we arranged a lunch—just the three of us—at a café on the West Side. The lunch was the least amount of awkward that such a lunch can be.

"So, honey, this is the woman I'm going to be living with for a month."

"Whatever."

Why does she trust me so much? Men should not be trusted in these situations! Does she think I am somehow not man enough to cheat on her during this road trip? She probably *does* think that. And she is probably right. Damn her.

Meghan arrives at Mom and Sandy's a few hours after I do. She is late, caught in traffic. Over a text message she apologizes and warns me that she is a "hot mess," which is a term she uses to describe anybody or anything that is unkempt, bedraggled, or drunk. When she finally shows up, she does kind of look like a hot mess. She's wearing an outfit I can only describe as "nouveau *Flashdance*": an off-the-shoulder gray sweatshirt, black headband, and black leggings.

The conversation is kind of stilted at first. We talk about politics a little, and my mom's sexual history a little—this is not a conversation I initiate, by the way, because that would be weird—my mom's health (poor), Sandy's grandson (a genius), the problem with Florida (everything), and all manner of topics large and small. Mom thinks judges are legislating from the bench. Sandy thinks there's too much religion in politics. I make a joke about them being elitist liberals for serving sparkling water, which goes over very well, and also a joke about how I used to get a lot of ass before I was married, which does not. Everybody is lovely to everybody else, but the whole thing is odd, neatly summarized by my mother, who says after about an hour of small talk, "So I still don't understand exactly what it is you're doing."

I don't either, Mom. I don't either.

Yet here I am, three thousand miles away from home, about to embark on a cannonball run across the United States in an effort to figure out what the hell is up with Lady Liberty. It is a noble endeavor, I think, albeit a half-baked one. What do we possibly think we can accomplish doing this other than having a helluva good time? I tell Meghan the trip will only be a success to me if one of us gets arrested.

"It'll be you," she says.

"I don't think so."

After the tension in the room has dissipated a bit, I make the choice to do something I almost never do, which is to allow myself to go barefoot. The reason I almost never do this is because I really do have bad feet. My toenails have that gross foot fungus that makes them thick like Ruffles potato chips, and the bottoms of my feet are all dry and crinkled. But I figure if we're going to be traveling together for a month, I might as well just throw caution to the wind. My Crocs are not off my feet for a minute before Meghan looks down and says, "You have the gnarliest feet I have ever seen."

Well, excuse me, Miss Perfect! If I wanted criticism about my appearance from a female, I could have stayed home with my wife. Maybe I'm making a terrible mistake here. Maybe I'm about to hit the road with somebody I can't stand. My mom is right: What *are* we doing here? Needless to say, I never allow Meghan to see my bare feet again. This whole idea is a hot mess.

Prescott and Sedona, Arizona

Tarantulas and Scorpions

Meghan: I never imagined that the first man I would officially bring home to meet my family over a Fourth of July weekend would be Michael Ian Black. My family has met my boyfriends before, in a sort of roundabout way, but I have never brought a man home to meet them and spend the weekend at our cabin in Sedona. Before we started off on this adventure, I only had a vague knowledge of who Michael Ian Black even was—in college the VH1 show *I Love the '80s* was particularly popular, and I remembered seeing him do commentary on it during the weekly group viewings in my dorm lounge area at Columbia University. Now here I am, sitting next to a virtual stranger with his tour manager friend, Stephie, in the backseat, driving along the same dusty highway to Sedona that I have driven thousands of times before.

I spent what feels like every weekend of my childhood trekking up on Friday afternoons and coming home on Sunday evenings to our cabin. I am trying to concentrate on how wonderful and tranquil our place in Sedona is, to calm my nerves instead of focusing on the fact that I am bringing complete strangers who not only my family doesn't know, but I don't know, to our cabin. After spending time with Michael and his family in San Diego, I still wasn't feeling exactly comfortable, and I think they were just as skeptical about me as I was about them. Neither Michael nor I were exactly letting loose and being ourselves yet, and on top of everything else we were having a complicated time explaining to everyone just what the hell we were doing together this summer. If I were Michael's mom, I would have given me the third degree too. I mean, what exactly was I doing with her happily married son on a road trip for the summer? By the end of that visit it was pretty apparent to everyone in the room that Michael and I really only had a #twitterelationship.

Even by my impulsive standards, starting at my family retreat, was up there with weirdness. I spent much of my formative years hiking, fishing, watching scary movies, and making forts with my siblings at our cabin in Sedona. Our cabin is tucked away in a canyon and is especially private and secluded, something I used to hate, but now relish. After the election, it was where we all hid out, recovering in the aftermath of Obamamania. If I ever decide to get married, it would be on the banks of the creek where I used to catch crawfish, the hundred-year-old willows shading the ceremony and my dad walking me down the sage-covered aisle.

I'll admit, though, it was a bit of an odd childhood spent in Sedona, with the likes of Henry Kissinger, Don Imus, and Warren Beatty passing through my memory like famous ghosts, gnawing on my father's unsurpassed grilled dry ribs on the deck. But mostly Sedona was a safe haven where, no matter the good times or bad, we could reconnect as a nuclear family and keep the prying eyes of the media world at bay.

I glance over at Michael. He's wearing two-tone Crocs and linen pants. He looks ridiculous; he should really be wearing jeans and cowboy boots, or at least just jeans. A cool chill passes over me as I imagine Michael getting out of the car and meeting my mom. Famous families in America are notoriously guarded with their privacy, political families are borderline militant with their privacy, and my family is no different. Everything about this scenario goes against the grain of how I was raised to protect the inner circle and our privacy, and at the last minute I am overcome with anxiety about the ridiculousness of this scenario. A scenario that I am completely complicit in creating.

I have never minded taking risks when it comes to my own life— at times I have even relished testing the boundaries of the things I can get away with—but I'm feeling stupid and guilty that I might be putting my family in the path of someone I barely know and have reasons not to trust; he's exactly the kind of Left-leaning comedian who loves to skewer people like us for gatherings just like this. What am I doing bringing this random guy and his road manager into the McCain lair, simply with the intention to observe and judge? What the hell have I gotten myself into? No, seriously.

Michael: Some clarification: although I have said that we're traveling the country by RV, that's not entirely true. Our first few stops will be reached by airplane, then we will pick up the RV and meet our peculiar RV driver Cousin John, in Austin, Texas. Neither Meghan nor I are well-organized enough to choreograph this dance, so we've also hired my friend Stephie to accompany us as tour manager. With our input, she's been putting together the itinerary, booking hotel rooms, contacting various people we want to meet, badgering Congressmen, and making the trip actually doable instead of the absurd Ambien-fueled fantasy it started as.

I met Stephie a couple of years ago when my friend Michael Showalter and I hired her to be our assistant on a TV show. She was just out of college then, an aspiring writer and producer. The word most people use to describe her is "adorable," because of her small size and big, moony eyes. My nickname for her is "Nermal." Regular readers of "Garfield" will recall Nermal as Garfield's nemesis, an impossibly cute kitten. That's Stephie: impossibly, annoyingly cute.

In many ways, she is Meghan's opposite. Meghan is brash and outrageous. Stephie is demure and shy. Meghan is a honky-tonkin', gun-totin', whoopin' and hollerin' cowgirl. Stephie plays videogames and eats raw spinach out of a bag. As of this point, they have only spoken by phone. When they actually meet this morning, I am worried about how they will react to each other. I'm not sure how my little Nermal will do in a cat fight.

"Hiiiii!" squeals Meghan when we find Stephie at the airport, wrapping her in a hug. I've known Stephie for three years and have never hugged her. I don't think I've ever even touched her. Because girls other than my wife scare me.

They start gabbing right away: How fun this is going to be, how excited they both are, Stephie's fiancé Chris and their wedding plans, *blah blah blah* girl stuff *blah blah blah*. They're just falling all over each other, instant BFFs. This is bullshit. Stephie's *my* friend!

I pout my way to the parking lot, where we pile into an SUV. The plan is to spend the night in Sedona, the Arizona Hamptons, that New Agey, feel-good, richy-rich Sun State oasis where the McCains have their country compound. Meghan keeps warning me that the house in Sedona is nothing fancy, but I don't believe her. "Nothing fancy" in her world is, I suspect, something pretty f-ing fancy in mine.

Arizona is gorgeous. Even when it's 108 degrees, as it is now, it's gorgeous. There's just something about the vast red desert and crumbly distant mountains that stills the mind. Everything out here is baked down to its essence, an entire world lived in a microwave oven. As we drive, I notice that it looks cloudy towards the horizon. Maybe it will rain, but I don't think so. I don't think it ever rains here. No wonder there were so many gunfights back when this was the Wild West; people must go crazy in these conditions. All this sun is just unnatural. It's beautiful, yeah, but I can't imagine living here. What are we even supposed to do while we're here other than die from dehydration?

Meghan: The only plan I am completely sure of going in, is that my brothers are going to take Michael into the middle of the desert and teach him how to shoot a gun. This is something Michael has requested, and there seems to be a lot of momentum gearing up around this piece of our trip. We'll go to our friend's house in Prescott tomorrow, but first we are going to Sedona to meet my mother and the Harpers, who are longtime family friends and neighbors. My intent is to give Michael a glimpse into my upbringing, show him a bit of Arizona, and give him a chance to meet the woman who made me who I am. In the same way that I felt it was important to meet Michael's wife, I think it is important for Michael and me to meet each other's mothers. I had a better understanding of Michael after meeting his mother, and I want him to have a better understanding of me. I also want to give my mother peace of mind regarding the strange comedian I will be traveling with for the next month. For the record, my mother is not as enthusiastic about this little road trip/social experiment as I am.

I think a lot of times people have a different idea of what my family is like for all of the obvious and clichéd reasons shoved down your throat by the media and gossip blogs. Unfortunately, the older I get and the more people I meet, I find that a lot of the stereotypes about famous people turn out to be true, especially those about famous politicians. I have always felt lucky to have parents who love and support me unconditionally, but also ones with a very low tolerance for bullshit or any indication of spoiled brat behavior. Their strictness used to make me crazy growing up but now, as I am heading into my late twenties, I couldn't be more grateful for the kind of childhood and sheltering my parents gave me. My parents somehow miraculously gave me a normal childhood and instilled morals and values in me while still letting me be my own person and make my own mistakes. I have no idea how they did it; they are incredible parents who did an incredible job, all within the ridiculous world of politics. I'm a lucky and blessed woman.

I pull the car up to our cabin in Sedona—or more accurately in a canyon in Cottonwood. It's not so much a ranch house as a collection of cabins clustered around a few ponds, on the banks of Oak Creek. I know, it's all very *Little House on the Prairie*–sounding, but I love it here. That being said, I'm worried that Michael will somehow be disappointed that it doesn't look more like a great lodge, or is more put together and architecturally well designed. The best way I can describe the cabins in Sedona is that they are super-homey, with all of the pictures, paintings, mementos, scratches, and imperfections that have collected around us as a family. It is unbelievably comfortable, cozy, and the kind of messy where no one feels like they have to dress up or worry about where they sit. As my mom says, "You can do anything to this place and not hurt it."

At this point, I don't know if Michael is a diva about hotels or some kind of pillow princess. Most important, though, I'm nervous about how he will interact with my mother. She has tweeted him saying she is glad he is going to be spending the Fourth with us. Michael's wife, Martha, later told me how freaked out he was when both my mother and my father tweeted him. Something about this made me happy. At least I wasn't the only one freaked out about this particular portion of our voyage.

As soon as I pull up to the house, my nerves calm. It's like wading into familiar waters. The wraparound porch beckons with its wide, inviting staircase. Inside it's cool, but not air-conditioned, and Mom is sitting in the living room watching the news. She clicks it off and brightly welcomes Michael and Stephie, asking if they would like a tour of the place. I exhale, proud of her ability to put every single person she meets instantly and genuinely at ease.

As messy as the cabins may seem, they are situated on a beautiful and somewhat expansive area—picturesque in all of the ways one hopes a cabin in Sedona to be. A beautiful creek, orchards, chicken coops, ponds, ducks wandering around, weeping willows, the whole bit. We stroll through the grounds while the sun sets hot pink against the mountains in the distance, and all I can think about is Michael's outfit. It might be the only time anyone has shown up in Sedona wearing linen pants who wasn't a middle-aged woman.

During dinner we settle into a friendly rhythm, for which I am grateful. My mother tells Michael about her work in the Congo, the Harpers catch me up on what their children are doing—they grew up next door and are as close as cousins. I feel happy to be here and for the first time think that this trip might actually be a good idea. Michael and Stephie fit right in and all of the tension starts to slowly fade.

Michael: Meghan wasn't lying about the McCain country home. It's modest. Simple. Homespun. It's a shithole. (I'm kidding.) What

I anticipated being a gated desert fortress is just a pleasant and well-loved series of small cabins tucked into a gorgeous valley floor. When we pull up to Camp McCain, I shake loose myself from the SUV and prepare to meet Meghan's mom.I'm pretty freaked out to meet Cindy McCain. My impression of her from the media is that she's an ice queen. Cold and remote and perhaps the proud owner of a fur coat made from 101 Dalmatians. I could not be more wrong.

From the moment we step inside, Cindy goes out of her way to make me feel welcomed and relaxed. What I (and I think much of the country) took as aloofness is actually poise and, I suspect, shyness. I never really considered before how difficult it must be for political spouses to willingly put themselves in the public eye just because their husband or wife has political aspirations. That would suck.

At dinner, I sit beside Cindy and listen to her describe her work with women in the Congo. It's work she's passionate about and committed to, spending weeks at a time touring the war-torn African country, hardly the sort of thing a spoiled senator's wife would devote herself to. Why did I have that muddle-headed impression of this lovely woman? Where did that narrative come from? And why was I so willing to believe it? This is annoying: the first new McCain I meet is already forcing me to rethink my stereotypes.

Meghan: Later that night we drive into Sedona and stop into this bar called The Olde Sedonan and watch the locals perform karaoke. I do my best not to make any jokes about the fact that Michael is dressed like Paula Deen, and Michael does his best not to talk to me about guns. He is clearly nervous about meeting my well-armed military brothers in the morning, and I have half a mind to let him sweat through his girly pants. Instead I patiently explain that other than the terrible, insane shooting of Representative Giffords, Arizona has been a place where people for the most part know how to keep safe around their guns. That we are taught from practically birth that guns are for protection, hunting, and, yes, sometimes target practice. I can tell he's not buying it, though, and decide to wait until he has one in his hand to wait for his final judgment. That always changes things. Even the most daisy-toting peace lover will get all excited by the feel of steel.

Michael: Arizona has some of the loosest gun control laws in the country, so much so that if you prefer people not bring their guns into your drinking establishment or house of worship or medical clinic, you need to post a sign requesting that people leave their firearms elsewhere.

While we sip some whiskey in Sedona, Meghan tells me about her brothers and their guns. She's got an assortment of siblings, but it's her two younger brothers and sister that I'm meeting tomorrow: Bridget is a sophomore at Arizona State University; Jack is a navy captain; Jimmy is a former marine.

"They've got a lot of guns," she says, checking my eyes for fear. Then to clarify lest I don't understand what she means, she tells me, "No. *A lot* of guns."

"Do you have a gun?" I ask.

"Yes," she says as though it's a crazy question. "But they've got *a lot* of guns."

This is one thing I am quickly learning about Republicans: they are afraid. Democrats are afraid too, I think, but it's different. Democrats are afraid for the future. Republicans are frightened for the future also, but they are equally or more terrified of the RIGHT NOW! In the Republican worldview, menace lurks around every corner. Whether it's zombies coming to eat our brains or robbers or rapists or immigrants or liberal politicians, they believe there is a nightmare army of evildoers out there whose only objective in life is to take what's theirs. That's why they are "conservatives." They want to conserve their shit from the bad guys. What's the most effective way to do that? Guns.

I explain to Meghan that growing up in New Jersey, I never fired a gun. Never even saw a gun that wasn't attached to a policeman's utility belt. Gun culture just isn't the same kind of thing on the East Coast. I'm not sure why. If anybody should be afraid, it's us. If you've ever seen *The Sopranos* you know why. The whole state is mobbed up and corrupt and filled with angry meatheads who blew out their knees playing high school football and never mentally recovered. Yes, New Jersey is also "the Garden State" and home to Princeton University, but mostly it's just kind of douchey. Honestly, we probably need some of Arizona's guns in New Jersey, because living there can be a scary experience for anybody not named The Situation.

Meghan: It's the Fourth of July, and I wake up early and walk over to the cabin Michael and Stephie are sharing. I'm nervous and anxious all over again. Michael's sitting on the living room couch, holding a mug of coffee and contemplating a bench covered in pillows adorned with my father's smiling face. They were decorations at a dinner party held in Dad's honor during the 2000 convention in Philadelphia, and are every bit as funny and slightly ridiculous as you might be picturing. The only sight funnier is Michael in his pajamas and Crocs—clearly the one time he took his Crocs off in front of me was embarrassing enough for him to now sleep in them.

Soon after, we leave for Prescott, which is about an hour away from Sedona. The plan is to stay at our friend Jackie White's horse ranch, where we will meet up with the boys, shoot some guns, and then attend the "World's Oldest Rodeo."

At this point Michael and I are still in the get-to-know-you phase of our relationship, and although we are getting along just fine so far, we haven't exactly crossed the threshold of the RV stage of our road romance, and the inorganic nature of spending time in closer quarters is beginning to once again loom large.

On the tense drive up to Prescott we stop in a small, former mining town called Jerome. It's a place mostly known for the local mining boom in the late 1800s and was proclaimed "the wickedest town in the west" in 1903 by the *New York Sun* for its scandalous reputation for prostitution and gambling. All of that wicked merriment is a thing of the past, and these days Jerome can only boast the random ghost story and the feat of residing five thousand feet above sea level. We stop to get lunch at a vegan-friendly—oh, Jerome, how far you've fallen—restaurant because it looks nice and Stephie has an extremely sensitive stomach and strict dietary needs. While we are eating, the screeching tones of "God Bless America" waft through an open window from someplace down the street. We initially try to ignore it, but soon realize that we need to investigate. I'm as patriotic as the next guy, but this song needs to be put out of its misery.

Michael: After eating, we walk up the street towards the source of the music. About five blocks away, we spy a speaker set up in an open garage. Sitting in a lawn chair, wearing a sash and a tiara, is a girl around ten years old. She's got a card table set up. On the card table is a tangle of homemade jewelry and a pile of CDs with her picture on them. This is what's been interrupting our digestion.

"Would you like to support me going to States?" the girl asks us.

It turns out she's a beauty pageant contestant trying to pay her way to the state competition the following Friday. But here's the thing, and I am going to say this in the most delicate way I know how: her singing sucks.

She tells us the beauty contest is a "natural" competition. No makeup allowed, no skimpy clothes. "It's nothing like *Toddlers and Tiaras*," she says proudly.

A beefy middle-aged guy comes out of the building and sits behind the card table. "Tell 'em why you're doing it," he says.

"Because I want to raise money for the pageant so I can buy, uh, food for like the . . . help me get the food and it will help me, like, pay for all my expenses."

Left unexplained is how "getting food" will help her pay whatever terrible expenses she has incurred. Regardless, I suspect she will need to work on her oratory skills a little bit before States. When she finishes her version of a world peace pageant speech, I buy a CD for five dollars and wish her luck because I love this little beauty contestant with her screechy, off-key voice, plain looks, and terrible speaking skills. I want her to win States. She's got my vote just for sitting in the sun in her limp sash and playing her patriotic caterwauling at full volume through all Jerome on the Fourth of July.

Leaving her behind, we stroll farther up the road to a souvenir shop where I buy each of my kids a present.

For my son, a tarantula encased in resin; for my daughter, a scorpion encased in resin, both recommended by Meghan as treasures from her own childhood. I think the gifts will freak the kids out, which is an appealing idea. The cashier is an older, wiry guy wearing a baseball cap that reads VIETNAM VET.

"You're a Vietnam vet, huh?" I say.

"Sixty-eight," he says.

"Her father was there too," I say, nodding at Meghan.

"There were a lot of us." It's clear he doesn't want to talk about his service, so I don't push. As he's ringing me up he holds up the tarantula paperweight and says, "I've got a family down south who does these for me," he says. "They send their kids out at night with flashlights to get the tarantulas."

"Their kids?" I ask. "How old?"

"Young," he says. I get the impression he means like eight or ten years old, which is how old my kids are. I do not think of myself as a pantywaist parent, but I cannot imagine a scenario in which I send my children out into the night to catch tarantulas.

"After they turn over the critters, the mom does the resin work," he says as though this is a normal occupation. Is this the Addams Family?

"How did you find them?" I ask.

He shrugs. "They found me."

Which makes sense, I guess. If you're in the encase-tarantula-in-resin business, you probably have to do a little outreach.

Are these the real Americans we hear so much about from politicians? Natural beauty queens, Vietnam vets, kiddie tarantula catchers? What about me, parading around Jerome in my city slicker clothes? What the hell is a real American, anyway? Can a country that prides itself on individualism actually have an identifiable type to hold up as exemplar of all that is America? Is John Wayne more of a real American than John Waters?

Meghan: Once we're back in the car, Michael threatens to put Little Miss Natural Arizona's CD in the stereo, but I cut him cleanly off at the pass. It's a short drive to Jackie White's ranch from here, and I'm not going to make it any longer by listening to the cat-screech stylings of a ten-year-old, no matter how adorable Michael may find her.

Along with being good friends with my mother, Jackie is also the mother of my college boyfriend, and luckily we have been able to keep a good relationship despite the fact that her son and I have not been a couple for a long time. He is still good friends with my brothers and remains one of the few exes that I have maintained a friendship with post-breakup—and if you want to get technical, he is the one guy I had brought around my parents, but only because I originally met him when he was hanging out with my brothers around our house. Jackie is an ER nurse and horse trainer, in addition to being hands down one of the toughest women I have ever known. She can best be described as a modern-day Annie Oakley or, as Stephie coined her, "Tough-As-Nails Jackie." Michael calls her "what he imagined a pioneer woman being like." Jackie's ranch is more barren, spread out, and set deeper in the mountains than our cabin in Sedona. It is much dustier, and surrounded by cactus and a large horse corral. It is probably more of the stereotypical setting one would have of cowboys roaming in the Arizona desert.

I am both very excited and curious about how Michael will be at the shooting range. There are really no better people to supervise Michael's first foray into shooting than Jackie White and my brother Jimmy. I remember the idea of gun slinging with my brothers came up rather early, back when we were writing our tour plans and book proposal. I found Michael's enthusiasm and willingness fascinating, though maybe this is another lesson in not prejudging people. I had pretty much figured it wouldn't be something he would even want to attempt, let alone in the middle of the Arizona desert with my navy pilot and former marine brothers.

Gun culture is hard to describe or rationalize to people who have not been exposed to it in any way. One of the things I was most surprised about when I first moved to New York City was the strange and almost visceral anger a lot of East Coast people have towards both guns and the protection of Second Amendment rights. Now, I hate stereotypes, but I've learned that it is a subject to avoid broaching with anyone who is not a gun owner, or from a state where gun culture has an intricate history of being something steeped in survival and pride—not to mention connected to a person's ability to protect and provide for a family. Gun ownership is not just rednecks and hillbillies sitting on a front porch with a shotgun-draped lap; it's also the man or woman who goes out and hunts in order to put meat on the table, or the people who sleep more soundly at night knowing they have a way of keeping their family safe from intruders or predators. Sure, there are also people who own guns just for the pleasure of going to a range and taking target practice, but is that really any different than hitting a small white ball with a club at a hole hundreds of yards away? Don't tell me that you can't kill a person with a golf club. I'm looking at you, Michael Skakel.

My perspective on guns and gun culture is pretty well documented, and by far one of the most conservative things about my political dogma. I am a strong Second Amendment supporter and card-carrying NRA member. One of the things I was worried about when President Obama got elected was that he was going to undermine and possibly even repeal the rights set forth in the Second Amendment. Looking back on it, it seems reactionary that I would think that, but I was not the only one—gun sales skyrocketed after he took office. Ironically, President Obama has of yet not done a single thing to erode the rights of gun owners, and we're all quite honestly a little surprised. Not even the policies put forth in the wake of the Giffords shooting have resulted in any sort of legislation. It makes me think that there must be quite a few Democrats who love their guns too. In fact, in the midterm elections in 2010, the NRA backed fifty-eight incumbent House Democrats in the kinds of states where owning a gun is no big deal.

The one area where I sway from traditional NRA ideology is when it comes to extended high-capacity magazines, the kind that allow certain guns—specifically Glocks—to fire off more than thirty rounds at a time. It's the type of weapon that Jared Loughner used to shoot Congresswoman Giffords in the tragic Tucson attack. I do believe that there need to be stricter regulations regarding individuals who have the ability to obtain certain types of guns, especially high-capacity magazines that should really only be used by law enforcement officials. That being said, I don't think the responsibility of who guns are sold to should simply lay with gun sellers. There should be more conscious effort within communities and law enforcement, with a greater emphasis on flagging people who are risks to themselves or their communities.

I do worry on some level that if we start giving an inch with gun regulations, anti–Second Amendment rights supporters will take a mile. It just seems to be one of those issues, like abortion, on which it is difficult for both sides to find a compromise. I believe that Americans should have the right to defend themselves in any capacity but especially if, God forbid, anything ever happens to this country; people should always be allowed to be armed and able to defend themselves. After all, it is one of the main principles this country was founded on.

Michael: The NRA is a piece of shit organization. I don't mean to denigrate any individual NRA member, and I don't even object to an organization whose mission statement is being "the foremost defender of the Second Amendment." Where I have a problem, and where I think a lot of reasonable people have a problem with the NRA is with its rigidity. The idea that any gun control law is a bad law is just plain nuts.

I likewise have trouble with the notion that we need ammunition whose only purpose is to defeat a bulletproof vest, that we should be able to carry concealed weapons wherever and whenever we want, and that we should not require significant background screening on people who want to buy guns. If it isn't guns that kill people, but "people killing people," shouldn't we be a little more selective about who gets to wield a semiautomatic Glock capable of firing thirty-three rounds in under seventeen seconds? Because that's what Jared Loughner did, and if he'd had a chance to insert another magazine, many more than thirteen people would have been killed or injured that day in Tucson. It seems that we're more selective about who gets a LinkedIn invitation than we are about the people we let buy firearms. All that being said, I'm looking forward to shooting up some shit. Second Amendment, here I come.

The GPS takes us down a dirt road to Jackie's ten-acre ranch, where we'll be spending the night. The house is low and built from cinderblocks, the type of hardscrabble place you would expect in this part of the country. When we pull in, Jackie comes out to greet us, wiping her hands on her blue jeans. She's probably around fifty, lean, and tan. Jackie built this house with her own hands and dug the holes for every fence post on the property. If it comes down to it, Jackie could kick my ass.

We park and get out and say hi to everybody: Jackie, her daughter Jessica who is in the air force, and Jessica's air force roommate, Stephanie. I also meet Meghan's younger brother Jimmy and his girlfriend, Holly. Unfortunately, Jack McCain had to get back to San Diego because he is on duty, but his roommates from the US Naval Academy, Mike and Kyle, have stayed for the festivities. I'm happy to see that my buddy Cindy McCain is also here.

Meghan's brother Jimmy is twenty-three, handsome, and tattooed. He taught marksmanship in the service, and will be my gun instructor on the range. "Good to meet you," I tell him.

"Sir, good to meet you."

At first I think the "sir" is his way of subtly making fun of me for being a soft, liberal, Yankee pussy, but I soon realize it's his Marine training. He calls Stephie "ma'am," even though she is probably less than two years older than him and looks about five years younger.

Jimmy's been out of the Marines about a year now even though he loved it. When I ask him why he left, he says it's hard on your body to do what he did and he just got tired. He's in school now, at Texas A&M, and he started a nonprofit called HonorVet that helps veterans adjust to civilian life. He tells me about a fundraiser they just had.

"I had a navy guy walk up to me with a check for three hundred bucks and he's like, 'That's every cent I have but I believe in you guys so much and what you're doing.'" It's obvious how much Jimmy cares about the military, obvious how much pride he takes in what he used to do with them and what he does now. But all of it came at a cost, and it took him a long while to get his shit together. When he got out of the service he says, "Forever I just lived alone with my dog and I didn't have a couch, so I'd lay on the floor with him and watch TV and just drink all day."

He doesn't get too much into specifics about what he did in the Marines, but Mcghan tells me he served two deployments, including one in Iraq as part of the 2007 Surge. This was not a "senator's son" situation either, where he hung out at HQ playing video games. Jimmy was in the thick of things and he'll be the first to admit it cost him: as the day goes on, I notice him walking with difficulty. His back is fucked up, his stomach is fucked up, and his feet are fucked up too. Once, he fell into an open latrine pit and did not shower for four months. His feet and legs got infected and are beyond grim. Meghan tells me his feet look even grosser than mine. Cindy tells me that he will probably always be in some pain after his time in the Marines. Did I mention he's only twenty-three?

Meghan: Jackie's ranch sits on a few acres of land surrounded by stables with horses that she boards, and an area where she keeps rescued dogs. It is a classic ranch-style house: dusty and spread out, and also completely comfortable and low key. When we walk in, the television in the living room is showing *Lonesome Dove*, and scattered across the side kitchen table is what Michael describes as an "armory" of guns. The situation was not planned, but it's about as clichéd as walking into an Arizona ranch house can be. I look over at Michael and he doesn't seem weirded out or uncomfortable at all. Stephie looks like she might pass out on the floor, or at the very least run away. In fairness to her, there are a lot of people in the room sporting giant belt buckles and big Stetsons and other assorted versions of cowboy gear. It occurs to me that maybe people out East don't think of Arizona as the West, so maybe the setup is a bit over the top, even by Prescott standards.

Before they can run out the door and drive the SUV back home, the time comes to gather up all the guns for Michael and Stephie to give it a go.

First, a little background information on my brother Jimmy. He is twenty-three years old and has just recently left the Marine Corps after serving two deployments—he enlisted when he was just seventeen. Everybody loves my brother Jimmy. He is charming, smart, and a roaring good time. He is by far my favorite person to drink with on planet Earth.

I didn't know this until I told Jimmy that I was bringing Michael home for the Fourth of July, but apparently one of Jim's favorite movies of all time is *Wet Hot American Summer,* featuring one Michael Ian Black. When I told Jimmy that I was writing a book with Michael, he was almost giddy. "That guy! I love that guy!" was his official response. As soon as Michael walks in, I can tell Jimmy is excited because he is geeking out a little bit, and there's a part of me that breathes a huge sigh of relief.

When we gather up to go out to my brother's giant truck—and by "giant truck" I mean the biggest Ford truck that is available for purchase—Jimmy offers Michael one of the extra Stetson cowboy hats that are lying around. Michael puts it on his head and asks Jimmy how it looks. Jimmy keeps a straight face, answering sternly, "Sir, it's on backwards." I put my hand over my mouth and nose to keep from snorting in laughter.

Michael: The dining room table is piled with guns. Heaps of guns. I can't identify most of them because I do not know one gun from another, but there are rifles and handguns, and I recognize a big black M-16 semi-automatic assault rifle. There's even an enormous "elephant gun," whose shells are the size of small cigars. I ask what the elephant gun is used for. "Killin' elephants." Of course.

It truly is an arsenal in here. Jimmy, Mike, and Kyle have been cleaning the guns all morning in anticipation of taking us out shooting. Boxes of ammunition and holsters and mysterious firearm swabs and brushes are strewn about with the weaponry.

"Let's go shoot," says Meghan, and everybody seems fine with that.

The boys carefully pack up all the guns into hard plastic cases and a big green rucksack left over from Jimmy's Iraq deployment.

Stenciled on the flap are Jimmy's name and blood type and the words NO PREF.

"What does 'no pref' mean?" asks Stephie when we get out to the range.

"It means I don't have a preference which religion reads me my last rites," Jimmy says.

It's going to be hot out there in the sun, so Jimmy gives me a black cowboy hat to wear. I slide it on as smoothly as I can. I touch the brim and let it rest low on my head. For the first time, I start to feel a little bit cool, at least until he tells me that I have it on backwards, sir.

We drive a couple of giant pickups over bumpy dirt roads until we get to state land, where it's legal to shoot. We pull up in front of a small hill. One of the women drags an old wooden target from behind some brush while the guys unload the truck. I offer to help but they politely don't trust me to touch anything.

Jimmy hands me a holster with a big .357 in it. The gun hangs low off my linen pants. As inconspicuously as I can, I make the first move towards drawing the gun from the holster and realize I have no idea how to get it out in a crisp way. If we have a gunfight out here, I am going to die.

Tough-As-Nails Jackie gives us a stern speech about gun safety before we head to the range. She's serious. There is no screwing around with Jackie and guns. "Only one firearm is allowed to be on the range at a time. Keep your finger out of the trigger guard until you're ready to shoot. Never point your gun at anything you do not intend to kill."

Damn right. I am going to kill that target. Kill it dead.

They start me off with a .44–40 "mare's leg," which they also call the "zombie killer," because it's the gun Woody Harrelson used in the movie *Zombieland*. Republicans clearly do not understand that zombies are not real. It's a cool-looking gun, first designed for a Steve McQueen TV show called *Wanted: Dead or Alive*. Jimmy shows me how to use it: swinging the barrel up to his waist, he cocks and fires all in one smooth motion. Fifty yards away, a big black hole appears in the target. He hands the gun to me and teaches me to sight the target. I swing it up to my waist like Jimmy did, cock the hammer, and pull the trigger. A clod of dirt explodes somewhere in the distance. I have not come anywhere near the target. I try lifting the gun closer to my shoulder, using two hands to support it instead of one like Jimmy. I fire. Miss. God, I feel stupid, standing here among these professional soldiers. Five more times I shoot the zombie killer, five more times I miss the target. Finally, shame-faced, I surrender my weapon.

Meghan: In all my time around guns and people shooting them, I have never seen anyone shoot anything in the middle of the Arizona desert wearing Crocs and linen pants, with one of my brother's cowboy hats on his head and a Colt .45 in a holster around his waist. The most surprising thing about Michael's outfit is how good he looks in a cowboy hat and how weirdly comfortable he seems with a gun slung around his waist. Although I am somewhat biased and think most men look good in a cowboy hat, what can I say, Michael is pulling it off. Just avoid the Crocs.

I cannot believe Michael doesn't start shaking or crying or something. I have seen people freak out at shooting ranges before, especially first-time shooters, but Michael takes to it like a fish to water, and one after another my brother brings several guns for Michael to shoot. I lean over to my sister and say, "I can't believe he's this much of a natural," and she says, "I know, he doesn't really seem like a guy that would be."

I marvel at Michael's ease as Jimmy hands him guns, saying, "This is the gun that Woody Harrelson uses to kill zombies in *Zombieland*. We nicknamed this one the 'noisy cricket' because it's so small but so strong, like the noisy cricket in the movie *Men in Black*. This is the kind of rifle we carried around while we were on patrol in Iraq." Michael tries every firearm he is handed and seems to enjoy every single one. When he finally turns around long enough for me to see the expression on his face, he looks giddy.

I yell, "It's like the first time you got to second base, right?"

"Yeah, kind of," he yells back.

Stephie, on the other hand, does not love her turn at all, and we break soon after to give her an out. I'm thrilled that I get to hold Michael making it to second base with a Colt .45 over him the rest of his life, but equally okay with Stephie not even wanting to un-button its shirt. Stephie keeps the gun-loathing perspective in check and balances out Michael, our newest convert.

Michael: After shooting, we drive back to Jackie's for a late lunch of homemade enchiladas and beef red chili before heading out to the Prescott Rodeo, "The World's Oldest Rodeo," dating from way back to 1888. Of course, when you do a cursory check on Google to find out the date and location of the world's oldest rodeo, Prescott does not even make the list. Depending on which civic organization you choose to believe, the world's first rodeo was either in Payson, Arizona, in 1884, Pecos, Texas, in 1883, or Deer Trail, Colorado, in 1869. But I'm not going to quibble with the residents of Prescott because I am a guest in their town and because they all have guns.

While we're cleaning up after lunch, the conversation turns to health care, or specifically "Obamacare," which Jackie hates. Jackie hates Obama generally and his new health care law specifically.

Even Jackie, hard ass Jackie, is willing to concede that there are parts of the Obama health care plan she likes. The preexisting condition stuff, for example. But she worries that our health care system, "the finest in the world," will become like Mexico's. Or Canada's. Jackie doesn't seem to think the people she sees in her ER night after night—the illegals, the meth heads, the wife beaters—are going to purchase health insurance just because the government says they have to. If they don't have insurance, well that's just too damned bad. She doesn't want our entire system brought down by those people.

"But what about the coal miners in West Virginia who lost their jobs?" I ask. "What about Detroit autoworkers? What about students? What about people in the creative community? Should they be lumped in with the meth heads?"

"No," she tells me. "Everybody should be given a helping hand until they get back on their feet."

Except that these days a lot of people will never get back on their feet, I want to say. These days a lot of people are just good and forever fucked.

But I don't say it.

One of the things I've noticed among the Republicans with whom I've been hanging out is that there seems to be an underlying resentment towards some amorphous group of their fellow Americans who, they believe, are gaming the system. Jackie calls them the "pimps and gangsters in New York City." Having lived in New York City for ten years, I cannot recall too many run-ins with either pimps or gangsters committing Medicare fraud. I can, however, recall some Wall Street types raping the entire American treasury.

It's hard to argue with somebody against protecting what's theirs. The question is, are there really hordes of gangsters, pimps, meth heads, and welfare queens lying in wait to steal our stuff and shoot us dead? I didn't think so.

That said, I'm not willfully naive either. Jackie told us a story about a rancher to the south of her place who was shot to death near the border while riding his ATV.

"When they found him he was dead, the dog was dead. The ATV was still there, so they must've shot him from a good distance away. Fifteen hundred people came to that funeral."

How do you discount that experience? How do you persuade somebody that tragic things happen to everybody across all fifty states but that events like those, while horrible, are extremely rare? Or maybe they're not. Maybe I'm the naive one. But then how have I gotten through my first forty years without needing to fire a gun?

A little while later, some bad news. There is no rodeo tonight. It ended the night before, on the third. Everybody apologizes to us profusely, and I'm disappointed because I wanted to see some guys get thrown off some bulls.

Meghan: There is no apologizing for America. We're the greatest country in the world and, although we have our issues, overall it is not a country that needs a huge amount of changing. That's how I feel; that is what I believe. Michael and I apparently have different takes on this.

First rule of attempting to make any kind of logical argument politically with someone, especially when it's concerning your thoughts on the wars in Iraq and Afghanistan, is don't do it when either of you is drinking on the Fourth of July.

Since the rodeo is cancelled, we decide to take Michael to Whisky Row, a quaint, all-American strip of bars surrounded by small restaurants, ice cream shops, a classic bandstand (with the bunting and everything), and a giant courthouse, complete with clock tower.

We walk into the first cowboy bar, which is blasting Kid Rock's "Born Free," one of my favorite songs. Holly and I go to the bar and order a round of Jack and Cokes, plus shots of tequila for the whole motley crew—Jimmy, Mom, Michael, Kyle, and Mike. Everyone is wearing cowboy hats and cowboy boots except for Michael and me. We start drinking, shooting the shit, and having the kind of good time you would imagine having in northern Arizona at an old school town with a row of bars.

I'm dancing, playing pool, gossiping with Holly about my dating life and how things are going with Jimmy since they moved to Texas, ordering more shots, laughing, dancing, repeat. We all sort of mingle in and out of various bars, and somewhere towards the end of the night everyone reassembles at one of the last bars on the strip. Michael and I start talking about the military and the wars in Iraq and Afghanistan. Something tells me that drinking and talking politics do not mix, but people in America do have these discussions while not sober.

I don't know exactly how the conversation starts, but pretty quickly I am furious at Michael. He doesn't agree with either of the wars in Iraq or Afghanistan, even though pretty much his only exposure to anything military was when he dressed up as a Ninja Turtle and toured the country as a teenager. I, on the other hand, well, if you paid any attention to my father's career at all you would know the whole bit: my great-grandfather and grandfather were both admirals in the navy; my great-grandfather played a major role in the ending of World War II, and subsequently died of a heart attack a week after the war ended while standing drinking a glass of whiskey. My father was tortured for five and a half years in a filthy Vietnam prison. Both my brothers joined the military as teenagers. I love the military and support the men and women who fight so courageously for our country so I can be here at home and write a book with an alternative comedian who is making my blood boil with his "give peace a chance" hippie attitude.

Obviously, everyone knows that there was false information given to the American public to sell us on the war in Iraq. I'm sorry; it makes no difference at this point. We were there and we needed to fight the good fight. I am not going to go into the extremely specific and intense details of the wars or war strategy or why I think General Petraeus is a genius. I generally react badly to anyone criticizing the military or the wars in Iraq and Afghanistan when they have absolutely no exposure to any men and women who have served, and when most likely the only exposure they have had to any of this is listening to people like Keith Olbermann.

As I try to listen to Michael's argument, I feel like he really doesn't get it, like maybe he's just another delusional, elitist, liberal—and possibly a jerk. At some point I stop his stream of pacifist rhetoric and say, "Listen Michael, freedom doesn't come free."

He laughs.

Now, if you have known me for fifteen minutes, you would know these words are dear to me, as they are to most people who have a deep love for the military. I know this is a slogan, much like "These colors don't run" and "Live free or die," but I never say it lightly, and never to evoke laughter. Those mantras really do mean something to me.

When Jimmy was deployed the first time, I stood with tears streaming down my face thinking that he was fighting for my freedom and this was a sacrifice: *freedom doesn't come free*. I understand that it is a simplistic way to describe something that is much larger and deeply rooted in extreme patriotism, but I don't see how anyone could be blind to the truth behind the sentiment. I'm shocked by Michael's disdain for the blood that has been spilt for this country, regardless of the shoddy intelligence that got us over there. At the time that the intelligence was put forward, it wasn't a matter of questioning it and risking it being *right*. God forbid someone like Michael take a moment to contemplate the outcome of that path. It's far easier to point a finger and say, "You were wrong to do that," than to say, "What if we hadn't done it, and we were wrong?"

I look at Michael's smirking face and cross my arms. "Why did I agree to do this?" I sort of half yell in his face, because I feel like not only is he not understanding what I am saying, but because I feel he is possibly judging me. I sit forward and realize that maybe this conversation would be better continued without the whiskey, so I say, "A good general rule about me is never laugh when I say the word freedom." Because like it or not, Michael's freedom as an American, to have this conversation in this bar, with these war heroes around us, has *not* come free.

Michael: Meghan and I get into our first fight. It's about Iraq and at one point she yells at me, "Freedom doesn't come free," which is so trite that I have to laugh, which only pisses her off more. Cindy gently interjects on behalf of her daughter who storms away, and it's then that I realize maybe Meghan and I should get to know each other better before we really get into this debate.

But seriously: freedom doesn't come free? What does that mean? It sounds good, but to me it's the exact definition of the kind of bumper-sticker politics this book is meant to dissuade. Who's out there proclaiming that freedom *is* free? If there is somebody out there making a good case for American anarchy, I haven't heard it.

Everybody recognizes that nations pay a price for their own existence, be it in blood or treasure or both. Everybody in America understands that our military men and women sometimes pay that price with their lives. To defend the Iraq War with that statement just seems to be designed to cut off debate. It's the equivalent of saying if you are against that war, or any war, then you are against America, an argument that is, to put it as mildly as I can, fucking stupid.

After a while we head back to the ranch. Everybody peels off to sleep one by one. Jimmy, Holly, and I are the last to go to bed. Holly is a couple of years older than Jimmy. They met at a bar the night before he deployed to Iraq. Didn't see each other again until he got back. There is something about Jimmy that is different than other guys his age I've known. It's easy to say that being to war changes a man, but I don't know because I never knew him before. Meghan says he changed. She says the old Jimmy is only reappearing after a long absence. I don't know. He laughs a lot and seems fired up about everything: movies, music, comic books. But there's something behind his eyes that I can't quite explain. Something hooded. Holly keeps her hand on his arm for much of the night, and when it's time to say good night, I hug them both.

"Good night, sir," Jimmy says.

I go to bed hearing patriotic music in my head. I have trouble sleeping. Late in the night, a big storm blows over the desert, pinging the metal roof with raindrops. I wake up around dawn, the first one up. I slip outside and take a long walk by myself. As I pick my way over the rutted road and through the brush, I notice the ground has taken all the water from last night's storm for itself. On my way back, one of Jackie's horses looks up at me and then goes back to his hay. All around me people are sleeping, and it is dry and already hot.

Las Vegas, Nevada

Viva, etc.

Michael: We arrive in Las Vegas hot off the dusty Arizona trail, my testosterone still a little jacked up after squeezing off all those semi-assault rifle rounds into the desert floor. I've got a little more strut to my step, a touch more dust on my linen pants, a teeny bit more scruff on my Crocs.

Now that we're finally away from both of our mothers, I'm starting to feel like this trip is getting serious. It's hard to be "Road Mike" when my mom is around. But now she's in the rearview mirror, Meghan's mom is back in Arizona, and I am ready to let this monster out to roar. But first, a nap.

Meghan's got a hook-up at the Palms named Larry, one of those casino hosts whose job it is to keep high rollers and high-profile clients happy. Meghan apparently qualifies as "high-profile," because he sets us up in a couple of enormous, over-the-top suites. Each is easily as big as the first house Martha and I bought. There are multiple flatscreens, a big living room with a purple sectional on which to lounge, a vast dining table, small kitchen, plus a huge bedroom overlooking the Strip. My favorite feature is what Meghan dubs "the sex shower": a large tiled room just off the bathroom sprouting about ten individual showerheads, which can be angled to hit whatever body part feels dirtiest. There's also a dial that controls an intricate lighting system: you can choose between red, blue, or yellow lights, or any combination, either flashing or not. It's like a Christmas display gone porno. Over the next three days, I spend a fair amount of time in the sex shower, although always by myself, and there is never any sexual contact between anybody, including between me and me; I just like the shower.

I always feel a little bad when people give me nice things, if only because I don't believe that anything comes without a price tag. People don't just give you shit; they always want something in return. This, of course, includes the government. The current Republican Party seems to worry about this problem a lot. That's why they're always bitching about "entitlement programs." They fear that the people receiving benefits from these programs don't realize that they have actual costs that other people—themselves—have to pay. In effect, they argue, the rich are subsidizing the poor. That's what they're talking about when they spout the phrase "redistribution of wealth." The problem is that the wealth has already been redistributed—to the rich. The poor are actually subsidizing the rich, through globalization, lower wages, less benefits, and weaker unions. Both sides in the debate feel taken advantage of, which creates a lot of tension. Over the course of our stay in Vegas, I begin to believe that a lot of the unhappiness in this country could be solved if the government just started handing out sex showers.

Meghan: I love Las Vegas. I love, love, love Las Vegas. Whenever anything is spiraling out of control in my life, whenever I need a break, whenever I want to be someone else for an evening (or a weekend, or a week, or whatever), as clichéd as this may seem, Las Vegas has always provided an answer for me. It's pretty much the only place I frequent as a vacation destination, and I have been serendipitously intertwined in news cycles with the city throughout my adult life.

In 2010, I fled to Las Vegas in the middle of my book tour for my campaign memoir *Dirty, Sexy Politics*, after cancelling a speech at Juniata College at the last minute. I had been on the road for weeks, and my boyfriend at the time broke up with me over email the day after my book release party, citing no other reason than "I'm sorry, I can't do this anymore. I just can't. I'm truly sorry from the bottom of my heart." I was distraught, but instead of going into an emotional tailspin over it, because sitting around crying and watching Nora Ephron movies simply isn't my style, I went to Vegas on an emergency trip with a few of my close friends. It did not occur to me how harshly the student body would take my cancellation, nor how the media would crucify me for it. Listen, was this my finest moment or the smartest move I have ever made? No, of course not, but I was broken-hearted and exhausted from my media tour and not acting from an entirely rational place. I made a mistake, and when I make a mistake everyone in the world gets to judge it and leave a comment on the Internet about it.

To put it lightly, the student body was not pleased about my tweets from Vegas, and did as much as they possibly could to notify the media about what a bad person I was for canceling on them and spending the time in Las Vegas instead. The incident created a small media firestorm and the next thing I knew, I was on the home pages of CNN and Perez Hilton on one hand, while having bottles of champagne sent to my room from George Maloof (the owner of the Palms) thanking me for the publicity on the other. I was slammed for being reckless with my career and speaking tour. You would have thought I was running for president and had called in sick to Iowa. A few days later, after the furor died down, I sent a tweet that said, "Mi Vida Loca. Vegas is a religion. Casino is my church." It's not something I would do again, and in hindsight was irresponsible and stupid, but any person who has ever been dumped on their ass probably knows how hard that is, and you just want to make the pain go away as soon as possible. Vegas has always been a place where I have found solace.

When I'm down, when I'm up, when I'm feeling lucky, or out of luck, you will most likely be able to find me in the city of sin. One blogger wrote about me: "Live by the tweet, die by the tweet." Well, if that's another way of saying that I was out there with the unapologetic truth, well then, I guess I wear my tweets on my sleeve.

My suite looks like a pimped-out boudoir. I throw my two suitcases, purse, and shoulder bag on the sofa and immediately recognize the fact that it seems a terrible shame to be alone in a suite of this size and caliber.

After I get in and settle down, I log on to Twitter and see that Michael has already posted a video to his "Sad, sad conversation" YouTube account. He and some of his friends who are also actors and comedians have an ongoing video diary where they vlog about what is going on in their lives. For the most part, they talk about their not-Oscar-and-Emmy-winning careers in the entertainment industry. Some of the videos they make are sweet and endearing, others are depressing and cynical. Michael's video is from his suite, and he's saying that he has been upgraded because of my connections with the Palms. This is true, but it seems as if he is apologizing to his viewers and sounds somewhat *guilty* and embarrassed, as if staying at a gorgeous suite might somehow hurt his credibility with the sad people of the world.

I'm annoyed for being outed for helping him get upgraded to a nicer room, but more so because after years and years growing up in and fighting my way out of a conservative environment, not to mention years of Catholic school, I am not a fan of unnecessary guilt. Yes, guilt is an important emotion if it is warranted, but feeling guilty in Las Vegas, after simply checking into your hotel room, seemed excessive. Michael feels guilty about a lot of things, especially if it's something that has to do with having a good time. It's weird; of the two of us you would think I would have the guilt issues, but I only feel guilty when it's morally warranted. Life is way too short to feel guilty about necessary evils. When in Vegas, I always stay at the Palms and they are always incredibly accommodating. Seriously, if it's your first trip to Vegas—and I am not just saying this—it is the most fabulous casino to stay in. From time to time they upgrade me because of my loyalty to the casino, but Michael was acting like we had done something wrong that he should be publicly apologizing for over the Internet. I know a lot of people may think I constantly get upgrades at hotels, but I assure you it is very rare. In Las Vegas, however, it sometimes happens, but like I said, I frequent the city more often than most people do. I really just wanted to get Michael to relax and have a good time, and I was not sure what type of mood was being set after watching Michael's sad video. I mean, isn't the whole point of coming to Vegas on this trip to have a good time and explore what the city of sin means in relation to the rest of America?

Michael: After I get a couple of hours' sleep and have a quickie shower, we reassemble in the lobby. Tonight we are heading downtown, to old Vegas, the original Strip, where cowboys and Mafiosi first crossed six-shooters to build a desert oasis.

The old Strip has really gone to pot. All the classic casinos are still there: the Four Queens, the Golden Nugget, Binion's, and Fitzgerald's. But whatever magic and glamour may have been there in 1963 is long gone. The only connection to those days are the cocktail waitresses; most of whom look as if they never left. This is the home of the three-dollar blackjack table and the ninety-nine-cent shrimp cocktail. This is where Lady Luck went to kill herself.

Old Vegas is so much more exciting to me than new Vegas because it is the truer face of the city. It's scrappier and hungrier. Old Vegas is the gambler who lost everything but just knows he'll make it back if he can just catch a couple lucky breaks. Who knows, maybe old Vegas can get lucky again; just across the street from the seedy casinos, there is a new downtown revitalization movement happening, an entrepreneurial revival unnoticed by the tourists sucking down giant frozen drinks out of enormous plastic hookahs.

Stop number one on our tour is the Downtown Cocktail Room, or "DCR," as it's known to its hipster clientele. Yes, even Vegas has hipsters. Whether or not there are enough of them to turn around this grungy neighborhood I do not know, but they are definitely giving it a try. The bar was opened by Michael and Jennifer, who agree to have fancy drinks with us. The cocktail room is dark and luxe, radically different from the garishness just outside their door.

This is a place for serious libation. There are, for example, eight different varieties of absinthe on the offering, and concoctions with names like "Persephone's Pomme" and "Satan's Whiskers." Our waitress is dressed, inexplicably, like Malcolm McDowell in *A Clockwork Orange,* complete with bowler hat and fake eyelash. I order something fruity, as is my nature, and we get to chatting with Michael and Jennifer.

They're a great couple, the kind of young, practical, industrious people that America is rumored to be filled with. For whatever reason, they've decided to make downtown Las Vegas their mission. They're making Brooklyn in the desert here. Not only do they run the DCR, they've also got Emergency Arts, a coffee shop/art collective housed in an old medical center. Friends of theirs own a bar-arcade called Insert Coin, where we play video games and drink bubblegum-flavored vodka.

There's a lot going on here, but the entire downtown restoration only extends a couple of blocks. For every new bar or art gallery, there are ten vacant buildings. When the economy fried, Vegas was the first place to get zapped. The whole town has a kind of jittery vibe to it, the way people get when they've been up too late partying. Las Vegas looks like a girl who stayed out all night and now her dress is crumpled, she's lost a heel, and her mascara is all over her face. Las Vegas is a hot mess. No wonder Meghan loves it so.

We spend the rest of the night walking around Freemont Street, a long outdoor plaza covered by an enormous electronic canopy. The canopy stretches for about three city blocks and is illuminated with millions of LED lights flashing messages, advertisements, and the occasional patriotic light show. The effect is to make it feel as though you are living underneath a football stadium scoreboard.

The street is mobbed with badly dressed, lumpy, drunken tourists, sipping from novelty plastic grenades and beer bongs. Attractions abound. A zip line system runs just above our heads. There are multiple Elvis impersonators and people dressed as SpongeBob SquarePants. A local '80s cover band is set up at the end of the street. They all have identical black plastic hair wigs and skinny jeans, skinny ties. They look miserable bopping around up there, exhorting the audience to "Wang Chung tonight." The crowd looks equally miserable half-heartedly stumbling along in something that looks like, but definitely is not, dancing. We stand on the edge of the crowd feeling a little miserable ourselves, but we don't want to leave because we don't want to miss anything; there's too much white trash shit show to take it all in. Sometimes hedonism can feel like a lot of work. When we finally tear ourselves away, I leave feeling dirty and depressed. Thank God I have a happy-ending shower waiting for me back at the Palms.

Meghan: One of the main things I want to do with Michael while we're in Vegas is tour the Zappos headquarters. I am a frequent user of the Zappos website to buy shoes and sometimes clothes. Although that is what I use Zappos to shop for, you can find a huge variety of things to purchase on the site that extend past shoes and jeans. Everything the Zappos company touts itself to be is true. My shipments come when they are supposed to, it is easy to print out a return slip from their website, and the customer service is amazing, probably the best I've ever encountered. Everything is simple and easy, and the people I have talked to about an order seemed happy to help me. As weird as it sounds, it is really refreshing to do business with a company that seems to truly believe in customer service. For the record, I have no affiliation with Zappos other than as a customer. On top of that, Zappos CEO Tony Hsieh has established a substantial cult following as a result of the wild success of Zappos and its somewhat unorthodox business environment; or depending on your perspective, the working environment all other working environments should follow and replicate.

Zappos made *Fortune* magazine's annual Best Companies to Work For list and it grosses over a billion dollars in sales annually. In fact Tony Hsieh's book, *Delivering Happiness: A Path to Profits, Passion, and Purpose*, has been an overwhelming success, spending twenty-seven weeks on the *New York Times* bestseller list. His latest venture is to rejuvenate downtown Las Vegas, where they are preparing to move their headquarters to the city hall building, which was slated to become a homeless shelter until Hsieh stepped in. He is attempting to invigorate Vegas in ways that the city hasn't seen since Bugsy Siegel—investing his own money and the time and talent of his entire team in coming up with new ideas to pump fresh blood into the area. Some say he is trying to create a new Silicon Valley right in the center of town. I say, more power to him.

Michael: I have never ordered anything from Zappos and do not know anything about them as a company, but Meghan is excited to tour the company because apparently people come from all over the world to observe their amazing corporate culture. In my experience the words "corporate" and "culture" do not coexist well together, sort of like "chocolate" and "martini." People often put the two together, but why?

What's so special about Zappos that people are freaking out about the company and wanting to emulate its success? As it turns out: construction paper and tambourines. The Zappos corporate culture can basically be boiled down to "adult day camp." Everything about the place is FUN! The popcorn machine in the lobby: FUN! The free ice cream sandwiches: FUN! The big throne where you can pose for pictures while holding the scepter of your choosing: FUN! Everything is shiny and loud. As we take the tour, every time we pass a different section everybody takes out their tambourine or kazoo or whatever noisemaker is on hand and makes a racket of welcoming.

"This is our designer handbag team."

JANGLE! HOORAY! YIPEE!

"This is our spring apparel team."

WHOOPEE! YEEHAW! HUZZAH!

Everybody's cubicle looks as if it was decorated at arts and crafts. Even their legal department is covered in construction paper and cardboard tubes so that it looks like a comic book Hall of Justice. In fact, there is a homemade sign outside the legal department that reads HALL OF JUSTICE.

The whole thing is so goddamned chipper it creeps me out. Meghan looks creeped out too.

"I could never work here," she whispers to me at one point.

"I don't think I could even *breathe* here," I say.

And it's true. Everybody seems passionate and happy, but the whole thing feels too hunky-dory to be real. Can anybody survive this amount of enforced cheeriness? I know I could not. But Zappos is not for everybody, and our smiley tour leader tells us that they accept one employee for every thirty applicants. Everyone has to fill out personality tests and undergo a rigorous interview process. Then, after a couple of weeks at work, the new recruit is offered two thousand dollars to leave. Very few of the Zappoistas take the money. After all, they have no-pay lunch, assorted free vending machines, the kind of health care only Congress has, and the encouragement from above to make sure that everyone plays as hard after hours as they do during them.

"How do you know if somebody is a good fit?" Meghan asks our tour leader.

"You just know," he says, and I don't doubt it. He's got the glow of a true believer about him. The whole thing has a fevered Scientology vibe to it, and I'm happy when it's finally time to go. If Zappos were a child instead of a company, I'd prescribe some serious Adderall.

Meghan: Although I consider myself a Las Vegas veteran, coming to this city with the anthropological intention of figuring out exactly what role Las Vegas currently is playing in American culture still felt like a daunting task, and I thought I needed to call in a little backup. My friend Paul Carr is a British writer and journalist who notoriously lives only in hotels and has written several books about his nomadic and unconventional lifestyle. He has just spent a month living on the Strip in Las Vegas and stayed at every single hotel on the Strip while blogging about the experience for the *Huffington Post*. I asked Paul for advice on where Michael and I should go to experience the "real" Las Vegas and to make sure there was nothing we could possibly miss during our stay. He gave me a list of recommendations and asked if I wanted to meet some exotic dancers, then signed off our email exchange: "Viva, etc."

Strippers. Strippers. Strippers. What is a proper trip to Vegas without strippers? Or excuse me, exotic dancers. Well, actually I have had many trips to Vegas that did not include the presence of strippers or a trip to a strip club. Michael told me early on that he has never been a huge fan of strippers and maybe only been to a strip club once or twice. He described his forays as "uncomfortable" and "inorganic."

A trip to a gentleman's club with Michael and Stephie turns out to be something that sounded a lot better on paper than it does when we are actually getting ready to do it. Michael is happily married with two young children, and Stephie is getting married in the fall. She really doesn't seem comfortable with the idea of going to a strip club, and I do not necessarily feel comfortable twisting her arm. Stephie is probably the sweetest, most innocent twenty-five-year-old I have ever met, and I am more than happy to not be responsible for anything that is going to corrupt her.

The thing about exotic dancing is that I am *incredibly* conflicted about the industry. The feminist, empowered part of me finds the whole profession depressing, degrading, tragic even, and innately sad for the women who feel the need to resort to taking their clothes off for money in front of strange, and probably more often than not, perverted men. Any woman who elects to become a stripper will always in some fashion have a social stigma attached to her for the rest of her life.

The other side of me personally knows women who work in the industry. Some of them claim to feel empowered by making the kind of money that the high-end customers shell out. Some of them treat their profession as an art form, and work hard on new routines and exotic costumes. There seems to be a huge demand for it in America. I mean, let's face it, America is obsessed with sex, porn, and exotic dancing. It's a weird dichotomy that in such a conservative culture there would also be such an intense appetite for all elements of the sex industry. Sex, porn, strippers—I think whether or not I approve of the industry, or partake in any element of it, all of these things will continue to go on. So from my perspective, I would rather have an open conversation about what the sex industry should be in America and how it should be better regulated than simply shutting down everything entirely.

I think there are bigger questions at hand: why our obsession with sex and the sex industry only seems to grow, and why exposure to pornography through the Internet also only continues to grow and become more readily available. Instead of ignoring the conversation and having the attitude that all sex is evil and wrong, we need to have a more open and honest dialogue about the sex industry in America if we are ever going to really address its issues.

As I write this I can already hear the bloggers firing up their laptops: "Meghan McCain supports the sex industry—this girl loves her some strippers." This will be an easy thing to take out of context and use to somehow exacerbate the already "wild child" reputation that for many reasons I do not deserve; but I still am a Republican and the daughter of one of the most famous politicians in America, so anything having to do with stripping and the sex industry is heightened to an unreasonable taboo level. What I really find comical about this entire scenario, though, is that Michael seems ready to throw up even before we leave the hotel. Of the two of us, he is the one who seems to be losing it a little bit.

I need to bring in more reinforcements, so I call my friend Josh Rupley and his boyfriend, Kasey Mahaffy. If you are an intense and longtime follower of my life and blogging career, you'll know Josh is my confidant/hair fixer who traveled with me during the presidential campaign. Josh's longtime boyfriend, Kasey, is an actor and one of the sweetest, most sensitive guys I know. He also loves whiskey as much as I do, which was an early bonding tool for us. I love Josh and Kasey dearly. They can also drink me under the table, which is what I need if I'm going to take these greenhorns out on the town. I think they will be perfect for breaking the ice with

Michael and accompanying us on our tour of the underworld of exotic dancing.

Michael: Here's something you might not know about Vegas strippers: they pay to take their clothes off. Strippers are not employees of any club but are rather "independent contractors," who give the clubs a house fee for the privilege of taking off their clothes in front of drunken bachelor partiers and handsy conventioneers.

Think about how genius that is for a second: the Sapphire Gentlemen's Club, which bills itself as "the world's largest Las Vegas strip club" (whatever that means), claims to have up to four hundred girls dancing there *a night*. House fees start at forty dollars and increase twenty dollars an hour from 7:00 P.M. until 10:00 P.M. That means a girl can spend a hundred dollars just to go to work, and with four hundred girls on the floor that means Sapphire is generating tens of thousands of dollars before they even turn on the smoke machines.

Meghan's buddy Paul has arranged for us to meet Sapphire's own Daisy Delfina for an "X-rated tour of Las Vegas," but first we go to dinner with my buddy Phil Gordon, an Internet entrepreneur turned professional poker player. Phil is far more active politically than I realized. He's a libertarian, which makes sense for a professional poker player. They are a "live and let live" breed, and in fact he and his professional poker buddies are in the middle of a battle with the federal government over the poker website they started, Full Tilt Poker, whose assets were frozen by the government. Phil has millions of dollars tied up in this venture, so politics affect him in a very direct, very consequential way. And here's the thing: it's *all* politics.

Gambling—or "gaming" as the industry prefers to call it—is an industry like any other. They've got their big players—the big casino owners and operators—and they didn't like the idea of a start-up operation like Phil's poker thing raking in money; money that could be going to them instead of to a band of poker players and their backers. The casinos were happy to let online poker sites exist when they were young and unproven. Once the market matured, it became a threat. So they had it shut down. Is that the free market at work? Or is that corruption? Is it influence peddling? I don't know. I just know that it smells shitty and my buddy got hurt.

Phil, to my surprise, tells us he's thinking about running for Congress from his district in Washington State. He's got the money to do it, he's brilliant, and he's got a compelling personal story. But he's not sure he wants to subject himself or his family to the professional and personal rigors of a campaign for office. This is something we hear a lot on the road. Good people, the kind of people we like to envision running for office, don't want to do it. God knows I would never do it. Not that I ever could. Unlike Phil, I don't have the money, am not brilliant, and there are enough comedy videos of me featuring dildos out there that I am most likely unelectable. Probably only one dildo video is enough to prevent you from holding elected office, though by the time this book is published, somebody is bound to have proven me wrong.

Meghan: Much to my surprise and satisfaction, Michael's good friend Phil Gordon is not a Democrat. In fact, he didn't vote for Obama, which means he voted for my father. When Phil reveals this, I think Michael is going to spit a spring roll out of his nose.

When we finally finish dinner and make our way to the Palms bar, I start scanning the place for Daisy. There are tons of women scattered around the place in various states of drunkenness, but no one that resembles the woman I saw online. In her Twitter picture she is wearing a red bikini with her cleavage as the focal point, giving a "come hither" look on her face. Finally, in the corner I spot a young woman with long brown hair wearing a baby-pink A-line dress that is tight at the top and swings out at the bottom. She's drinking a glass of white wine and typing on her BlackBerry.

I walk over and ask, "Are you Daisy?"

She stands and says, "Hellloooo, so nice to finally meet you! I have been looking forward to going out together for a while!" and gives both Michael and me big hugs. Now, Daisy is gorgeous and I don't know what the stereotypical image of a stripper may be, but she is the most conservative-looking stripper I have ever seen in person. She's wearing minimal makeup and from what I can tell she isn't wearing extensions (which could only be said for one of us because I rarely go anywhere without extensions in my hair anymore); she could be any professional woman sitting at the bar.

As we order a round of drinks, two of Daisy's colleagues join us at the bar: Jessica Janson and "G-Cup Bitch." Jessica is very tall, with very, very long blond hair, and looks like she's about twenty-one. She's wearing very high heels (even by my standards) and a very tight bandage-style dress. G-Cup Bitch is more petite, with red hair and glasses and, yes, G-cup breasts that are shelved nicely in a tight, black strapless top. The three women are very pretty, and really friendly, albeit very curious about why we want to meet them.

Sapphire is the gentleman's club of choice, and our next destination. It is supposed to be the best of the best that Vegas has to offer, and as Daisy calls it, "the Costco of strip clubs" because of its size and variety of options for both strippers and "rooms." Sapphire sends us over a long stretch limo with neon lights that outline the ceiling, and we all pile in: me, Michael, Stephie, Josh, Kasey, Phil, Daisy, Jessica, and G-Cup Bitch: one big happy family. The ride over is initially a little tense, what with Michael's inability to stop tape-recording and writing stuff down. I sit in the back with the girls and have girl talk. They are curious about my life in politics; I am curious about their lives as strippers. We talk about great bra brands, men, and the world of politics. They are sweet and friendly and seem to genuinely want to show us a good time and insight into their world. I have met many tour guides before who were not nearly as hospitable hosts. Does this feel weird? Of course it feels weird. I am heading to a strip club with some strippers and Michael Ian Black. The purpose of this trip is to discover different parts of

America that we don't normally encounter and to talk to Americans who we probably would not normally have conversations with. Quite frankly, I am extremely curious about the adult industry and the women who subject themselves to it. So far, the women have surprised me. They seem to be happy and well adjusted. Their attitude towards their clients is that they are manipulating them. None of them want to work a job that pays them minimum wage, so they have chosen this path instead.

Michael: Honestly, I'm bad at talking to strippers. Maybe I'm a prude, but I can never quite find my bearings talking to women who use their bodies in this way. Part of it is intimidation, I guess, and part of it is that they make me ashamed to be a man, to be so easily manipulated. As a result, I find myself on guard with them and unable to relax. This will continue for the rest of the evening. I think of myself as shy. But that is not how Meghan describes me.

"You're acting like a little bitch," she says, and I cannot disagree. The only consolation I can take is that Stephie is just as uncomfortable. She looks like Alice after falling into Wonderland.

Daisy is thirty-two, well spoken, and gorgeous. She grew up in Bed-Stuy, Brooklyn, the first college graduate in her family. Her relationship with her family back in New York is strained, not because she dances, but because she left the neighborhood. "They think I should have ten babies and be on welfare." She sighs with frustration and pats her flat stomach. "No babies," she says. She is a proud, self-made woman, and she wants us to see her as an American success story. "Gucci," she tells me, pointing to her wallet. "I earned it."

G-Cup Bitch says she mentors younger dancers. "When girls are shy, I tell them to look at men and see wallets."

"It's all a hustle," says Jessica. "They should teach classes on how to hustle."

"What would be the first lesson?" I ask.

She thinks about it for a second. "To get as much money as you can by doing as little work as you can."

We drink at the bar for a while. Meghan's friends Josh and Kasey join us and coo over the girls. Gay guys and strippers are a great combination. One complements the other perfectly.

Sapphire is huge. Seventy thousand square feet, according to the owner, Peter Feinstein, who takes us on a tour of the property. Peter is from New York, probably in his mid-fifties, who started out in the health club industry. He developed a bunch of big gyms in the city until he and his partners realized they could make more money in gentlemen's entertainment. I guess it's not so different from the health club industry. Both have changing rooms.

When we are walking around, Jessica pulls me aside and tells me to breathe in deeply. I do. "Do you smell that?" she asks.

"Yeah." It's a weird, musty smell. Kind of unpleasant but not terrible. "What is that?" I ask her.

"Strip club," she says.

So it is. I have another term for it: "dirty pussy."

The club is so massive that on slow nights like tonight they draw an enormous curtain across half of it and it's still huge. Peter sets us up with a table in the back and a bottle of Grey Goose vodka, and we proceed to have an evening of drinking and lap dances.

The lap dance thing is lost on me. Having some half-naked lady gyrate on my lap for money in public is, for me, more terrifying than titillating. Not that I don't like naked girls. I do. But I don't like naked girls pretending to like me. Then I just feel like one of those wallets G-Cup Bitch was talking about. If that makes me a little bitch then so be it.

Josh and Kasey are having a grand time, throwing back vodka cranberries and whooping it up with the girls. Nermal has never been to a strip club before, and she is wide-eyed, maybe with fear, maybe with fascination. I can't tell. Before we left the hotel, Meghan, Stephie, and I jokingly agreed on a safe word if we found ourselves in a situation we could not handle. When somebody said "puppies," it was time to go. I fully expect Stephie to puppy up at any moment. Unless I get there first.

Meghan: We pull up to Sapphire and meet the manager and owner, who gives us a tour of the club. We walk past the caged area where patrons check in, and into the back room where all of the calls and requests come in for casino pickup limo service. Stephie and I are invited to tour the women's dressing area, which looks like the women's locker room at Victoria's Secret. We meet the "house mom," Sandy Berrigan, who was once a dancer there. She seems protective of her girls and suspicious of Stephie and me.

Daisy and the girls whisk all of us to the top floor, which overlooks the entire strip club and has a giant pole at the top with stairs that lead down to the main floor. When Daisy tries to get everyone dancing, and to go onto the strip club ramp with her, Michael looks like he's back in seventh grade, frozen at the prospect of dancing with a hot girl. I'm the only one game enough to dance with her on the long, lit-up ramp. It's awkward, but I don't want her to feel bad or like I am not down to enjoy this experience in its entirety. Also, I want to add to anything that is going to make Michael feel even more uncomfortable.

We finally make our way downstairs and it's game on. Daisy takes us to a special reserved area and suddenly *everyone* is at the junior high dance, standing around waiting for someone to make the first move. Michael, Stephie, and Phil huddle at a table in one corner and Josh, Kasey, and I take the opposite end, with the dancers intertwined between. I immediately start pouring everyone drinks from the vodka bottle and various juices and Red Bulls that have been placed in front of us. Josh whispers in my ear, "Drinking will get all of this moving along faster."

My attitude at this point is that we're here. We are in Vegas, we are here to have a good time, and we are here to experience another side of America and Vegas. When in Rome, right? And goddammit, Michael and I need to start bonding.

A lot of the dancers make their way towards Michael and circulate around him. Next I see that all of them are sitting there . . . talking. Leave it to Michael to get all of the dancers to start opening up about their emotions instead of doing their jobs. They all look like they are deep in conversation about something very important. I am perplexed about why Michael seems to be avoiding getting a lap dance to such an extent. If he expects me, Josh, and Kasey to carry the weight, he is delusional.

Josh buys Kasey the first nonintellectual lap dance and, although Kasey is gay, apparently when you put a half-naked stripper on his lap, you can't really tell the difference. Kasey is as Waspy as they come, but he looks like a slathering pig in a tub of butter. Suddenly Phil starts ordering dances, and then Josh out of nowhere has two girls grinding on him.

I sit on the top edge of a booth, between Jessica and G-Cup Bitch. Jessica leans over and asks me if I want a dance. I say, "Not yet, waiting it out for the right girl." It's not that I'm particularly picky with my strippers, but tonight feels like a good night to watch and wait.

Jessica says, "Well, at least Phil is getting dances. I told the dancers to go for the professional poker player and not the comedian." Suddenly Josh runs up to me and yells that he's found our girl. He points to the highest part of the stage where an incredibly tan stripper with long, blond extensions is doing a contortion on the pole that can only be described as Cirque du Soleil worthy.

I say, "She's perfect, Daisy, we want her. Would you mind getting her?" The dancer's name is Phoenix and she's from Arizona.

Josh gets the first lap dance from Phoenix, which was probably his third of the night, and I get the second one. I apparently took it like a pro, although the entire thing is actually very uncomfortable for me. In the middle of the dance I ask Phoenix if she's wearing Peace, Love and Juicy Couture perfume, because that is the same perfume I wear. She is. The whole thing feels awkward and just absurd. I mean, I just want to get it over with, but I also want to maintain my pride about the fact that I, the conservative senator's daughter, handle myself better than Michael does at a gentlemen's club. I start to feel a little guilty and, dare I say, dirty. Phoenix is a cute girl, with excellent taste in perfume. Once again, all I really want to do is ask her how she got here and if she likes her job.

I pay Phoenix and point at Michael, instructing her to give him a lap dance. I hand her more money and insist that she is not to let him leave that booth before giving him one. "Seriously, he's going to fight you. I don't care what you have to do, give that man a lap dance."

Michael: As immune as I like to think I am to the whole stripper thing, when a twenty-two-year-old blonde named Phoenix with an amazing body is grinding against you and blowing in your ear, even a professional cynic like me can find himself, shall we say, interested. At one point, she surrounds my (fully clothed, fully limp) penis with her mouth and kind of circulates warm air on it. I am mortified and my little friend stays exactly that: little.

Over the course of the night, I come to admire Daisy and her friends. I don't know what dark shit they have in their lives, hopefully none, but they seem like a nice group of women: smart, confident, able, not so different from the suburban mommies I hang out with back in Connecticut. Each of them talks about how their job is a business, like any other. The difference is that they are out on their own, every night, in uncertain work environments, catering to a clientele that is often drunk or high or aggressive or whatever they are. The women say they almost always feel safe at work, although they each have a story to tell about a time when they were not. The owner, Peter, puts it this way: "Guys are animals." As a guy, I don't entirely agree, but there were enough animals in the club that night to convince me he knows what he's talking about.

I am trying very hard to have a good time. I drink several drinks, and I try chatting with some of the girls, but my efforts fall flat. "So where you from?" just doesn't sound right in that environment. After a few hours, there just isn't that much more to see and Daisy asks us if we want to move on.

Yes.

Meghan and I are embracing the spirit of "yes." To every suggestion, the answer is yes. This will be the mantra for our tour. Yes
to everything.

Daisy suggests we go to the Green Door, a club where people
have orgies.

No.

I'm not ready for that. I don't think I will ever be ready for that.
"How about the Palomino?" she asks.

All of us pile into a taxi and head for an even seedier part of
town. The Palomino is one of the older strip clubs in Vegas, dating
to 1969. The girls are all really young or really old, and are all butt
naked. They all also seem wasted, and most of them sport some sort
of Hello Kitty paraphernalia: bracelets, tattoos, earrings, bags. Why
Hello Kitty, I do not know, but it certainly gives the proceedings
an even nastier taint.

As aggressive as the girls at Sapphire were, the Palomino girls are
worse. Hovering on the other side of desperate. They are on us from
the moment we walk through the door. One girl in particular is a
real problem. She is at least forty, probably Filipino, and like a
shark. As soon as we are seated, she sidles up beside me, resting her
hand on my thigh. "Why you not move your dick?" she asks me.

"What?!" I have no idea what she's talking about. I mean, I do,
but I don't.

"Why you not move your dick?" She is slurring and has her
hands all over me. "You want an upside down pussy?"

"No thank you," I say. I do not need to know what an upside
down pussy is to know I do not want one.

Meghan is ready with her twenty dollars, and before I know
what is happening, the girl has her head between my legs, and *her*
legs spread-eagled by my face. Her naked vagina is about an inch
from my chin.

As advertised, her pussy is upside down.

As if that isn't awkward enough, she then starts rocking her
pelvis back and forth so that it is bumping into my collarbone.

Hard. Like, really hard. Painfully so. It's like she's trying to fuck my clavicle. "Ow!" I mouth to the air. I want this to stop but I am too embarrassed to say anything because I don't want to hurt her feelings. The upside down pussy is so much more painful than firing the M-16 back in the desert. The gun had far less kickback.

"Puppies!" I say, but nobody can hear me over the music. "PUPPIES!" Nothing. I'm just going to have to ride this out. After an interminable amount of time, she stops her gyrations and asks me if I want more.

"NO!" I yell.

"Can I have a drink?"

We've ordered a bottle of booze from them for, get this, FOUR HUNDRED DOLLARS! And now Upside Down Pussy wants to drink it? No way.

"Yes," I say, because I am not a man. I am a little bitch.

Stephie has remained wisely sober throughout the evening and, as three o'clock in the morning approaches, she asks if I meant it when I said "puppy." I nod, shell-shocked. Meghan and her friends are continuing to have a great time, getting lap dances, laughing, drinking. But I am a puddle of goo. I need to get back to my kennel.

We stumble into the night: Meghan, Stephie, Josh and Kasey, the strippers, and me. They want to know what's next?

"The Green Door?" someone asks.

I shake my head no. I can't. I just need to go to bed. Kasey wants to go back too, but Josh still wants to drink. Josh convinces him to go out with him and the girls. Stephie, Meghan, and I take a taxi in stunned silence back to the Palms. I feel like I have a yeast infection.

Meghan: From there it just gets later and, well, darker in every sense of the word. I'm sitting with strippers, on strippers, laughing, drinking, and sharing more life stories and bra tips. I'm dazzled by the liveliness of it all, and start to realize this is why I run to Vegas when I'm low—it's the one place I can truly let go and not think about being judged by the people around me. As they say, you really can be whoever you want in Vegas. There are no bloggers in this room, and there are no pundits. No one is calling me a wild child in any other way than as a compliment. I'm an anonymous American, having the kind of good time that goes all the way back to the founding of Vegas in 1905 as a stopping off point for the railroad to refuel and play a few hands of cards.

I end up genuinely liking the girls we are hanging out with. They are warm, friendly, and nonjudgmental, so I'm nonjudgmental in return. They do not seem at all ashamed of their industry and give me a new perspective on exotic dancing. Again, I am not the biggest proponent of the industry, but these girls are really sweet and don't seem to think of themselves as victims in any way.

As evolved and innovative as I have always felt that America is as a country, our cultural attitude towards sex and women remains something that is extremely unhealthy and puritanical. Is it possible to be an exotic dancer in Las Vegas and find the experience and the profession one of empowerment? I do not know and, like I said, I myself remain conflicted about the industry as a whole. All I know is that Daisy, Jessica, and G-Cup Bitch are each fun, respectful, and thoughtful women who share real insight with us into what it's like working in the sex industry. They do not come off as victims and seem to understand that they have a level of control over the people who request their services.

Whatever any pundit or politician wants to say, there is no real way to be a woman in the media and not have your relationship with sex in whatever capacity harshly judged. We seem to be regressing as a culture, or at the very least have plateaued, in that subjects such as birth control and a woman's right to have access to birth control have returned to the forefront of the political landscape. Of all the issues facing America right now, my right to have access to birth control is pretty much the last thing I would have imagined would be a discussion in this election cycle. I mean, isn't this something we as a country already passed during the feminist movement?

On a personal level, my relationship with what sex on the broader landscape means to me is probably the most difficult subject to deal with and talk about publicly. Unfortunately, the problem is that in America, women in the media are still treated as either Madonnas or whores. Men still run the media and are threatened by strong women with strong voices; and the easiest and most predictable way for a lot of men to deal with a strong woman with strong opinions is to automatically call her a slut and immediately call into question her morality and life choices.

Being a woman in America right now is confusing and scary, at least from my perspective. I did not wait to have sex until I got married. I do believe that everyone should have access to birth control, and I still worry about the kind of mixed signals that continue to be sent to young women in this country. Arguably the biggest celebrity on the planet, Kim Kardashian, got her start essentially by releasing a sex tape with Ray J. Right now she is a multimedia mogul, with a hugely popular television show, different types of clothing, perfume, and endorsement brands, and is frequently on the cover of most weekly magazines. So on the one hand, as a culture we celebrate celebrity figures, even if they have compromised themselves to the point where they have a sex tape available for viewing on the Internet, and on the opposite hand, the debate over whether or not women should have access to birth control is still part of the national dialogue. Why is there no middle ground between virgin and sex tape?

In my life I want it all, and I hope that I am allowed to have it all. I want to be a strong, empowered, smart woman who speaks her mind but can also maintain a strong connection to my sexuality and femininity. Unfortunately, in my experience women are not really given room to have both: to be smart and strong in the world of politics and own their sexuality. I hope we get to a point as a country where the repression and attitude towards all things related to sex are not so taboo. I hope we can have more open conversations about sex and the dangers of sex without the attitude that if you are talking about sex in a real way, you are automatically judged and stereotyped. I do not know what the answer is. All I know is that I myself feel like, from time to time, the media has tried to shame me for talking openly about sex and not trying to lie and hide who I am or the kind of life I lead, which at the end of the day really is not so controversial.

The problem with the current attitude in American politics towards women and sex is that it is not a subject that has really evolved much. Being gay is still considered a liability to many people in and out of politics, which is why so many politicians stay closeted. How many times have we been faced with the hypocrisy of egregious political sex scandals, which more often than not involved people who rallied the hardest for a return to moral values in this country? Times are changing, and this generation has an entirely new accessibility to the Internet and sex; as a result, we have to stop turning the other way and acting like this is still the 1960s. I always try to strive for balance in my life. I want America to have a healthy yet realistic relationship with sex. I want women in this country to have the opportunity to be three-dimensional human beings. I want women to be accepted as smart, powerful, intelligent, and in tune with their sexuality without automatically being labeled "sluts" for having those qualities. I want there to be more middle ground, instead of just being put into one extreme category or another. As Michael and I continue to spend an evening delving into the sex industry in Vegas, it continues to bring up weird feelings for me. Getting lap dances and exploring strip clubs with Michael serves as an easy way to reflect on America's attitude towards sex. I mean, would it be necessary for strip clubs to even exist if there were less rampant repression in this country?

Michael: Here's my thing about sex: you should have it when you want it, how you want it, and with whomever you want it. Our bodies are our own to do with what we like, and if you like hanging out with strippers, great. If you like being with dudes, great. If you like being in a situation where there are two ladies and you, and then there's another lady in a Wonder Woman costume eating ice cream out of a carton but not letting you have any because you've been a baaaad boy, but then she puts caramel all over your tummy and all three ladies lick it off while you watch, well that's fine too. In fact, that's more than fine. That's awesome.

Now that I'm a father, maybe I'm supposed to be more censorious about sex. But I can't be. Because it's not how I feel. No, I don't want my son and daughter to have sex too early in their lives, but nor am I going to be the one who determines when is the right time for them to start. I was fifteen when I lost my virginity. Writing this as a forty-year-old man, I think about how young that seems to me now. I think about how worried I would be for my own kids if I knew they were sexually active at that age. But here's the thing: I don't regret it.

My girlfriend and I had already been together for over a year when we finally decided to take each other's virginity. We discussed the matter for months before doing it. Honestly, if I'd given my studies as much care and consideration as I gave to the appropriate time to start having sex, I would have been a straight-A student. The most important feature of our decision was also the simplest: we were in love.

There are adults who question teenage love, but I remember the intensity of my feelings for her, and I do not know any other word to express how I felt. We were careful, we were informed, and we made, for us, the right decision. Twenty-five years later, we're still friends.

That's all I ask from my children; that they first have love before they first have sex. As they mature, their sexual lives will probably expand to include people they do not love. That's okay. Human beings are sexual creatures, and I want them to know the act of sex as one facet of their lives as sexual beings. Sex should never be used to repress or punish or manipulate. It is a gift you give to somebody. Sometimes it is a small gift and sometimes large, but it is always a gift.

But sex is also a gift you take. I want my children to know that accepting a gift requires more responsibility than giving one. Giving is easily forgotten, but when we take, we carry a tiny bit of the giver with us. Hence: crabs.

Who we love is less important to me than *that* we love. I hope they feel comfortable enough with their bodies that they are able to talk about sex with their partners, that they are brave enough to know who they are sexually, and to never be ashamed of themselves for what they want.

Sex is powerful, physically and emotionally. When young people don't know how to handle its power, they are more likely to make mistakes. When we make sexual mistakes as young people, we tend to make them again and again as adults. When my kids decide to have sex, I want them to be well informed, safe, and ready.

I hate that sex is so politicized. It maddens me when politicians try to insert their own values into my bedroom (or the back of my sweet custom van). We are a nation founded on liberty, so let us agree that our orifices are our own, into which we should have the liberty to insert whatever we like. In fact, one of my favorite love-making songs is Ray Charles's version of "America the Beautiful." Nothing gets me going like the image of all those fruited plains.

Meghan: I think back on how mad I got when then-candidate Obama publicly dissed Las Vegas at a town hall in New Hampshire, saying, "You don't go buying a boat when you can barely pay your mortgage. You don't blow a bunch of cash on Vegas when you're trying to save for college. You prioritize. You make tough choices." President Obama's comments received a lot of backlash from the city of Las Vegas, which had already been one of the hardest hit by the sagging economy. The city has built a reputation as America's playground, and though I'm not bringing a kid here anytime soon, it's only because I don't plan on having any. One of the most amazing sights here these days is families on vacation. Many people don't even enter a casino while they're here; instead they come to shop at stores they can't find in the Midwest, and eat at big city restaurants while still feeling like they're in a pretty small town. Add to that the lure for new business being led by Zappos, and you begin to understand how terribly wrong President Obama was to sling shame in this direction.

I was among many voices that came out publicly defending the city. Americans need to take breaks, and no other city provides the benefits and deals that Las Vegas does. Ever since that incident I feel an even larger responsibility to promote the city, and to defend any of us who find a void filled by the entertainment here. And hell yeah, I'm having a good old time tonight, but Vegas doesn't exist just as an excuse to party. The city is a symbol of many things that are great about America: innovation, impulsiveness, the American Dream of hitting it big, our gambling nature, and that we are a country that would build an entire city based simply on the notion that what happens here promises to stay here. I mean, come on, President Obama, "Viva, etc."

Salt Lake City, Utah

The X-Men

Meghan: I always hate leaving Las Vegas, or worse, waking up to leave Las Vegas very early in the morning. As beautiful as the Strip is at night—all lit up, sparkly and seductive in its excess—the city looks depressingly barren and naked in the sunlight. Without all of the neon lights to highlight the architecture of the casinos, it seems monotone and bland, like all the glitter of the showgirls and tinkling of ice cubes have gone to sleep for a well-earned twelve hours. There's a reason why I usually do my gambling in the daytime, when I have a clear enough head to walk away from the table up a few. The city doesn't really come out to play until the sun goes down.

Our flight to Salt Lake City leaves at eight, and after two hours of sleep it is only by the grace of God that I'm able to leave my hotel room and make it downstairs to meet Stephie and Michael. My pimp suite ended up crammed with Josh and Kasey, due to a glitch in their own reservation. With all the suitcases and rollaways scattered around the room, packing and winding my way out the door is no small feat.

I drag myself, hung over and makeupless, into the lobby a few minutes late, and Michael's already there, tapping one Croc on the marble. I feel guilty and embarrassed for some reason, an emotion completely alien to my relationship with Las Vegas.

He asks me from behind his sunglasses, "How late did you stay out?" At almost six feet, Michael towers over my five-foot-two frame, which makes me feel like I'm back in high school and my parents are asking me where I spent the night.

"Somewhere around four-thirty, I guess," I say sheepishly.

"I stayed up all night playing poker, so neither of us got any sleep," he says with a commiserating laugh.

It should make me feel better, but as we get in the taxi for the Las Vegas airport, I am nauseous and uncomfortable. I'm thankful that Stephie's in the car. Michael's idea of including her on the road as our tour manager and guide is my hangover's saving grace: she is the perfect buffer between the two of us. Even so, I feel a looming sense of "what have I gotten myself into?" yet again. The trip is really about to start and I no longer will have my own Stephie in my corner. No more cabin. No more hometown. No more Jimmy. No more Kasey and Josh.

To say it feels strange to get into a taxi, leaving Las Vegas after spending a night together exploring strip clubs, the world of exotic dancing, and buying each other lap dances is an understatement. It's like everything is going backwards. Michael and I are experiencing things together that normally only close friends would do, but the ugly truth is that we don't know each other at all. Usually when I meet someone I either love them instantly and we are bonded for life, or I feel more cautious and we end up just acquaintances. The thing with Michael is I still have a difficult time gauging how he is feeling or what he likes. I can't believe that after watching a bunch of women dance naked together, we could still feel so darn awkward with one another, and this worries me.

Michael: The next morning we meet outside the Palms at eight o'clock for our flight to Salt Lake City. Meghan comes downstairs in sunglasses. She does not meet my gaze.

"How'd it go last night?" I ask her.

"Fine," she says in a voice pitched a little too high.

"Did you get any sleep?"

She shrugs. She didn't. She's embarrassed.

"Did you?" she asks.

"Yeah," I say, but I'm embarrassed too, because after I dropped off Stephie in the lobby, I played poker all night, trading chips with obnoxious tourists until dawn. I am exhausted. There's a quiet moment when neither of us says anything. We just stand out in the sun trying to blink ourselves awake.

After a few moments of silence, Meghan asks, "Are you having fun?"

"Yes," I say. "Are you?"

"Yes."

"Are you sure?"

"Yes," I say. "You?"

"I'm having a great time."

Each of us is trying to convince the other that we are having a good and/or great time. The whole trip is starting to feel like a first date, a really odd, really long first date. I'm not saying it's a *bad* first date, but it's got that kind of charged atmosphere where each person is hoping to make a good first impression even if they're not necessarily interested in seeing each other ever again. The problem is that our first date is going to be a month long.

A few hours later, we arrive in Salt Lake City just as Brigham Young and his band of followers did 160-something years ago: exhausted, bedraggled, and filthy. The difference is that, unlike the early Mormon settlers, we are arriving after a night at a nasty-ass strip club.

The thing about Salt Lake City, which makes it different from every other major American city, is that it's still pretty much a theocracy. America has had its share of religious communities, but Salt Lake City is the only one that was founded by a prophet, flourished, and still retains its theocratic roots. This is Mormon country. And Mormons make me nervous.

If you've ever seen the *X-Men* movies, you know they're about a group of mutants who are the next wave of human evolution. They've got special powers, and if left unchecked they will eventually wipe out humanity as we know it. That's how I feel about Mormons. They just seem to be a slightly *superior* breed of human: they seem taller and more bright-eyed. Mormon kids have straight teeth. The women are all pretty. They are a wholesome, better breed of people. Never mind that Mormons wear more than their fair share of Dockers. Never mind that Utahans consume more porn than anybody else: that just speaks to their superhuman testosterone levels. Mormons are taking over. It's the fastest-growing religion in America, and now they are even running for president. Who knows? By the time this book comes out, one of them might actually *be* the Republican nominee. Salt Lake City is Mormon Mecca, spiritual and administrative home of the Church of Jesus Christ of Latter-day Saints. SLC is LDS, and being there can make you feel like you are on LSD.

Meghan: We land in Salt Lake City and drag our hot mess of a trio to rent a car and go explore the land that Joseph Smith built. When we are standing in the rent-a-car line there is a group of little boys clustered around with their mother, all of them dressed identically. They have matching blond bowl-haircuts and matching blue eyes. They look like any and all idyllic versions of small all-American little boys, except maybe all-American little boys from the fifties, given that their outfits are some spotless, tucked-in version of light-blue shorts and button-down shirts. Their hair perfectly gelled in a sort of Beaver Cleaver coif. If Norman Rockwell had married Maria von Trapp, these would be their kids.

Michael whispers in my ear, "I'm betting they're Mormon."

"I know," I say. "Why do they dress their kids like that?"

Just to be clear, I have no problem with Mormons, with neither their religion nor their culture. In fact, every Mormon I have ever encountered has been nothing but kind, if a little on the quiet side. I support Mitt Romney's run for president and think he has a really good shot at winning the whole thing. It is fascinating that we could possibly elect our first Mormon president before we have elected a woman.

Mormonism has of late been hitting the mainstream pop culture. The Broadway play *Book of Mormon* is a huge, huge success, both critically and commercially. In addition to Romney, fellow Mormon John Huntsman made a primary bid for the Republican nomination. *Time* and *Newsweek* magazines have both run features on what it means to have Mormons running major corporations and possibly even the free world. It's a religion I've been around my entire life, representing an estimated 5.8 percent of Arizona's population. Congressman Jeff Flake, who is currently running for the Senate to fill Jon Kyle's old seat, is highly respected—and a Mormon.

I was amused to learn that long before the railroad tycoons settled Las Vegas, a small band of Mormon missionaries set up an outpost in a small adobe fort near a spring-fed creek. The mission failed and they returned to Salt Lake City. The juxtaposition now for us going from Las Vegas to Salt Lake city is purposeful, with the intention of going from one extreme of American life to another and, depending on your perspective, going from a place of good to bad, or bad to good.

Michael: One of the games I have always enjoyed playing when visiting SLC is "spot the Mormon." It's easy. You just look for anybody who looks happy. I can't explain it. Maybe it's the lack of alcohol. Maybe it's just that structure makes people happy. Maybe, ironically, in a country that prides itself on being the freest in the world, strict guidelines actually make people happier. Mormons have a lot of rules. No caffeine, no alcohol, no premarital sex, have lots of babies once you do get married, work hard, be self-sufficient. These are all pretty good rules, and maybe if you are able to live by them you can be happy. Of course, people are still people and a common joke about Mormons is, "How do you keep a Mormon from drinking all your beer? Invite another Mormon."

I'm also told there is a higher percentage of interest in breast augmentation surgery here than anywhere else, which stumps me until I find out that the state also leads the country in births per mother. The theory goes that women here have more children at younger ages, and ultimately wear out their milk factories. Who wouldn't want a little lift? What's more curious is that the general plastic surgery rate is also higher here than elsewhere in the country, which makes me wonder what other body parts are being improved upon and why. As my new Vegas buddy Kasey says, "Repression breeds obsession."

Of course, people in Salt Lake City want to emphasize to visitors that their town is about more than Mormonism, but I personally don't care about their jazz festivals and hiking trails and whatever else they've got. When I go to Salt Lake City, I have only one destination in mind: "Show me the Mormons."

Meghan: The entire purpose of visiting Salt Lake City is to explore further the Church of Jesus Christ of Latter-day Saints. Although I have exposure and knowledge of the church and Mormonism, both Michael and I want to know more: why Mormonism seems to be such a point of fascination in the media, and to get a better insight into why Mormonism is currently the fastest-growing religion in America.

As I look around the rental place and see so many shiny, happy faces, I start to wonder if maybe this is the religion I'm missing. Maybe this is my church. I have had such a tumultuous relationship with organized religion that I refer to myself as a "liberal Christian," a term I stole from the wonderful Kristin Chenoweth. In general, however, I am conflicted about many religious concepts. Much like my politics, there is a lot of room for gray. I enjoy going to church and have found much comfort in it. I pray every day, but I believe that all of us are praying to the same divine force—the God that created us, looks over us, and protects us.

I don't believe that there is a right God and a wrong God, that one religion's image of God is better than another. The biggest conflict I have had with my childhood church is how it approaches the issue of homosexuality. I believe people are born gay, and I don't accept that God makes mistakes. I also don't understand where the hate comes from when all versions of God and Christ say that we need to love one another and not spread hate. Because of my church's position, I am constantly feeling like I'm missing out on something by not having one specific religion to join and claim entirely as my own. Who knows, maybe on this trip I will find out that Brigham Young is the man who will bring complete and total enlightenment to me. At this point, I am open to anything. Maybe I will want to convert to Mormonism by the time we leave Salt Lake City. I mean, it's not out of the question, and the thought crosses my mind . . . but the thought also crosses my mind that my behavior the night before probably automatically precludes me from being allowed into the Mormon church.

Michael is an atheist. I don't understand atheism, and this core difference between us strikes me as one of the most profound. I don't understand not having some kind of faith in something or believing in some form of God. The absence of a higher power of *some* kind, or there being some sort of divine plan just doesn't make sense. Really, nothing comes after this? And there was nothing before this? I refuse to believe it, and I find atheists arrogant. Arrogant and simpleminded. It's one of the few deal breakers when it comes to the men I will date. No atheists. No atheists and no vegans. I'm still a red state girl at heart and I like my men to eat red meat and love God. Faith is such a huge part of my life that it is hard for me to conceive of what it's like for someone to get out of bed every morning and not have faith in their life.

I really didn't think I could connect with an atheist until I met Michael. My closest friends and the people who have had the most intense impact on my life all have the common denominator of a strong sense of faith in some form of a higher power. Michael believes in nothing. He doesn't believe in God, he doesn't believe in an afterlife. I don't understand this. I don't understand how a husband and father of two can believe in nothing. Michael is so full of life in so many different ways, I am perplexed and even borderline angered that he finds faith in nothing. It makes me sad for him and I've already tried to convert him to *something,* or as I jokingly said, "Turn him into a believer."

Michael has his own reasons for not believing in a higher power, but all of his reasons only make me sadder. I always assumed atheism would come with some kind of emptiness or loneliness in an individual, but Michael doesn't display any of that, so maybe I am wrong, but for the rest of Michael's life I am going to continue trying to pull him over to my side and make him a believer. One of the many things he will have to deal with about me until he dies and goes to heaven.

Michael: Meghan does not seem to understand my feelings about religion. Yes, I'm an atheist. No, I do not believe in an afterlife. But atheism is not the same thing as nihilism. Nor is atheism (at least my version of atheism) a lack of spirituality.

My belief system basically boils down to this: I believe the world is more mysterious than we know and maybe more mysterious than we ever *can* know. Answers reveal questions that reveal answers, forever, like an endless game of *Jeopardy*. Our search for meaning is what defines us as human beings. To me, that search is our spirituality. Maybe the thing we seek is what some people call God.

I am not opposed to religion. Far from it. I'm for anything that gives people peace. That's why I am also for hot tubs and compact discs of whale songs. Anything that soothes the soul is fine by me.

Where I get upset is when people presume to tell me how to live my life based on their religious beliefs. I don't care what you worship or how you worship. Jesus, Vishnu, Satan: it's all the same to me. But please don't shove it in my face. You keep your gods in your backyard and I'll keep my lack of God in mine; that way we can all go to Applebee's together without a problem.

Which doesn't mean I'm not interested in religion. I am. I love to learn about people's faiths, which is what brought us to Salt Lake City in the first place. Of course, we're only staying for the day because belief systems are fascinating, yes, but only in small doses. We've got to use our time here wisely.

First stop is the most popular tourist destination in Salt Lake City, Temple Square, home to the Church of Jesus Christ of Latter-day Saints. It's exactly what it claims to be: a huge square in the middle of town, where they've built an enormous temple. I've seen plenty of churches, cathedrals, and synagogues in my day, but they all shrink in front of this granite monolith. I'm excited to go to the temple and get a better sense of what makes Mormonism a compelling religion. Before that, though, we've got to get something to eat.

We try to zero in on a restaurant near the temple, but nothing sounds good. Everything is "Eat at Brigham Young's House!" "Eat What Brigham Young Ate!" "The Joseph Smith Burger!" Instead of tucking into a "Coca-Cola Pork Loin," surely created by one of Brigham Young's fifty-five wives (notwithstanding the tiny detail that Coke wasn't invented until eleven years after Young's death), we end up at some bagel shop right across from Temple Square.

Right away, it's obvious that the clientele here is not typical LDS. For one thing, the guy at the counter has tattoos and those big ethnic earrings that make it look like you stuck a donut in your earlobe. He's some sort of punk rocker, I guess, which seems out of place for the area. The other workers at the shop all have a similar vibe. Salt Lake City basically has two looks: door-to-door salesman or homeless guy. These guys aren't selling encyclopedias. After Meghan and I order our sandwiches, Stephie hangs out to wait for her order. She gets to talking with the counter guy and mentions that we're writing a book about politics.

"You want to meet some anarchists?" he asks.

"Are there a lot of anarchists in Salt Lake City?"

"You're talking to one."

He asks Stephie if we want to hang out with his anarchist posse. I nod hell yes! I've never met an actual anarchist, let alone in America's most religious city. This is great news. We'll tour the temple, have dinner with our hosts, and then hook up with the anarchists for a wild night of Molotov cocktail–making and nihilist theory. Perfect!

"Great," he says. His name is Omar. He instructs us to meet him back at four when his shift ends.

I suppose I shouldn't be surprised that of all the places to run into an anarchist, we happen to meet one in America's most religious city. Anarchy, or at least the desire for anarchy, is the natural response to feeling stifled and rule bound. The more rules a society has, the fewer rules its citizenry wants. (*See under:* Tahrir Square.) Anarchy is just the political expression of that feeling. Of course, *actual* anarchy can't exist because a lack of law would only allow the strongest and most brutal to take over, thus creating even more totalitarianism. They say Somalia is as close to anarchy as the world has at the moment, and I don't see a lot of young Omars boarding planes for Mogadishu. Even so, it'll be cool to hang out with a bunch of anarchists for the night to see what they actually do. If we don't light some things on fire and steal some cars, I'm going to be very disappointed.

Meghan: The area surrounding the Mormon temple is a difficult thing to describe. The only other place I have seen such meticulous grooming of plants and flowers is the White House. The square is teeming with different flowers, plants, and a small, raised marble stream that filters around the entire surrounding areas. It's gorgeous. Stunning even. Tranquil, beautiful, calm, serene. Everything you would hope for and imagine for a religious setting. Michael and I look like black flies on a white wedding cake. First of all, we are disheveled from our taxis, planes, and cars, not to mention dragging from our mutual lack of sleep. I am in leggings, long black top, and a denim jacket. Michael . . . well, I think you know by now exactly what Michael is wearing. I'm starting to think that he's got ten pairs of identical linen pants in his suitcase. At least it's what I *want* to think. With our messy hair and large, dark sunglasses we stand out. I wish I had stopped to put on a nice dress and do my hair before we visited the temple.

There are small crowds of people walking around, talking, visiting, and taking pictures. One man who looks to be the leader of a small church group, comes up to Michael and asks him why he looks familiar. The man is dressed in a crisp button-down shirt, nice slacks, polished shoes, and wears his hair slicked straight back.

Michael gets very uncomfortable if you approach his celebrity in this way. Here's a tip for all you Michael Ian Black fans out there: If you are out on the street and you recognize Michael, if you do not also recognize his work, do not approach him. If you recognize him, talk about his appearances on Comedy Central, *The State*, or *Stella*. Do not talk about his work on VH1 or *Ed*. Michael could never be a successful politician; he is incapable of the smile and nod.

This is how the back and forth goes at the Mormon temple with the nice Mormon man:

Nice-looking Mormon man: "You look familiar."

Michael: "I don't know, I'm an actor and a comedian."

Nice-looking Mormon man: "Where would I have seen you?"

Michael: "I've had a few shows on Comedy Central."

Nice-looking Mormon man: "No, that's not it."

Michael: "I dunno, I'm an actor and a comedian."

I can't take it anymore, so I barge into the conversation. "Sir, you've seen him on the show *Ed*."

"Yesssss, of course. That's it!!!" The nice-looking Mormon man practically high-fives me. "My wife and I looove that show. Watched it every week."

Michael and the nice-looking Mormon man proceed to have a conversation about *Ed*, why we are visiting the Mormon temple, and why the nice-looking Mormon man is also visiting the Mormon temple with his group of students and followers that day. Michael looks like he would rather be eating a pile of worms. I get it: being recognized but not "recognized" is awkward. I'm just trying not to burst into uncomfortable laughter at Michael being recognized in the shadow of this huge temple, by an *Ed*-loving Mormon. Michael clearly wants my help getting out of this endless conversation, but instead I just stand there and nod along with the nice-looking Mormon man's monologue. Maybe if Michael had been more forthcoming I'd be more sympathetic, but he's getting pretty much exactly what he deserves. Red America loves *Ed*. Michael should be proud!

Michael: The Mormon temple anchors the ten-acre site, but there are a bunch of other related buildings, including two visitors' centers and the tabernacle, which sits like a foil-topped Mormon

Superdome behind the temple. Temple Square is a huge tourist destination, drawing millions of people every year. I'm not exactly sure why they come, because there's not much to do. No rides, for example. No deep-fried Twinkie booth. Just flowers and quiet water features and cheerful-looking people strolling around taking pictures of stuff.

It's lovely, but weird. Like Canada. Everything is familiar but just off enough that I feel out of place.

Meghan also says she feels uncomfortable.

"Why?" I ask.

"I don't know," she says. "It just doesn't feel spiritual to me at all."

I know what she means. There's nothing mysterious about the place, nothing grand, nothing that stirs the soul. As holy as the place is to the LDS community, to me it feels less like a religious site and more like an upscale conference center: a Holy Land as designed by the Ramada Corporation. Maybe that's why Mormonism is so popular in America right now. Americans love their corporations. What better, then, than a corporatized religion? I mean, has there ever been a better representation of both Mormonism and corporatism than Mitt Romney? He doesn't just come across as a guy who drinks milk; he comes across as a guy who *is* milk. Skim.

Meghan: Much to our disappointment, the temple is closed for renovations. We sit down and just people watch. There's a really cute couple who look to be about sixteen taking wedding pictures. The girl's wearing a wedding dress that is so modest her grandmother could have worn it. They play with different poses, hugging, standing up on a ledge to get a better shot of the temple, and pecking kissing.

I start daydreaming about what my life would be like if I had been raised Mormon. I'd probably be married by now—in these parts, I am definitely an old maid. To prove my point, along comes a grandmother who can't be more than fifty, with a gaggle of grandchildren. The way their outfits match gets me to thinking that the stores must sell these things in groups at a discount, a kind of Mormon Garanimals.

"Now, smile, this is for your dad's race," Grandma says and my ears perk up. These are a politician's kids—I can feel it in my DNA—and this must be the day they're taking pictures for what I assume is their father's campaign. I prod Stephie to go ask what their father is running for. Grandma jumps back a little when Stephie approaches, then seems to dismiss her. I look down at my clothes, at Michael's, at Stephie's, and I realize that we are dressed like people who shop in a non-Mormon store. We don't all match. It's one of those moments when I want to say something to prove my Red State bone fides, but my politicking radar is receiving the message loud and clear: We Don't Talk to Strangers.

Michael: Meghan and I watch as the grandparents try to blow Stephie off, and the kids goof off in their button-downs, narrowly missing pushing one another into the fountain. One of them, about six years old, keeps frowning and squirming. He clearly doesn't want to be there.

"That's the gay one," I joke to Meghan.

"Come on, this is for Daddy's campaign poster," Grandma says to the kids as she turns her back to Stephie, and snaps off a photo. Meghan sends Nermal over to pry some information out of these people. Sweet, unthreatening Nermal—the perfect spy.

"Excuse me," she says, "I couldn't help overhearing that your son is running a political campaign. Is that right?" I can tell she's about to explain that we're writing a political book, but the grandfather cuts her off.

"No."

No? Didn't Grandma just say this is for daddy's campaign poster?

"Yes," says Grandma. "Our son is running for the Nevada state legislature."

"Oh," says Grandpa somewhat begrudgingly. "Yeah."

Why did he just lie to Nermal? Nobody lies to Nermal! Stephie starts to ask some questions but the grandparents deflect them all. For whatever reason, they don't want to talk about their son the maybe-politician. Maybe they think we're press or something. Maybe we are.

They are polite but firm. They don't want to talk, and after a couple more sentences, they gather the children and stroll away. I swear the six-year-old looks at us with pleading eyes as they walk through aisles of perfectly manicured flowers. *Take me with you,* his eyes seem to say.

LDS are a guarded people, which I understand. Their early history is about persecution. In fact, the reason they are in Utah at all is because they were chased across the country by people who didn't want a bunch of religious nuts settling in their hometowns, which is weird considering our country was founded by a bunch of religious nuts. The religion's founder, Joseph Smith, was murdered in 1844 by some locals who didn't want this newfangled religion setting up shop in their hometown of Nauvoo, Illinois.

We learn this after going to one of the square's two visitors' centers. When we walk in, we are greeted by two young missionaries in knee-length skirts and button-down shirts. One is from Germany, the other from South Korea. Each wears her home country's flag under her name tag, just like hotel clerks do at some of your more international Ramadas. They ask if we'd like to take a tour. You bet we would. The Korean girl goes off to find a tour guide for us. I ask the German girl about her missionary work.

"We come for eighteen months," she says.

"Do you get to pick where you go?"

"No."

"Are you disappointed that you ended up in Salt Lake City?"

She hesitates. "I love Asia," she says diplomatically.

I want to hear her talk smack about Salt Lake City but she is a well-trained missionary and, despite my prodding, does not bite. The most disparaging thing she will say about Salt Lake City is, "It's slow."

Meghan: A tour seems like the most logical next step. Since the Mormons can obviously sense that we are here to observe, and not to worship, we might as well start acting like tourists. We are assigned two very young girls who are on a mission. Clearly any woman who is married is at home having babies, so they need to populate the inner temple with super-fresh single girls.

Sister Hicks and Sister Other-Mormon-Girl are wearing long blue skirts and blouses. They are both cute, clean-cut looking, and carrying Bibles. One of them has dark curly hair and is from California; the other has long, straight dark hair and is from Mexico. Otherwise they are spiritually identical in their aura of calm and striking self-possession.

The visitors' center is basically a medium-sized convention center dedicated to describing and explaining the Mormon faith. There are different sculptures, dioramas and exhibits set up to portray the entire history of Mormonism. We go through the center via a sort of maze that guides us through each chapter of the history of Mormonism. It's kind of like a religious Epcot Center. . . .

I once heard a friend of mine, who is also a famous comedian, describe a visit to Salt Lake City. He said that being around Mormons was like going to Japan and being ensconced in Japanese culture. "Everyone is very nice, well-dressed, and friendly, but you feel a little out of place." As I stand here on our tour in Temple Square with our very cute, sweet, friendly, clean-cut guides, I am overcome with extreme self-consciousness that to a lot of people here at Temple Square, to a lot of people in my own religion that I was raised in, and hell even to a lot of people in America, I am a heathen sinner. I am who these people think are what's wrong with the world. In their eyes, I will more than likely end up burning in the fiery damnation of hell, or in the infinite abyss, or whatever. The gist is that I am not going to the good place, given the kind of life I am leading: I am going to the really bad one for all of eternity.

Granted, I am standing at the center of Mormon faith, among individuals who have dedicated themselves to living a pious life led by Joseph Smith. I am not dressed appropriately and am still feeling the left-over parts of a hangover and, yes, coming off of a bender with strippers in Vegas, but I admit that as I listen to the sisters and go through the tour, I feel strange and almost ashamed of myself— almost. I want to make clear that it's not as if our guides have any sort of pious attitude, in fact they are surprisingly open to our prodding about their lives and questions as to why Mormonism is the right religion for them. I assume they are used to being given the third degree by curious visitors about their faith.

The thing about the Mormon faith—and really any religion that relies on strict rules and doctrines—is that on a very basic level, I don't really understand how they can do it. I do not understand how these sisters have the type of discipline to lead the style of lives they lead. It's kind of like the way I sometimes feel in a room full of extremely conservative Republicans. I don't understand what it's like to believe that one way, one thing, one person has all of the answers and that if you don't abide to those strict rules and doctrines, you are, well, burning in hell—or considered a bad Republican.

I periodically have moments when I wonder if my life would be easier or different if I could just calm down and stop being so rebellious and impulsive. My natural instinct about life has always been one of discovery and questioning. I have a moment in that visitors center, standing next to the Mormon sisters, surrounded by beautiful, clean-cut, Beaver Cleaver family look-a-likes: I am almost envious. It makes me wonder: if you apparently have all the answers figured out, is life is any easier or do you at least know the path to redemption in the afterlife?

Michael: The sisters are unfailingly sincere as they lead us through the visitors' center, kind to the point of insipidness. I don't trust nice people, but I also recognize this as a personal character flaw and not as an indictment of nice people. As pleasant as they are, however, I stay on guard. These are salespeople; I do not want to walk out of this place in magic underwear.

They show us around. Their early history is no different from an episode of *Little House on the Prairie,* except that none of the early Mormons had the star power or sexy hair of Michael Landon. We see lots of department store manikins in pioneer clothes. They show us a stone used to construct the temple. Not interesting. A wagon that transported the stone. Not interesting. A guy cutting stone. Not interesting. Then they explain that Mormons can convert dead people to Mormonism in order to get them into heaven. Interesting.

"Wait," I say. "What?"

"Yes." Sister Hicks explains how they baptize their long-dead relatives who "never had a chance to accept the truth" so that they can enter heaven. "Do you understand?" she asks.

"Not really," I say.

There's a short video they play that explains it for me. Basically, Mormons believe nobody can enter heaven without being baptized in the faith, but because the religion is so young, it means all of their relatives born before 1844 are currently suffering in hell. To rectify this situation, they've come up with a scheme where they can baptize people after they've already died, the way you might postdate a check.

"You might have heard that Mormons are very into genealogy. This is why," Sister Hicks tells us without further commentary or any hint of skepticism.

I *had* heard that. Now that she mentions it, I'd also heard Mormons were going through the rolls of the dead killed in the Holocaust and baptizing the victims. When word of this got out, it was a *wee* bit controversial. I guess various Jewish groups didn't appreciate those killed solely because of their religion having that religion changed without consultation. The Mormons didn't see anything bad about it; they just want to make sure that all spirits have a shot at their celestial reward. There have even been rumors that they've posthumously baptized the likes of Anne Frank and President Obama's mother. After the shit hit the fan, the church agreed to keep their baptizing within their own genealogical fountain. They really get enough bad PR without digging up the graveyard for more.

Apparently, Mormons really like Jews, something I'd never known before. I just assumed they disliked them because it seems like that's kind of the norm but, no, the Mormons are into Jews because they co-identify, believing their fold to be one of the lost tribes of Israel. You know, the lost tribe that left Israel and sailed to America in 600 BC. Yes, America. If you haven't heard about any archaeological evidence about such a lost tribe, it's because there isn't any.

Meghan: Mormonism is one of the fastest-growing religions in America. Whatever criticism is made concerning some of the more atypical Mormon traditions, radical undertones, and beliefs, no one can suggest that this religion isn't hitting some kind of chord with Americans. If it's anything beyond just feeling good about God, it might have something to do with what the faith offers as a culture.

The appearance of being an extremely conservative throwback to a time when America was different seems to be the defining characteristic of the Mormon lifestyle, one that appeals mightily in a world where everything can feel a little too fast and somewhat scantily clad. Maybe American culture has gotten to the point where we are so overstimulated, sent so many sexualized messages from the media, and desensitized in our reaction to overtly bad behavior, that in comparison Mormonism can appeal as something that is safe.

Probably one of the biggest Mormon names out there is Glenn Beck, and he is nothing—and I mean nothing—if not obsessed with the idea of a better time in America, and bringing it "back to that time." It's interesting that Beck converted to Mormonism after a long battle with drugs and alcohol. The religion obviously gave him some answer to his problems. On the other hand is Stephanie Meyer—a good ol' Arizona Mormon—who has managed to completely desexualize vampires though her *Twilight* series. Perhaps you've heard of it. She claims that she's not pushing her faith's adherence to chastity, but at the same time you have to wonder if that's not exactly what teenage girls and their moms find so appealing about Bella Swan.

As the tour ends, I'm left with an oddly nostalgic feeling about Mormonism, as though I've just left my grandmother's house, or closed the cover of a historical novel. I liked the tour, I liked the experience, I felt underdressed. Mormons seem like shiny, happy people and it seems like a shiny, happy faith. I respect their religion and what they believe in; I just don't think it's gonna be the one for me. It is just a bit too organized and structured, but I will hold out that I can't completely rule it out until I go to the temple and sit through a service, because I don't feel like God was talking to me anywhere I've been. I don't feel overly inspired at Temple Square. My bouts of extreme faith and inspiration have hit me at different times in my life, but I felt more connected visiting temples in Bangkok than I do in Salt Lake City. My feeling towards God and faith is that it should be something overwhelming and visceral.

Sometimes when I go home to Phoenix and I can't sleep, I will get up and go to the roof of my parents' building and watch the sun come up over the desert. Watching the sunrise in Arizona is what I imagine having God whisper in your ear must feel like. That is the feeling I would need to get at Temple Square for me to connect with the temple.

I find God in weird places. I find him in moments that make me feel like the world is so spectacular and beautiful, it's absolutely overwhelming. Anyone who has a strong sense of spirituality in their life knows what I mean. God for me is found everywhere; in my family, in the desert, in first kisses, in smiles, in laughter, in friendship, in cheesecake, in red wine, and above all else in love. God for me is not something simply found in a church or temple. God as he relates to me is found in everything that makes me feel grateful to be alive. Maybe I will never find that perfect faith, or perfect religion, and I don't know if I will ever be able to simply define it, but for me, God and faith have no borders or limitations.

Michael: I'm not sure why Mormons are all Republicans. Is it just the gay thing? Mormons *really* don't like gay people. We didn't ask about it because there was no point. They don't like gay people almost as much as they used to not like black people. To give you a sense of the LDS's former attitudes about our more melanin-enhanced brothers and sisters, here's a quote from Brigham Young: "You see some classes of the human family that are black, uncouth, uncomely, disagreeable, sad, low in their habits, wild, and seemingly without the blessings of the intelligence that is generally bestowed upon mankind."

Quotes like that don't make them seem like the most racially sensitive religion. Lest you think the early Mormons were just products of their time, consider the fact that until 1978 blacks weren't even allowed to be Mormon priests.

Out of curiosity, I ask Sister Hicks if there are any Democratic Mormons. I associate the LDS community so strongly with the Republican Party that this seems like a good question.

"Oh yes!" she says brightly. "I think one of the other missionaries is a Democrat." Keep in mind there are *hundreds* of missionaries here.

"Which one?" asks Sister Other-Mormon-Girl.

Sister Hicks mentions a name.

"I don't know her," says Sister Other-Mormon-Girl.

Meghan asks the sisters if they are allowed to date while doing their service. No. She asks why there seem to be only female missionaries.

"They used to have boys too, but they were kind of . . ." she trails off.

"Immature," says Sister Other-Mormon-Girl.

Makes sense. The last thing you want is a bunch of horny teenage boys messing up the temple tours. As we finish, Sister Hicks asks if we would like to have somebody visit our homes to continue the conversa—

"No!" I blurt out before the sentence is even out of her mouth. No, this was quite enough, thank you. As pleasant as everybody here at Temple Square has been, I'm just not in the market for a new religion. Especially one that's so *clean*. As filthy and depressing as Vegas is, those feel more like my people: the dispossessed and desperate. I wish it weren't so, but it is. I wish I could be more like all the good-natured people here at Temple Square sitting among the bright flowers eating their box-lunch turkey-and-mayo sandwiches, but it's just not me.

One of the great things about any religion is the certainty it gives you. These Mormons all seem so *certain* about everything. They *know* what they are doing is right, they *know* Joseph Smith was a prophet, they *know* they are going to heaven. I wish I had that kind of certainty in my own spiritual life but I don't and doubt I ever will. I'll just never be one of those people who can decide to believe something and not look back. I wish I could. I wish I could be a Mormon. My wardrobe choices would certainly be a lot simpler. Dockers and polo shirts. Every day.

For eternity.

After we bid the sisters goodbye, we make our way back to the bagel shop to hook up with Omar. We're about fifteen minutes early, so we figure we'll just hang out there and decompress with some highly caffeinated beverages. The Mormons eschew caffeine, so a Mr. Pibb Xtra is just what the atheist ordered.

On our way back over, Meghan keeps talking about how Mormonism left her feeling cold. I'm not sure I really understand why. To me, LDS is no different from any other strain of Christianity. They're all equally weird to me. I get the sense that even though Meghan considers herself a Christian, she is kind of struggling with what she actually believes. To me, that's a good thing. Why are spiritual questions so removed from political discourse, but spiritual certainty is so embraced?

I'm always wary when presidential candidates start talking too much about their faith. Wrapping little baby Jesus in the American flag does a disservice to both. I would prefer that my political leaders practiced their religion however they see fit in private and shut the hell up about it in public. Spirituality has always felt to me as private as sexuality. We don't go waving our wieners all over the place and we shouldn't wave our gods around either.

Meghan: I think anarchists are even stupider than atheists. That being said, the only anarchist I've known was a guy in college who wore dark sweatshirts and guyliner and went around saying that he was an anarchist, and from everything I observed didn't do anything else other than say he was an anarchist. I am almost certain he never acted on his impulses to overthrow the government from our Ivy League dorm. I don't even really understand what it means to be an "anarchist." What does an anarchist do? How do they exercise their anarchist tendencies? Who do they vote for in election cycles? Do they vote? Probably not, because they hate the government. How do you hate the government in America to the point where you think lawlessness is the right answer? Is it weird being an anarchist in the middle of Salt Lake City, Utah? Is it weird being an anarchist across the street from the Mormon temple?

Jackpot. This guy! Omar the Anarchist! Omar the Anarchist had all of a sudden evoked a flood of questions in my brain. I was so glad we met Omar, because he was fascinating. Finally, an anarchist, and in Salt Lake City no less! This will be fantastic. He exchanged numbers with Stephie and we decided to meet up with him when he got off work.

We go back to the deli an hour and a half later to meet Omar the Anarchist. Much to our disappointment, Omar the Anarchist has already left work and hasn't waited for us even though he said he would. For the record, we are only ten minutes late. He and Stephie proceed to have a text conversation that goes like this:

Stephie: Hey Omar, its Stephie, one of the 3 you met at your work. What are you up to tonight? Michael and Meghan, the other 2, are writing a book about politics and America, and talking with an anarchist would be pretty great.

Omar the Anarchist: Well word i would be very down but you kinda caught me at a really shity time i have to move out tomorrow so

Omar the Anarchist: And yea so i kinda wanted to chill here and party so is this the cute one with shades

Stephie: This is the brunette with glasses, so I believe you are referring to Meghan, the very cute blonde. That's too bad— we'd love to talk to you tonight.

Omar the Anarchist: And no sorry i didnt mean her i meant you i just suck at multi tasking and texting they get mixed up but yea i meant glasses so

Omar the Anarchist: Just come party tonight with me

Stephie: Where will that be?

Omar the Anarchist: And yea sorry the blonde is not my type at all ha ha

Omar the Anarchist: My house ha well whats left of it

Stephie: Well I'll see how the guys are feeling later. Thanks ever so for the invite.

Omar the Anarchist: Ha for sure i kinfda wanted to get you more so

Then, six hours later . . .

Omar the Anarchist: Hows your night

The anarchist could meet up with us but doesn't want to get up off his ass to do so. This conversation is probably the best example of why anarchy has never really worked. They apparently cannot organize themselves enough to even explain why they don't want a government, let alone overthrow it. Dictionary.com's definition of anarchy reads: "A theory that regards the absence of all direct or coercive government as a political ideal and that proposes the cooperative and voluntary association of individuals and groups as the principal mode of organized society." Omar pretty much summed up what I would expect from a so-called anarchist in Salt Lake City. I assume he just calls himself an anarchist because it sounds cool and is a way of rebelling against the straightlaced ways of his surroundings.

Michael: I don't know if Meghan is at all insulted that "the blonde" is not his type. Not that Omar is *her* type, but still it's nice to feel pursued even when the pursuer is a dolt. Whatever the reason, she is kind of dour during dinner. This is the first time I've seen Meghan shut down, and it worries me a bit.

She really is a hot mess. One minute, she is the life of the party: tossing twenties at strippers, knocking back shots, whooping and hollering. But the next she can be quiet, demure, and a little sullen. When we walk into the restaurant where we're meeting our hosts, I notice that she immediately clams up. It's one of those *nouveau* American joints where specials are written on chalkboards and liberals come to swirl wine around in long-stemmed glasses. In fact, our hosts are good Dems one and all. We are dining with—stay with me here because this gets a little complicated—Stephie's dad's sister's husband's cousin and the cousin's friends. In other words, I don't know who the hell these people are, but they are gracious hosts and good conversationalists.

Most interesting are the friends: Patrice Arent is a Democratic Utah state legislator and her husband, Dave, is some sort of investment guy who is also former LDS. Patrice is Jewish and I think Dave converted to Judaism when they married. Needless to say, there aren't a lot of Utah Jews, but Patrice's family moved here a century ago, back when it was still rough and tumble and didn't have nearly as many nouveau American wine bars, so she considers herself as much a native as anybody.

There's a lot of small talk about our trip, but Meghan remains strangely subdued. She excuses herself to go to the bathroom and is away for about ten minutes. It occurs to me that, after almost a week together, I am learning for the first time that Meghan McCain is *shy*. Especially, I will learn, around Democrats. When she returns to the table, she gives one-word answers to questions about the trip.

"How's it going so far?"

"Fine."

"Are you learning anything interesting?"

"Yes."

She mumbles and spends a lot of time studying the menu. What happened to the old Meghan? Party Meghan? I miss Meggy Mac, a nickname bestowed upon her by her friends, which she *hates*. This new, nervous-as-a-fawn Meghan is just kind of wigging me out.

Eventually she gets a Bud Light or two into her and relaxes into the conversation a bit, but I am struck by how the tough blond chick I believed myself to be traveling with is a lot more sensitive than I had assumed.

"You okay?" I ask her at one point.

"Fine." She smiles at me, but I find myself worrying about her throughout the meal. Shit: did I just adopt a little sister?

Meghan: During dinner I don't have much to say. Before you jump to any conclusions about Omar the Anarchist, the short answer is that I can be shy. The weirdest part about Michael is the fact that I get the impression he has never been around a woman like me before. I do not know the kind of women he surrounds himself with other than his lovely wife, but he seems perplexed when I start turning into a three-dimensional person.

Stephie's family friends are more than lovely and I have a nice time at dinner. It is awkward for me, however, to meet new people who within the first few minutes of conversation start talking about how in the last election cycle "they were inspired for the first time in their lives to volunteer and get involved in a meaningful way." Listen, everyone is entitled to their opinions and political beliefs. I never understand, however, when people seem to want to go out of their way to tell me how inspired they were by Obama, or how much they hated Sarah Palin, or really anything of that matter.

It's not that I didn't like our hosts; I always just feel less inclined to be conversational when someone opens a new conversation after we meet by talking about how President Obama is the messiah. My last name is McCain, my father is one of the most famous politicians in America, and I should be used to people being insensitive without meaning to be, but a lot of times it just makes me introverted.

Also, I was exhausted and still a little hung over. Like I said, they were perfectly nice people who were extremely welcoming to Michael and me; it just wasn't the most "on" I have been over dinner, which apparently came to Michael as quite a surprise. Lots of things throughout the trip would come as a surprise to Michael. Like the fact that I don't like to leave the house (even to get on an RV) without makeup on. Things like that, that honestly I think are pretty normal for a lot of women, would shock Michael. I freely admit I am not the most low-maintenance woman, but it was like Michael had never met a woman in her twenties who was on television from time to time.

Michael: After dinner, we go to Patrice and Dave's house for some more conversation about Utah politics. Patrice is circumspect when the subject of the Mormon church comes up. She has to work with them in the legislature, after all, and does not want to accidentally say anything that could come back to bite her in the derriere. Dave has no such constraints, and expresses his opinions about church leadership a little more freely than she might like. Being former LDS himself, he's got a lot of opinions.

Patrice is the first politician we meet on the road (Meghan's mom doesn't count because she's not technically a politician), and I have to say I am struck by Patrice's decency and sense of purpose. She is somebody who practices politics because she believes she can make a positive difference in her community. She's not sleazy or condescending or self-important. She just kind of seems like a mom.

I sit out on the porch with Dave listening to him talk about LDS member Glenn Beck and the White Horse Prophecies, which Joseph Smith preached and which state that "the Constitution will be hanging by a thread, and they [elders of the LDS] will be the ones who save it." I ask him what that means. What does it mean to "save the Constitution?" He doesn't have a good answer for me, but it sounds uncomfortably like the X-Men swooping in to save the world.

Meghan is more at ease now, and she joins us out there along with everybody else. We stay up late talking about the things every American—Mormon, Jew, atheist, anarchist—talks about: baseball, music, family, and friends. It's a good night, all of us enjoying the warm air and the big Rocky Mountains off in the distance.

We are up early the next morning to catch a flight to Austin, where we will spend a day with more of Meghan's friends and finally meet up with Cousin John.

"I can't wait," says Meghan. She has been looking forward to meeting Cousin John for weeks now, ever since Stephie interviewed him by phone for the driver job. He's Meghan's cousin's cousin, a former rafting guide from Tennessee who now lives in Aspen, Colorado. None of us has met him in person, but as far as we are concerned, he has three qualifications for the job:

1. He knows how to drive an RV.
2. He once lived in an RV for a summer.
3. He had an orgy with a famous comedian.

I will not name the comedian, but as soon as he tells Stephie this nugget during their phone interview (unprompted, by the way, and certainly not in response to that standard interview question, "Have you ever had an orgy with a famous comedian?"), Stephie responds with the only two-word phrase she can possibly say: "You're hired."

Meghan has been talking about Cousin John ever since Stephie relayed the interview story to her. She is buzzing to meet him. I worry. Cousin John could either be an amazing addition to our little group or an incredible mistake.

Austin, Texas

A Blue Dot

Meghan: I love Texas. I know, it seems like I love it everywhere, which is kind of true. I really love America, especially red states, and I really love everything about Texas. I don't mean this to come off like a cliché; you know, American girl loves America, but it's true. I spent so much time on the road during my father's campaign that I came to fall in love with America and Americans in a big way.

Texas is still very much the Wild West and not a hugely different culture from Arizona, so it's second nature for me to like the independent, God-fearing, freedom-loving stereotypes that abound here. In particular, I love people who "cling to their guns and religion," as President Obama so famously said (and then backtracked from) while campaigning for president. I love unapologetic attitudes, unabashed patriotism, long-neck beers, longhorn beef, big hair, big makeup, giant Ford trucks with THESE COLORS DON'T RUN bumper stickers, Second Amendment rights supporters, and pretty much every Texas stereotype that exists. It's a culture I'm familiar with and understand. I also think it's a culture that is gravely misunderstood and poorly portrayed by many in the media.

Michael hates Texas, and I had suggested going to some cities other than Austin, but because of scheduling issues, it wasn't possible. Also, Michael is much more comfortable in hipster-friendly cities and Austin is one of the best. Don't get me wrong; I love Austin as well, but it isn't exactly representative of the culture within the majority of the state.

Michael: My generosity as an American citizen is probably at its lowest when discussing Texas. I have been known, on occasion, to refer to the entire state as a shithole. Not because I actually believe that, but because Texans are so inordinately proud of being Texans that I sometimes feel the desire—more like a *need,* actually—to do my part to deflate those Texas-sized egos, even if it's just the teeniest bit.

The Lone Star State has an attitude unlike any other in the union because Texans have never really, truly believed themselves to be part of the union at all. In fact, from 1836 to 1845, Texas was actually the Republic of Texas, a freestanding country. Sure they joined the union, but I've always had the feeling that Texans sort of consider themselves to be slumming as Americans. For proof, you don't need to look any further than the Texas state flag. One star, one red stripe, and one white stripe. In other words, it is exactly like the American flag minus the rest of America.

Most state capitals are bores: Sacramento, Albany, Tallahassee. Has anybody ever actually *been* to Harrisburg, Pennsylvania? Not Austin. Austin is a freak show. It is the only state capital I can think of where tattoo artists come to live. And local butchers, organic bakers, and hippie candlestick makers, plus the whole panoply of Texas weirdoes who have no other place to go. It is, as they say, a blue dot in a sea of red.

I can't wait to get there because it will be our first truly "blue" destination. Even Las Vegas, for all its hedonism, is conservative in its way. It is the corporatized vision of decadence, not decadence itself. Austin is the opposite, with its sweet-tea-steeped grassroots weirdness. And after a day of the chipper but dreary Salt Lake City, I am ready for some grunge, grime, and barbecued pork.

Meghan: The morning that we leave Salt Lake City, I start singing "God Blessed Texas" by the band Little Texas on the car ride to the airport. The lyrics to the song cover a lot of Texas-loving ground, to an infectious country-swing backbeat. Possibly my favorite line says, "If you wanna see heaven, brother, here's your chance." Texas is so expansive, so freewheeling, so full of its own greatness, that, yeah, it's definitely a certain kind of heaven.

That's exactly how the majority of Texans feel about their state. The lyrics go on in a sort of line-dance-friendly anthem to all things Texas, amounting to a pride-felt battle cry. Also, it's just a catchy, fun song that I always find myself singing whenever I visit Texas. My little brother Jimmy attends Texas A&M in College Station. When he first got to school, we had a conversation about how he had met some people who felt like Texas should secede from the Union because the rest of America is such a mess. When they drink, instead of "cheers," in some places they say "secede." I don't think anyone really believes that Texas will actually secede from the union, but just the fact that this is a warning of sorts is simultaneously absurd and amazing. This kind of posturing is inherently, fabulously American. It is something that I used to think was just sort of ridiculous patriotism from Texans, but it is easy to understand how people can fall back on ideas that let them feel as though they have options. It's like anything else, just another option to try and make life possibly better or easier.

Michael: We're going to spend the next couple of days with Meghan's buddy who lives in Austin, a film critic turned screenwriter who has promised to show us a good time. His name's Cargill, and I am dismayed to learn that he and Meghan met, of all places, on Twitter. I thought I was her only Twitter friend. I don't know if Cargill is his first name or his last name or just a made-up name that sounds cool. Cargill. It is the kind of name somebody from Austin should have. Hopefully the image lives up to the name.

Cargill does not disappoint. When we descend the escalator to baggage claim at the airport, there he is, bearded and rumpled and gravel voiced. He looks like a younger version of The Dude from *The Big Lebowski*.

"You made it," he rasps when he sees Meghan, who squeals and throws her arms around him. They immediately begin chirping about people I don't know, including his wife, Jessica, who was going to meet us but is feeling a little sick. It's just as well since there's not enough room in Cargill's crummy little beater for the four of us *and* Meghan's luggage.

Meghan is traveling with the heaviest suitcase in the history of heavy suitcases. It is *Flintstones*-heavy and enormous. A good-sized person could live in that suitcase. I've seen smaller Japanese hotel rooms. Before we left, she was bemoaning all the stuff she had to leave behind. I have no idea what she could have possibly left behind because to my eye, she brought *everything*. Everything in the whole world.

We shove ourselves into the car and head to Cargill's. As unlikely as it seems based on his Dude-ish appearance, Cargill is actually a Republican, a "philosophical Republican rather than an ideological Republican," descended from a long line of military men.

"I'm the eldest son of an eldest son of an eldest son going back seven generations," he says, speaking of his family's tradition of service. The fact that he never served seems to weigh on him a bit and he relates a heart-to-heart conversation he had with his father, a twenty-six-year air force veteran, as they drove to the airport one dawn.

"It's like five-thirty in the morning, you know, and I say to him, 'We never talked about this, but I know you're disappointed that I never joined the military.'

"And he said, 'I'm not disappointed that you never joined the military. If we're disappointed in you at all, it's that you never became a stand-up comedian.'"

There would be a lot fewer books written about hard-assed military fathers if more of them were like Cargill's dad.

Meghan: I travel so much I have accumulated friends all over the country. One of my most favorite parts of visiting Austin is getting to spend time with my friends Cargill and Jessica. It's a little embarrassing to admit how many friends I have made over Twitter, but there are quite a few in my life. One of my followers became so adamant that I start following Cargill, that I just had to tweet him. Cargill's real name is Christopher Robert Cargill, but I have never heard anyone else call him anything but Cargill. I started following Cargill on Twitter, and it was only a few days before he started following me, after he saw my appearance on *The Colbert Report*. I guess our friendship was just meant to be.

Cargill is a screenwriter and movie critic for the website Ain't It Cool News, which has a cultlike following of movie nerds. We immediately started tweeting each other about our favorite science fiction movies, and eventually, after finding out that he was happily married to his gorgeous high school sweetheart, I started asking him for dating advice. We are both insomniacs, and I started coming back from bad dates and venting my frustration to him over direct message. He started giving me relationship advice and still, to this day, I solicit it from him. We also bonded over our mutual frustration with the more conservative side of the Republican Party. Like me, Cargill is frustrated with the way many of its philosophies have been hijacked by special interests.

The thing I love most about Cargill is that he really is who he is. He's a film nerd and sci-fi geek who loves his wife, loves Austin, and is also just living the American Dream. I have since become friends with his lovely wife, Jessica, and find her to be equally, if not more, charming. I often joke that if there were ever some huge political scandal in my life—the worst kind of scandal that I could fathom— I would go to Texas and live in Cargill and Jessica's guest room until things blew over. That's the kind of friends I have. I have been lucky in my life to attract genuine friends, even over Twitter.

Michael: Maybe it's the military thing that binds Meghan and Cargill, or maybe it's just the fact that he's a really good time in a nerdy kind of way. He and Jessica just returned from Convergence, a sci-fi convention in Minneapolis. They go every year. I've never really understood the appeal of sci-fi conventions. He says there are panels all day "on everything from your favorite science fiction show to comedy to fantasy literature." And then at night, "They give out alcohol and you just wander from theme party to theme party and it's just getting drunk, having crazy times, and then going to your room, having sex, coming down, getting more drunk, and then you wake up somewhere." Well, I guess when you put it that way, I can maybe understand the appeal.

"Do you dress in costume?" I ask. Keep in mind this is a man in his late thirties.

"Yeah, I usually take a costume every year."

I love this guy.

We go to their home to meet up with Jess. It's a small ranch house, decorated with movie posters and memorabilia everywhere. Jess is an adorable brunette, her voice a little gravelly from whatever small ailment she has. We sit around their living room and shoot the shit.

"Show them your office," says Jess.

Cargill opens a door and we enter Nerd Paradise. There are hundreds, or possibly thousands, of small lead figurines from the role-playing game Warhammer 40000, which I think is like Dungeons & Dragons except it takes place in the future. But it's basically the same thing: a bunch of dudes (and I am going to make a wild assumption here that it's almost all dudes) sitting around rolling dice, smoking pot, and killing Orcs.

Cargill's Warhammer dudes fill every surface area of the office. Inside the closet are even more. He has assembled a tiny army here, thousands of creatures of every conceivable form. It is the dorkiest thing I have ever seen.

If it sounds like I am making fun of this, I am, but only a little. I played D&D as a kid, and my own father was into painting lead figurines. I remember him huddled over a giant magnifying glass with a tiny paintbrush trying to get a wizard's robe the perfect shade of periwinkle. Cargill also has a giant magnifying glass. Seeing it almost makes me tear up with nostalgia.

Meghan: The first time I ever really hung out in Austin was with Cargill and Jessica for an event called Butt-Numb-A-Thon, a twenty-four-hour film festival where the attendees watch consecutive movies hand picked by the "Head Geek," Harry Knowles. Let me tell you, the tickets are hard to get and you have to be invited and approved by Harry, but if you get the chance, go. It was one of the most fun times I have ever had, especially watching movies. My dirty little secret part of myself (actually, there is nothing dirty or little about it) is that underneath it all I am a huge nerd. I love sci-fi and horror movies, video games, everything. I apparently passed the "geek/nerd" test by Cargill when I told him *District 9* was my favorite movie from 2009.

I'm so happy to be in this house of old friends with my new friends that everything starts to feel like it's back in balance. Although I think Michael is hilarious and pretty much feel like I had to pass the Michael Ian Black seminar while preparing to go on the road with him, I'll admit that I don't always get his snarky humor. A few cracks he's made along the way about me being a rich girl and my father being old, I have to assume is just his way of showing weird affection for me as a friend, even though I don't really find personal jabs of this nature to be funny at all. It's probably our biggest obstacle so far, my not really knowing if Michael is joking or being serious. Like most comedians (or at least the few I have known), so much is shielded with humor that I find myself asking Stephie if Michael is laughing at me or with me. But now, here, with Cargill and Jessica, I feel relaxed and safe, as though they'll be able to soak up some of my self-consciousness with their more affable brand of humor.

Michael: There is a certain kind of American who just does not give a shit what the world thinks. They do what they do, and if anybody has a problem with that, they can go take a flying fuck. It feels like a quintessentially American attitude, and Cargill and Jess have it in spades. They like what they like—movies, sci-fi, karaoke, good eats—and they have created a life for themselves here in Austin that allows them to do what they like and be left alone.

This is one of the common threads among the people we meet on the road; they just want to be left alone. Not isolated, not separate and apart from their communities. But they want to preserve the

freedom to live their lives however they see fit with as little inter-
ference as possible. It was true for Jackie out on the ranch, and the
entrepreneurs we met in Vegas, true (I assume) for Omar the Anarchist, and now here it is again in the form of Mr. and Mrs. Cargill.
And it's true for me. It is a classically Republican philosophy: self-
reliance, individualism, freedom. Yet Cargill is reluctant to call himself a Republican, at least as it's currently defined.

"I'm a philosophical Republican rather than an ideological Republican," he says, complaining about the state of his party. "It's
really frustrating when they're fiscal *radicals* who are like, 'No,
we're not budging on taxes.' That's actually a very radical fiscal policy. Fiscal conservatism is actually about balancing the budget and
figuring out how to pay for everything."

He says there's nobody in the Republican field he likes and that
"at this point, I'm probably going to vote for the president right
now."

Yet he would never call himself a Democrat.

Almost nobody wants to own the label "Democrat." That's another thing I'm learning. Even I, the "liberal" on this trip, have a
hard time saying I am one. Because I don't know what the Dems
stand for. It's easy with the Republicans. Whether you agree with
them or not, at least they are ideologically consistent. So ideologically consistent, in fact, that nobody is pure enough for them. I
think that's what Cargill means when he says he is a "philosophical" Republican, as opposed to an "ideological" one. Philosophy
implies reason. Ideology, as applied to the current political scene,
implies rigidity. Like Meghan and me, and nearly everybody else
we meet, Cargill is sick of political rigidity.

But enough about politics, and on to drunken karaoke.

First up is a big meal at Casa Chapala, a Tex-Mex joint in a nearby
strip mall. "Don't let the location fool you," Cargill warns. I don't.
It's amazing. I order the Mexican thing with the stuff in it. Deli-
cious. As we are leaving, Jess and Cargill point out the photo of
President Bush the Younger on the wall. As it turns out, President
Obama also has eaten here, but there's no photo of him.

Meghan: Cargill and I are really on the same page with things. For as long as I can remember, he has referred to himself as a "philosophical" Republican versus an "ideological" one. I refer to myself as a progressive Republican and have even been harassed by Glenn Beck for, you know, being a bastard mutation in the original Republican "ideologue" design. This is the thing, and I'll say it as often as I have to: I really do identify myself as a Republican, and I firmly believe in the core ideals on which the party is based.

One of my bona fides that many people outside of the Republican circle haven't heard is that my mother was pregnant with me at the 1984 Republican Convention in Dallas, where President Reagan accepted the nomination from our party. It's my most badass Republican street cred, and I have attended every single Republican Convention since.

I flat-out love everything about it: the converging of the best—and, yes, worst—minds of the Republican Party in one happy room. No one's there to talk smack about our platform; they're all there because they believe in what we stand for, with passion and commitment, without a bunch of nitpicking naysayers attacking our vision for including diverse opinions. I'm not naive; I know that there are also bad apples on some branches who are there seeking their own power and glory, but from where I'm usually standing I have a treetop view of all the good that can be done when people with conviction work together for America. Until you are on that convention floor, talking to people from every corner of America, you cannot begin to understand just how beautiful the spirit in that room really is. Television cannot do it justice, trust me. It is a *party*, of the very best possible kind. Yes, even better than Vegas—unless, of course, it's being held in Vegas.

Unfortunately, Republican politics really started getting more radicalized in the last eight years. I want to live in a Big Tent Party, and I believe we should be reaching out to younger voters by finding flexibility within the platform. I have never thought being a Democrat was cool, and anyone who believes in big government doesn't really understand what big government means. On a philosophical and cultural level I connect to the Republican Party, and there is no scenario where I could fathom myself ever voting for a Democrat, or joining another party. Yes, even in instances where the party would lean more conservative. I am a moderate Republican and I am more comfortable with a little sway more conservative than liberal.

While we are eating, the issue of Michael's and my cultural differences over our party alignments flares up once again. I start to see that much of our arguments tie back to cultural rather than political differences of opinion. As stereotypical as it may sound, I think that being a Democrat implies being a pacifist: someone who is out of touch with the rest of America, or more specifically someone who compromises to the point where they end up with little of what they started out with. Being a Democrat, in my experience, doesn't mean "ride or die," or fight until the end. It means "Anybody gone into Whole Foods and seen the price of arugula?" another one of my favorite President Obama quotes. Michael's arguments to the contrary don't sway me in the least, but I'm happy to have this conversation as many times as it takes for him to see my point. I know there are lots of naysayers about my specific "brand" of Republican, but I have found that those types of Republicans are living in fear of the changing world we live in. The face of America is changing and the Republican Party needs to start evolving, not giving up the basic principles this party was founded on and stands for.

Eventually the topic turns to horror films, and we find plenty of common ground before going back to our hotel for a couple of hours to relax until leaving for our next destination.

When I get up to my room, one of my close girlfriends calls me to check in.

"How's everything going with the comedian?" she asks.

"It's going actually really great, but it's only a matter of time before I really freak him out," I say. It's true, I'm just waiting for the time when I will drink too much and say too much, and Michael second-thinks this trip. I'm hoping that my impression of Michael being the kind of guy who rolls with the punches is holding true.

Nothing has really shocked him so far, and he's been awfully amiable about guns and strippers. Maybe he's more understanding of my point of view than I realize. I tell my friend that I wish I could be more like that, and promise myself to try.

Michael: The fastest growing party affiliation in America is "independent." People no longer wish to identify with either the Republican or Democratic parties because many of us feel like those parties don't identify with us. Party loyalty, in my opinion, is a joke.

Why should I be loyal to one party over another? These are businesses, pure and simple. The business they are in is the big-money business of government. Any company that wants my patronage has to provide a better product than the other guy. For me, right now, that company is the Democrats. I like their product better. Not much better, but better. I think of it like this: Pizza Hut makes a better pizza than Domino's, but they're both pretty shitty pizzas. Well, what if Pizza Hut and Domino's were the only two pizza places in the whole country? That would be awful, and that awfulness pretty much describes our political system right now.

The two party system seems antithetical to our whole notion of a free market. The game has been rigged in such a way that it's almost impossible for a third (or fourth, or fifth) party to get off the ground. We wouldn't stand for that in business, yet we don't seem to have too much of a problem with it in our governance. Monopolies (or duopolies) are bad in the private sector and they're also bad in the public sector.

I wish we had more political options. I wish the "marketplace of ideas" was really that, a marketplace. The problem is, even if we had a third party, it would be co-opted by big money just as fast as the first two parties have been. Money is the toxin running through our political bloodstream. Everybody knows this but nobody who can do anything about it is doing anything about it because they are the beneficiaries of all of this radioactive cash.

One of the things I will always admire Meghan's dad for is that he tried. The McCain-Feingold Act of 2002 attempted to regulate the use of money in political campaigns. The bill was challenged in the Supreme Court and largely upheld, but it hasn't achieved anything. What we're left with now, ten years later, are Super PACs and ever-growing gobs of greasy money flowing into the system like raw sewage.

Why are all these big money donors giving so much? I don't think patriotism is driving them. The only thing driving them is big, fancy cars. And big, fancy private jets. And trophy wives with big, fancy tits.

So, no, I'm not loyal to the Democratic party. I'm loyal to my beliefs. Right now the Democrats come closer to embodying those beliefs than the other guys, but I don't trust them because I don't trust power. At the moment, the only thing I trust is that Cargill and Jessica are going to show us a good time.

Meghan: Later that night we all go hang out at a bowling alley/bar/karaoke place called Highball. It is one of the better places in America to have multiple kinds of good clean, albeit drunken, fun. Before I met Michael he insisted that he didn't drink, and when I first met Stephie she said the same damn thing. I told them that I had spent two years on the road on my father's campaign, and if there was one thing I knew about a good road trip, it's that at some point everyone starts drinking.

When we get to the karaoke place with Jessica and Cargill and a few of their friends, I know that drinking is on the agenda if we are all gonna get up there and sing. I am, without bragging, the worst singer in the world. Truly, no one should be subjected to my singing, but when in Rome, one must partake. About two beers in, I am ready to get my Lenny Kravitz on, and get up to sing probably the worst version of "American Woman" in the history of bad karaoke.

More rounds of Bud Light are ordered, and Michael sings a hipstery Radiohead song that I think was popular in the nineties, mostly showcasing just how different he and I are, though honestly we have quite a bit in common on the tone-deaf front. Next up,

Cargill does an insanely fantastic rendition of Digital Underground's "Humpty Hump." But I am most pleasantly surprised when my girl Stephie lets her karaoke hair down. She even starts drinking a little, and kills on Carrie Underwood's "Before He Cheats" with me. She is awesome, and I think finally really getting comfortable with me. No one should let Stephie's adorable, innocent, Nermal good looks fool them; this is a girl who is down to have a good time and play. She's like Michael, rolling with every situation. I look around at them and tilt my beer towards a toast, happy that our little crew is starting to feel like a family. Buzzed off beer, in a sweaty karaoke lounge with some film nerds in Austin. Is there really any other place this could happen?

Michael: The thing about Austin is that it's the kind of town that *would* have an all-in-one bowling alley/cocktail lounge/performance space featuring a mentalist/poker room/karaoke emporium. If that sounds like hipster nirvana, it is.

The Highball is populated entirely with guys sporting ironic facial hair, and girls in vintage sundresses. Needless to say, everybody has clever tattoos. I might be the oldest person there, although to be fair, I am still *very* good looking, even at my advanced age. Actually, now that I think about it, I might be the oldest person in all of Austin.

This is definitely a young city. Cities with big art scenes usually are. The average age is 31.2, as compared to 35.5 for the United States as a whole, which is impressively young considering the state government is located here and politicians, as everybody knows, are old farts.

The Cargills have invited some of their Austin buddies to join us at the Highball. We occupy one of their seven karaoke theme rooms and get to the serious work of belting out off-tune versions of the greatest hits of the '70s, '80s, '90s, and today. Meghan, of course, sings a spirited version of "American Woman." ("Spirited"=terrible.)

I sing a note-for-note, perfect, heartbreaking version of Radiohead's "No Surprises." When I am finished, not only does the entire karaoke room stand in unison to applaud, but so does everybody within the entire state of Texas.

That isn't true. What is true is that I am a horrible singer and were it not for the enormous quantities of Bud Light in my system, I would not have the courage to sing at all. If you're wondering how many Bud Lights it requires to get me to sing Radiohead at your next function, the answer is two.

Yes, I am a lightweight, a source of considerable amusement to Ms. McCain, who drinks her Bud Lights with a sense of purpose. Until this trip, I almost never drank beer at all because I do not like the taste, and I certainly never drank Bud Light because it seemed kind of Whisky Tango to me. But here's the thing I discover at the Highball: I *like* Bud Light. In fact, it might be the only beer I actually do like. Meghan *only* drinks it because she has some family allegiance to the brand. She is the one who gets me into the stuff and I have to say, if you're only going to drink one watery kind of shitty beer that will still get you buzzed, Bud Light is definitely the way to go. I love it.

After hours of pitiful rock 'n' rolling with Austin's least talented singers, we finally tumble from the Highball at closing time. Cargill and Jess drop us at the hotel and I doze off, excited to meet up with Cousin John the next day.

Yes, tomorrow is finally the day we pick up our RV and driver. No more flying. No more soft living. From here on out, it's the open road for us, every single mile. Hard road living, that's what we're going to do. I mean, not so hard that we won't spend every night in a comfortable hotel because sleeping fourwide in a rented RV when your driver likes having orgies with famous comedians is taking things a little too far.

The RV place is located on a depressing strip of highway somewhere just outside of Austin. We drive past it twice before realizing the used car outlet we keep passing is the place. There they are: a short line of white Cruise America RVs aligned along the baking asphalt.

Cousin John is already there, standing next to a particular model and patting it like a dog. He flew in from Aspen this morning, and he greets us as we get out of the car. He's a big guy, probably about six feet, 220 pounds, dark wavy hair, and a broad round face.

"How ya' doin'?" he booms as he wraps his beefy hand around mine before launching into a story about the hotel job he just quit, his trip to the airport, the flight, the lady sitting next to him, finding the place, the heat, and his bike, which he thought about bringing but did not, and maybe he'll just pick up a fifty-dollar bike somewhere on the road so that he can bike because he's been doing a lot of biking, in fact that's how he gets around Aspen, biking, fifteen miles back and forth along the Rio Grande, if you touch his ass you'll see that it's made out of granite. I do not touch his ass.

Throughout this monologue, Meghan cannot stop laughing. She has to turn away and cover her mouth because she is laughing so hard. When he finally stops speaking, her face is scarlet from the effort to still her uncontrollable mirth.

"I love him," she whispers.

Stephie appears to be in shock. Her normally globular eyes are practically bugging out of her skull. As for me, I am bewildered. What the hell is this guy talking about?

Before we leave the parking lot, Cousin John has one more thing to add: "Rule number one on the RV. No number twos."

That I understand.

We say our goodbyes to Cargill, and then we are off to Houston for a quick stopover before going on to New Orleans. We are officially on the road good and proper. From here on out, we will bump along every single mile, the four of us in our foul-smelling RV, whose air-conditioning seems to barely be functioning on this hundred-degree day. The road!

Cousin John gets lost leaving the parking lot.

New Orleans, Louisiana

We Got This

Michael: We spend the first hours in the RV getting acclimated to our new home. We stop at a Wal-Mart to stock up on Pop-Tarts and pretzels and cans of Pringles and a plastic bag of spinach for Stephie, who is an insufferably healthy eater. Meghan and I wheel a big squeaky shopping cart around the store. "You want to go see the guns?" she asks. She's obviously taunting me, thinking I'm going to say something about how pissed off it makes me that Wal-Mart sells guns.

"Absolutely."

Over by the ladies' underwear section is the big spinning rifle case. Meghan explains to me the differences between the various firearms, but they all pretty much seem the same to me. They're all big pointy sticks that go "boom," just with different paint jobs, different attachments and scopes and butt stocks (I think that's a rifle term, but if it's not, it's just funny to say "butt stock"). Maybe some liberals get all bent out of shape over Wal-Mart selling guns but I don't care. As long as Wal-Mart's not selling anything illegal, more power to them. If they decide to open a double-headed dildo section tomorrow, I'll be okay with that too.

(It would actually be interesting to see if the same conservatives who defend Wal-Mart's right to sell firearms would be equally accommodating if it were to start selling double-headed dildos.)

We catch up to Cousin John wandering around the bedding aisle. He's bleeding all over one large flip-flop. I don't know how, but he somehow cut open his big toe sometime between the parking lot and the Wal-Mart. There's more blood than there should be and it doesn't seem to be letting up.

"Part of my brains are coming out of my toe," he says, sopping up the blood with a paper towel. "Don't worry about it."

"Are you sure?"

"I'm an EMT and I'm fine."

We are already unsure of Cousin John's competence. Seeing him bloodied less than three hours into our time with him does nothing to alleviate our concerns.

While we load our groceries, Cousin John fiddles with the GPS. He plugs in the address for our hotel in Houston and we set off. I fall asleep for a little while and when I awaken, we are off the main highway, driving along a narrow, bumpy road through some dingy Texas town. The sun is going down.

"Where are we?" I ask.

Meghan shoots me an evil look.

Wherever we are is not Houston. Cousin John pulled off the highway a while ago because "the GPS told me to," and now we are somewhere. Not lost exactly, but taking the slowest possible route to our hotel.

"This GPS isn't worth shit," says Cousin John. He unplugs it from the lighter and hides it in the glove box.

Nobody says anything as John navigates the big RV over two-lane Texas roads. We pass low cinderblock houses and Sonic restaurants. We are only a couple of hours behind schedule but the mood is turning grim. John turns on his iPod's selection of good-time stoner music: Bob Marley, the Eagles, Dave Matthews. Worse, he sings along.

"I've got a peaceful, easy feeling . . ."

Meghan looks like she might punch him in the throat.

My own emotions are mixed. On one hand, it will be horrible if we are stuck with an incompetent pothead driver for the next two and a half weeks. On the other hand, it will be hilarious.

"What are the odds that he crashes this thing?" I quietly ask Meghan.

"Thirty percent," she answers.

"That sounds right."

Meghan: As much as I've enjoyed spending time in Austin, I'm thrilled to be on the road to New Orleans, and even though we are working our way through a brief stop in Houston, I'm already drawn by Nola's indescribable energy. I've heard New Orleans referred to as "the only European city in America," which really captures the city's old-world charm. New Orleans is completely intoxicating and a little mysterious. There's an aura and a swagger to the city I have never found anyplace else.

Over the years, I've had extremely special and even life-changing experiences in New Orleans. The first time I got my heart badly broken I had to be in New Orleans a few weeks later. While I was there still reeling, I skeptically visited a voodoo doctor who had been recommended to me by my airport cab driver. I don't really believe in psychics or fortune-tellers, but I thought a voodoo doctor might be an interesting experience. I really didn't think anything was going to help, so why not give voodoo a try? At the very least it would be a distraction from my broken heart. To my great shock, the doctor gave me such insight into my life and my recently ended relationship that I truly can say I got closure, and my heart started to heal in New Orleans. Everything the voodoo doctor told me would later come true and I found the experience unbelievably cathartic. Believe what you want, say what you will, the voodoo doctor gave me closure and I will always be thankful to her for that.

Although I am a woman of Christian faith, I have always been open to the advice of others, and that woman was a great help to me during a difficult time. If there is some kind of looming crisis in my life that I can't seem to shake, and I have the opportunity to travel, Las Vegas may be the city where I go to forget, but New Orleans is the city where I have learned to move on. This all may sound very poetic and idealistic, but that's the kind of person I am and the way I like to look at life and politics.

Katrina and the aftereffects of the hurricane still linger there, not only around the Lower Ninth Ward, but in pockets throughout the rest of the city as well. It is tragic that so many years later there is still so much evidence of the devastation wrought by Katrina; the work still needed to restore the area continues apace. New Orleans is a city of intense beauty and rich culture, haunted by the repercussions of the shortcomings of the worst kind of American partisan politics. I have come to view Katrina, and the subsequent disastrous way in which it was handled by our government, like the canary in a coal mine. Hurricane Katrina was a warning sign about so many other areas of weakness within us as a nation and within our government. It showcased how bureaucracy can come between the handling of a natural disaster in a morally culpable way. It was an example of the worst America has to offer, a dark spot in our nation's history. All of that being said, part of the reason why I am eager to visit New Orleans on this trip is to further explore the dichotomy that is this city: the gorgeous and sophisticatedly rich culture scarred by dark parts of our history. But first we have to freaking get there.

Michael: Houston doesn't have much to recommend it unless you are curious to see where oil executives work. Answer: big buildings. We thought about touring NASA, but that would have required waking up a lot earlier than we were prepared to do, so we just said, "Fuck it."

It is our first night with Cousin John, so we take him out to dinner at a Mexican joint called Gringo's, an appropriate choice since we are all, in fact, gringos. He spends the meal regaling us with stories about his upbringing in Tennessee, his tour of duty as a tow-truck driver in Aspen, his various romantic misadventures, his political leanings ("I don't feel like I've abandoned the Republican Party; I feel like the Republican Party abandoned me"), his initial impression of me ("you could be my uncle Pat's twin brother except my Uncle Pat has a glass eye"), his future plan to get a sheriff's badge tattooed on his ass in homage to Bob Braudis, the "live and let live" former sheriff of Pitkin County, Colorado, and his life philosophies ("you guys are all caterpillars who are still living inside your own head; I'm a butterfly who lives anywhere I want to be"). He also compares himself to a freight train ("you can't stop a freight train, and my freight train is a freight train of love and understanding").

"We needed you on this trip," I tell him. "We didn't know it until now, but we needed you," I say, kind of meaning it and kind of just saying it because his earnest, mixed metaphors are making me squeamish and I feel the need to say something appreciative.

After dinner we head back to our hotel. Part of our deal with Cousin John is that we are not paying for his hotel. That was made clear right out of the gate, but now that we're actually at our first hotel with him, I feel pretty shitty about it. We're not paying him very much as it is, and I feel bad that we're asking him to sleep in the RV. He says he doesn't care, but it's really hot out there, and, as I said, the AC barely functions. He's going to sweat his balls off. But if I offer to buy his hotel room tonight, maybe he'll expect me to do it every night and I am way too cheap to even consider that option. So I keep my mouth shut and the girls and I check into our comfortable, air-conditioned rooms. The butterfly Cousin John cocoons in the hotel parking lot. I feel terrible. But I take an Ambien and soon forget all about the freight train of love.

The next morning, we clamber back into the RV around nine. There's a man-sized wet spot on one of the cushioned benches, Cousin John's residue after a hot night. We are all a little grossed out. Cousin John is chipper, though, and ready for the day's six-hour drive to New Orleans.

"Weren't you hot?" I ask him.

"Man, this is nothing," he says. "I used to live in my car."

Fair enough. Nobody wants to sit on the salty outline of our driver. It looks like the police outline of a murder victim. The back of the RV has a bedroom, and it's unclear why he didn't just sleep on the bed, but I don't ask and neither do Meghan or Stephie. No-body wants to call too much attention to the gross-out factor, I guess.

Meghan: By the time our RV pulls into the Big Easy, Michael, Ste-phie, Cousin John, and I are well on our way to becoming a family. I'm secretly pleased that Cousin John is here, because there is still a part of me that is annoyed that Michael has backup with Stephie in our small semblance of a culture war that was going on before we set foot in the RV. I have wanted another red state Republican along for the ride—or at least someone who didn't know Michael coming into the trip—and I'm pretty sure Cousin John could be that fourth element, an equalizer of sorts.

This is the thing about Cousin John: he really is one of a kind. He grew up in Tennessee but has conflicted beliefs about the South and southern culture in general. He lives in Aspen, Colorado, but for a time, he worked as a river guide in New Mexico. He is for all intents and purposes a self-made man, really living his life on his own terms.

It was surprisingly difficult to find someone to take on the job of driving our RV. People either weren't qualified or didn't want to spend a month of their summer driving us around for a cultural ex-periment. There was a moment where I was worried the trip would not happen at all simply because we could not find a driver. Luck-ily, I was talking to my friend Sarah Scully, and she suggested I get in touch with her cousin. I met Sarah on the campaign trail in 2007 before the New Hampshire primary. She was working for the Inde-pendent Film Channel, doing background interest spots about each of the candidates. I spotted her and her production partner, Will Raabe, outside of a town hall meeting, and I noticed we were all wearing identical Ray-Ban sunglasses; we have all been friends ever since.

I love Sarah so much that when she suggested her cousin as our driver, I figured anyone related to her would probably be amazing.

The thing is, I immediately do like Cousin John. He is nothing if not an additional colorful personality to our little clique. All of his statements normally end with, "Are you kidding me?" I love that he always wants things to be a joke. He calls us all "Gumdrop," for no reason in particular, but it's sweet in an absurd enough way that we all start using it, all the time. He is sweet and charming and sometimes a little offensive. He is also a big, burly guy who is more than happy to help me get in and out of the RV and help me with my "Flintstones-sized suitcase." He is a doll, and he clearly likes me a lot more than Michael, which makes me happy.

Michael: The first New Orleans landmark is the Superdome, its big white mushroom cap sprouting just off of I-10. The Superdome feels a little like the American Chernobyl. Something horrible happened there, but it's invisible now. Of course, New Orleans is still habitable and there are no radioactive wolves wandering around, so maybe the analogy is imperfect, but it's still kind of blood chilling seeing it there, a giant, puffy haunted house.

It's impossible now to think about New Orleans without thinking of Katrina just like it's impossible to think of Pearl Harbor without thinking of, well, Pearl Harbor. Coming just a few years after 9/11, the hurricane and its aftermath represented a new kind of American impotence, like we suddenly became that middle-aged guy who finds himself flaccid in bed going, "This has never happened to me before."

We watch the Superdome go by and nobody says much about it because what is there to say? I'm not one of those "George Bush doesn't care about black people" Democrats, but I do think that when a political party makes their bones saying the federal government is incapable of doing anything well, they often appoint people who prove their point. If W. is guilty of anything regarding Katrina, it's that. If he didn't think FEMA was capable of doing its job, why not appoint as its director somebody skilled at turning failing institutions around, instead of Michael ("Heck of a job, Brownie")

Brown, former head of the International Arabian Horse Association? I'm sure the IAHA has its own troubles, but I doubt the Arabian horses' troubles compare to hurricanes and tornadoes.

The stifling drive from Houston has left us all a little worn, so we each repair to our hotel rooms for a little while before heading out for an evening of dinner and carousing in the French Quarter. I have never liked this part of New Orleans, the boozy touristy district where out-of-towners go for rowdy displays of public intoxication and booby flashing. Most cities have those areas (minus the booby flashing), and over the course of our trip, we will pretty much hit every one in every town. Meghan, of course, loves the French Quarter because she is unembarrassed to be seen among drunken white people. After all, a lot of the time she *is* a drunken white person.

We take a streetcar not named Desire to the French Quarter as the sun sets, wandering along Bourbon and Royal and Dumaine Streets. Even in the middle of the week in July, the cobblestone roads are humming with music and street performers and a phalanx of colorful race cars from some coast-to-coast road race lined up and down the streets.

We amble along the storefronts, losing Cousin John almost immediately. I think maybe he wants to ditch us to do his drinking without fear of judgment. The day before he'd had a beer at lunch, which caused all of us to raise our eyebrows a bit. After all, he's our *driver.* One beer wasn't going to get the big boy intoxicated, but none of us were thrilled. Stephie had a private word with him the next morning, informing him that from that point forward, we would appreciate it if he did his drinking when he wasn't driving a thirty-foot motor vehicle containing us.

For dinner, we settle on an overpriced touristy fancy-pants restaurant, and each order some bizarre New Orleans drinks to accompany our meals. Mine is a concoction of fruits and whipped cream and coconut and maybe some caramel and there must be booze in there too, but I don't know because all I taste is the aching sweetness. It's delicious and I am buzzed immediately.

Since the Quarter is small, before too long we run into Cousin John, who tells us he just saw a one-punch fistfight, are you kiddin' me, and then he and Meghan get into a little spat because he won't shut up about her offer to come watch him get his ass tattooed. He's drunk. We're all a little drunk, I guess. They bicker while Stephie and I walk a few paces ahead, weaving among all the other inebriated tourists. Nobody flashes their tits at me, which is a disappointment, even though God knows I've seen my share of lady parts lately.

Meghan: As we scour Bourbon Street for nightlife with giant drinks in our hands, I try to refresh our dinner fight, but Michael's too happy. We find Cousin John, who keeps insisting that I said I would watch him get his ass tattooed. It actually crosses my mind that it would be entertaining to watch Cousin John get his ass tattooed and that all four of us might end up getting road tattoos as mementos from the trip. Then it occurs to me that I really do not want to get a matching tattoo with Michael; we would never be able to come to a meeting ground about what that tattoo would be anyway.

The next morning we head to the swamps for a tour. A friend of mine had gone on one recently and insisted that I must also do it when in New Orleans. I figure it is as good a way as any to get to know the local color, so we get up really early. The swampy air is about 900 percent humidity on top of all the rising heat and mist. I can't help feeling that the whole idea is quickly becoming a recipe for disaster.

Boat seats confirmed, we load onto an air-conditioned tour bus for the sticky ride to God knows where or why. I'm in no mood, so of course the minute my butt hits the cushiony blue seats, Michael starts spewing some nonsense about health care and we begin the morning by bickering like an old married couple. By now he must be fully aware that health care and national defense are possibly the two issues that I am most conservative and he is most liberal about.

Well, even though I'm pretty sure there's a big brick wall in my future, we start discussing Obamacare on the bus on the way to the swamp tour. Michael's argument starts with Republicans being heartless, and that we all need "to give a little more for the common good," and that "health care should be free to every American." I naturally feel like Uncle Scrooge when I say that universal health care would bankrupt this country if enacted into law. Of course I think all Americans should have access to health care, however, the concept of free health care is unrealistic. I wish I could be so idealistic as to think that if we "all just gave a little more," then everyone could have the same level of amazing health care, but it's just not that simple. It makes me feel like I come off sounding heartless, when in reality I think I am simply being pragmatic about the kind of world we live in and what our country can afford.

In reality, Republicans and Democrats will continue to argue about how many Americans are completely uninsured. One of the main reasons our health care costs have gotten so out of control is the outrageous cost of malpractice insurance premiums doctors have to pay. In reality, Republicans have often looked for affordable ways to provide health care for people, but the truth is we cannot just simply give everything away. Republicans have long advocated tort reform, which would put some reasonable caps on things that people can sue for. If a doctor operates on you and causes harm to you, you should absolutely be able to sue for it. But the truth is, there are a lot of people getting really rich off of irrelevant lawsuits. This is not simply a Republican problem; we have to take a red pen to programs that do not work in order to be able to afford health care for all Americans. Until we are ready to do the hard work of looking at programs that are quite simply broken, we should not be moving forward.

Beyond that, no one, not even Michael Ian Black, has been able to convince me that the quality of health care in this country would not suffer if we went so far as to enact free health care into law in America, which is my biggest problem with "universal health care." Anytime you give something away for free, the quality will inevitably suffer. The idea of universal health care seems very much like a first step towards radically socializing medicine in a country that is too large and complicated to support such a drastic move. Yes, I will concede that insurance and pharmaceutical companies are making money hand over fist, but I do not think you can penalize big business for doing what our democratic capitalist system is designed to do. Also, take into consideration that much of that money goes back into research and improving the outstanding level of care that we already have—so why should an award-winning hospital like the Mayo Clinic in Scottsdale, Arizona, have to risk becoming less of a leader in finding new solutions to medical problems by making it cater to anyone who walks in the door? I think it's pretty telling that world leaders and dignitaries from other countries come here for their care when the situation calls for it—we have the best health care in the entire world.

This is not to say that I don't think health care needs reforming; I think any individual with half a brain would agree to that. No one can deny that our health care system is badly broken and people in lower economic brackets have suffered. That is an embarrassment, and our government should be working harder to reform the system. That does not mean, however, that we swing the pendulum so far in the other direction that we give health care away for "free" and the overall quality starts to suffer.

I tell Michael, "At the end of the day, there is nothing in this world that comes for free."

"It's not like you could ever understand not having health care," Michael angrily replies.

This is not the way to argue with me. I've spent a significantly large part of my life trying to combat any bullshit "poor little rich girl couldn't possibly understand real life" stereotypes, and I'm in no mood to do so with Michael on a damp bus on its way to the swamps.

"Don't say anything like that when you meet my father. I'm still trying to explain to him exactly who you are," I say, even though I know it's an argument ender.

Michael curls his lip and snaps back, "Well, I mean he is *really* old."

I lift up my sunglasses and say in a very high-pitched mocking tone, "Oooo."

Michael and Stephie mock me right back in a Valley Girl accent, "Ohhheewww!"

I am furious. I feel my face getting hot and turn my head away from both of them and look out the window. We pull into the swamp boat tour and I pick up my purse, pushing over Michael and storming off the bus. I walk right across the gravel road into the swamplands. I take out my phone and text one of my girlfriends from Arizona: "I wish there was another Republican on this trip with me!!!!"

Michael: If you ever want to piss off Meghan McCain, the quickest and easiest way to do it is to imply that she is, in any way, spoiled. She hates that. HATES that. When we were in Vegas, she didn't speak to me for hours because I told her she "walks like a rich girl."

So when we get into one of our tiffs about health care, I am ashamed to say that my emotions get the better of me and I pull out that particular ace card. I tell her she can't understand what it's like to worry about health care because she's never had to worry about anything. It is an ugly thing to say and I regret it before the words are out of my mouth.

Even more shameful is that I (kind of, sort of) mean it.

She's never had to worry that a sore throat might mean an unaffordable trip to the emergency room, that taking sick days might cost her her job, that a serious illness might mean losing her house.

In truth, I haven't either, but there have been times in my life when I could not afford health insurance. Times when I had no plan for what would happen to me if I ever got sick. That was when I was young and single. Now that I'm a married father of two, the thought of going without health insurance fills me with panic. What would happen if one of my kids got sick? What would I do? Where would I turn? The entertainment business is notoriously fickle. At the moment, I have money in the bank I could use to take care of them, but it's easy to envision a scenario in which my occupational prospects dry up, and I deplete my savings to take care of a loved one. This is happening to people from every walk of life every single day. If you come from a wealthy family, as Meghan does, I do not know if it's possible to understand the fear that these circumstances might provoke.

Regardless, I shouldn't have called her out on her privileged life. She may be a rich bitch, but she's the most grounded rich bitch I've ever met. And I didn't call her father "old." I flatly deny that. I never said it. Although, to be fair, he is really old.

By the time Meghan emerges with her pout still on, the tour has assembled. Our guide looks like Larry the Cable Guy minus the charm. His name is Tater or Bubba or Gumbo or something ridiculously trite. It's probably not even his real name. He ladles on the Creole accent pretty thick as we skim along the swampy bayou waterways. Every few minutes we slow down and he tosses marshmallows into the water. I'm surprised that this is the alligator food of choice, but he explains, "Alligators are scavengers and they like to see what they're eatin' so we use marshmallows. Besides that they're marsh *animals*." I think we're supposed to laugh. When nobody does he says under his breath, "They like marshmallows."

He tosses handfuls into the water but no alligators come.

"C'mon! C'mon! Yeh-yeh-yeh-yeh!" he calls.

The alligators don't seem to be out, so he takes us to another spot. Tossing more marshmallows into the water, he calls again. "Yeh! Yeh! Yeh!" Then we see it, a squiggling hump in the water attached to a pair of eyes.

"There he is," Tater says with evident satisfaction. The gator snakes through the water to the bobbing marshmallow, opens its jaws and swallows. Soon other gators join the first, surrounding the boat in all directions. We gawk and take pictures. They're smaller than I would have preferred, averaging about six feet long. I wanted to see some prehistoric gator shit, oversized and preferably rabid. I want the boat to be attacked. I want dismembered limbs in need of quality, affordable health care. I want lives to be lost. But instead we just sit in our little boat and watch these shy, placid creatures swim for their marshmallows. They're about as scary as cockatoos.

"The only bad part about feedin' 'em is it's like havin' 'em on the payroll," Tater says.

Yeah, they're like goddamned Democrats, these gators, depending on the largesse of strangers!

Once in a while Tater gets out of the airboat and into the water, which raises the alarming and thrilling prospect that he will get chomped on, but of course nothing like that happens. These reptiles know better than to devour the hand that feeds them.

He's a good guy, passionate about gators. He tells us how the gators almost became extinct in the 1960s due to hunting and trapping. But then people like his family started a program of raiding the alligator eggs from the nests and bringing them to alligator farms where they could control the eventual gender of the babies through temperature. Then they toe tag them and release them back into the waters. Today, he says, there are 1.4 million. Good for the gators, good for the marshmallow industry. So that's a happy ending to our airboat ride.

Over the course of the tour, Meghan's temperature cools to the point where she will look at me and, eventually, speak to me. I should apologize, but I don't because sometimes I'm an asshole.

Meghan: By the time we finally make it back to our hotel, I am over it. O-V-E-R. I-T. To the point where I actually think this trip might have been a mistake. I am over Michael, over Stephie, over fighting about health care, over feeding marshmallows to reptiles. The constant in my relationship with Michael is that we seem to push each other's buttons on purpose and fight like brother and sister. Meaning that when Michael is angry with me, I'm just an overindulged rich girl who doesn't know anything about the world outside of my fancy shelter. When I'm angry with Michael, he's just an entitled, delusional liberal hipster who couldn't possibly understand the concept of "live free or die." None of that is true at all, but even the two of us at times fall victim to slinging stereotypes in place of understanding.

Unfortunately most of America behaves like this, especially when it comes to politics. There is a culture war infecting this country right now that seems to only be getting stronger. You are a red stater or a blue stater. You are a liberal, socialist, Obama acolyte, or a redneck entitled Republican who is scared of the changing face of America. Once again, neither of these descriptions is true or fair, but it's the world we're living in right now, and at times I'm worried that maybe Michael and I are just too different to come to some kind of an understanding, even if I am finally catching on to his dry sense of humor.

My friend Liz's friend Jonah has a friend, Glen, who is going to take us on a tour of the west bank of New Orleans and show us what "real" Nawlins is like. Any opportunity to get to experience a side of the city that tourists aren't able to normally access is appealing. For some reason, Michael gets irritated anytime I get shy or quiet, which is happening now that I'm in a new situation, waiting to meet a perfect stranger. For the record, Michael is not the first person to be surprised by this fact. I think people assume, if you are a television commentator or personality, that you're just as "on" in person and at parties as you are on a set, but with me that's not the case. Especially if the day has been going as badly as this one.

It is the kind of hot summer day that shuts me down, and in my haste to get out on the town dressed in something that could go anywhere, I threw on a long black maxi-dress with the hopes of being both cool and casual. While we wait for Glen, the back of my dress already feels soaked with sweat and I can feel both my eyeliner and confidence melting into the sticky early-evening air.

Michael: We're meeting a guy named Glen, one of the mysterious people Stephie has somehow found. He's a friend of a friend (I think), a musician, and a New Orleans native. That's all I know about him. Stephie and he have been trading text messages for a few days trying to arrange an evening of genuine New Orleans flava. I'm looking forward to it because the French Quarter wears thin pretty quick. Plus the whole area smells like somebody left a bunch of deli meat out overnight. That is the aroma you get when you cross stately Colonial French architecture with barf.

A few hours later, we're on the Canal Street Ferry, which connects the French Quarter with the Fifteenth Ward on the West Bank of the Mississippi. Glen is going to meet us on the boat. Actually we were supposed to meet him on the landing for the ferry, but he's nowhere to be seen. Stephie's been texting him. He keeps saying he's five minutes away, but five minutes stretches to fifteen, the ferry arrives, and he tells Stephie that he'll just meet us onboard.

We pass the time talking to a couple of Teach for America volunteers. They're young and earnest and doing it for all the right reasons. "It's a really good way to go to a place that you really love and do good work." They impress me, these two, in their desire to serve without it feeling pious or self-important. I'm reminded of Meghan's brother Jimmy and his friends we met at the ranch in Prescott. At the time, I remember thinking how mature they seemed, how confident. I get a similar feeling from these two. They certainly seem more self-possessed than I did when I was twenty-two or twenty-three. Both groups, the military and Teach for America volunteers, have purposely put themselves in unfamiliar and challenging environments. I can't help but feel a little jealous that I never went through a similar experience, unless you count theater camp, which I suppose you should not.

I start thinking about the concept of national service. So many other countries have mandatory military service, which I don't think we need, but I wonder whether some sort of mandatory national service wouldn't be a good idea for our country. Whether it's military or educational or mentoring or park service, the list of needs we have is great and we certainly don't lack for bored young people. I also worry that our culture is slowly becoming so fragmented that our national identity might get irretrievably diluted along the way. National service would bring together young people from every region, every background, and give them useful, purposeful work. I recently heard an interview with Tom Brokaw, who was proposing something similar, the formation of six public-service academies. My idea is a little more far-reaching than that, because it would get everybody involved, but I'm glad to see that Tom Brokaw and I share more than just gorgeous speaking voices.

Meghan: A few minutes later a very tall, handsome black man approaches and greets us with hugs, giving Michael the "guy hand shake," and I can't help but giggle because Michael clearly isn't as used to giving other guys bro hugs as Glen is.

"Hi, Michael, Meghan?" he asks and we nod. "Good to meet you. I'm Glen. Whose friend are you exactly?"

"You know, my friend Liz's friend Jonah," I try to say casually.

"Don't know a Jonah but it doesn't matter," he says, and I like him immediately, knowing that he's the guy to show us a good time. The ferry makes its way to the part of New Orleans on the west bank of the Mississippi, and Glen takes us along a patchy road that ebbs in and out of cobblestones. He talks about the history of his neighborhood and the racial tension that I am disappointed to learn still exists. Apparently there are still black and white sections of the areas that have not exactly been gentrified.

"Is it getting better, yeah," he says. "But do race issues still exist? Yeah, it's New Orleans."

I don't know why this is surprising, but I think there is some kind of cultural myth that because we now have elected our first black president that somehow all race issues have dissipated. As we make our way deeper and deeper into Glen's neighborhood, he suggests a quick stop at his girlfriend's house. She is apparently a professional boxer in training for the Olympics. We walk up to a modest-sized white porch leading to the door and he casually asks if we smoke weed. This is a loaded question for me, because there is no right answer to this in the political world. I am a truthful person and I hate liars, so saying no would be a lie. Saying yes in America basically makes me a scofflaw.

Let me put it right out there. Yes, I have smoked marijuana a few times in the past. The first time was on a trip to Amsterdam in college and I was surprised by how mild of an experience marijuana was (and in my experience still is). It is a plant that makes me mellow and giggly and, quite frankly, tired. Yet, depending on where you are in the United States, smoking is possession, and that is either a misdemeanor or a felony, depending on how much and whether it's your first time. Split that hair however you want, it's still a crime.

That being said, I believe that marijuana should be legalized in the United States. This is not a decision I have come to quickly or lightly. Over the course of the last four years, in discussions with friends pro and con, I believe the legal ramifications of possessing marijuana are egregious. For one reason, I think it is a substance that does no more damage than alcohol does, and second, if we legalized marijuana in this country and taxed the hell out of it, our economic problems would at least be temporarily helped a great deal. In fact, you could even use the revenue stream to pay for universal health care if you wanted.

Mostly though, I do not completely understand the allure and taboo associated with marijuana. The few times I have partaken in smoking pot it has been a mild experience. Yes, it is a substance that will alter your mind frame and judgment, but as someone who is high strung and has a natural tendency to get nauseated, I can see its appeal.

Michael: We walk along the cobblestone streets of Old Algiers. Glen says he's started something called the No Nigger Campaign, which is his effort to get people in the black community to stop using that word. I nod. He says it's damaging to people's self-esteem and that until black people start respecting themselves, nobody else is going to respect them either.

He shows us some neighborhood landmarks. "The Mardi Gras floats? This is where they build 'em." He then points out the invisible line between the black section of the neighborhood and the white.

"Is it still pretty segregated?" I ask.

"You know something? Unfortunately, New Orleans is. It's real fucked up. My girlfriend's white and what fucks it up is that people are people. They didn't vote for Obama here," he says, pointing to the neighborhood around us. "Only in New Orleans," by which I guess he means the other side of the river.

We get to his girlfriend's house, a cheerful little shotgun shack. The house is aligned along a narrow corridor. One room flows into the other: living room to what I guess would be the dining room to the kitchen. The reason it's hard to tell whether or not it's supposed to be a dining room is because there's a punching bag hanging from the ceiling, along with a bunch of other training equipment. It turns out Glen's girlfriend is a professional boxer named Tiffany Junot. Framed photos of Tiffany line the room. On the floor are a couple of belts, the kind boxers get when they win championships.

"She keeps her belts on the floor?" I ask.

"She doesn't give a shit about those. She's got a lot more. She could kick my ass."

Stephie asks if she's from New Orleans.

"Been in this house a hundred and ten years. Her great-great grandfather built it."

We talk about music and Glen's role as himself on the TV show *Treme*. It turns out Glen is an accomplished musician, a trombonist and vocalist who just scored his first major record deal. He's just come off the road with his band a few days ago. He mentions that his cousin is Trombone Shorty, and I nod, impressed. When he goes to the bathroom, I ask Meghan who Trombone Shorty is. She says she doesn't know.

It turns out we're the idiots because when I dig around later, I realize Trombone Shorty is one of America's greatest jazz musicians.

New Orleans jazz has a steep learning curve for those of us not cool enough to have cribbed before arrival.

Glen packs a small bowl with pot. I take a hit. Meghan takes some and then Stephie.

"You're SO hard core, Michael," Meghan says, trying not to cough.

"I *am* hard core," I reply, happy to see her coming back out of her shy shell. She's been a little moody since our pre-gator health care fight, and I've refused to coddle her out of her various snits. I wink at her, encouraging her fun side to come out and play.

Meghan: Does it cross my mind that entering a stranger's house and smoking marijuana might not be the smartest thing to do? Yes, of course it does, but I like Glen. In the forty-five minutes that I have known him he is making all of us laugh, showing us around his neighborhood, and opening us up to a side of New Orleans we would not have gotten to experience otherwise. He is also flirting with me and calls me a beautiful woman in front of Michael and Stephie. I like men who confidently flirt with women they have just met. Also, I do not want to seem like the Debbie Downer in this scenario. Michael immediately says yes to smoking a joint with Glen. I don't know—buy the ticket, take the ride, right?

As we continue down the cobblestone streets, Glen passes a joint. The thought does occur to me that someone could see us and we could get arrested, though if we went to jail I'm pretty sure it's Michael who would cry. Just the same, I'm not looking to find out.

I walk down the road, trying not to trip over my maxi-dress, and hold Glen's arm for support. Up ahead of us a car honks at Michael, he jumps a little, and a woman yells out of the window, "Stop toking and get out of the road!" I laugh myself in half at the priceless look on Michael's face, simultaneously freaked out and proud as a peacock.

Michael: We're all a little buzzed now as Glen tells us about the way Old Algiers was during Katrina.

"This neighborhood was under chaos because this is the neighborhood where the police committed all the murders," he says. "They got thirteen police charged for murder. Every fucking case of police misconduct was proven."

He tells us where we are standing was entirely underwater up to our waists. All of these proud old houses drowning under the muddy river waters. There are still water marks on some of the houses. You can see where the waters stopped rising, can see how somebody might have needed a boat to navigate, can see how people might have been forced to their roofs. It's eerie, and yet this neighborhood survived better than others. At least here there are still people on porches. Glen calls to them when we pass. He seems to know them all and they know him.

We wander over to a concert right on the riverbank, on a big stage ringed by concession stands that sell food and alcohol. There's an all-female brass band playing and I wonder for a moment about the difficulty of finding female tuba players. Glenn leads us through the patchy grass to the booths selling drink tickets. We buy some drinks for ourselves: water for Stephie, sweet tea for me, Bud Light for Meghan.

"What do you want, Glen?" she asks.

"Something hard," says Glen.

He seems to know everybody here. Every few feet he introduces us to another friend: musicians, locals like him, people from his block, business people. Lots of handshakes. We meet the leader of the next band about to go on. We walk up the banks of the levee and meet more people up there. Glen wipes his face with a white handkerchief while we walk, sipping a vodka cranberry, shaking hands. He introduces us to Dr. William Jones, recently relocated from Phoenix, proud possessor of a PhD in musical education. He's around sixty, African American, and talks like a civic booster.

"There's nothing like this New Orleans culture," he says. "The politics out here is great, and now it's up to all of us to bring our wonderful city back."

This surprises me because he is the only person I have ever heard who describes New Orleans politics as "great." More commonly used words are "corrupt," "racist," and "incompetent." When I come back a little later, Meghan is talking with Dr. Jones.

"I found a Republican for you," she says, pointing at him.

I laugh. A black Republican.

"I know it's not fashionable to be a black Republican," he says, glossing over my skepticism. "But I'm a proud black Republican." He says his wife gives him a hard time about it, and Stephie asks him why he's a Republican. He mentions something about Lincoln freeing the slaves, but then says, "But let's be real: if you want to get ahead, you roll with the big dogs. The Republican Party is the big dogs."

"I hear ya," says Stephie, which I think is her attempt at "being real," per Dr. Jones's advice.

Meghan: Front and center is a series of jazz musicians wearing traditional Mardi Gras Indian costumes. Glen explains to me that during the Civil War, when American Indians helped shield runaway slaves, the two oppressed peoples developed a bond that eventually found colorful outlet in the Mardi Gras tribes. Every year the tribes compete to have the most intricate and beautiful costumes, some weighing as much as 150 pounds and costing thousands of dollars. They are breathtaking. The men wear giant feathered headdresses, derived from the ceremonial attire of many Native American tribes.

I am somewhat ashamed to admit to Glen that after my times visiting New Orleans, I had never seen a traditional Mardi Gras Indian nor was I aware of the tribes that still exist in New Orleans. Glenn tells me all about how music runs in his family, being a trombone player, and working on the HBO show *Treme*.

Along about this time, we meet Dr. William Jones, who says to me, "We almost made it to the White House." I smile—I've been recognized for all the right reasons, and my prayers for a fellow

Republican are answered—he's also from Arizona, which makes me triply happy.

However, the look on Glen's face completely changes, as if the music playing between us stops and there's only one chair. He looks at Dr. Jones and says, "Are you kidding me? How can you be a Republican? What black man is a Republican?"

I pull Michael into the mix, hopeful that this man can help him see my points of view, and Dr. Jones does a wonderful job of laying out the principals of smaller government and fiscal conservatism. As excited as I am about my ally, it is clear that Glen and Michael are both stuck on the completely unimportant fact that a black man could be supportive of the Republican Party. Putting it mildly, the situation is a little depressing. I don't know Glen well enough to chastise him, nor do I want to make Dr. Jones any more uncomfortable than he already is. I want to roll my eyes at Michael and yell at him, *That's right, they exist—minorities who are Republicans! Don't believe everything Keith Olbermann tells you!!*

Instead I take the high road, hiking up my damn maxi-dress and taking Glen to get a piece of fried catfish.

Michael: Glen returns a few minutes later and explains new New Orleans politics to me.

"After the storm, the majority of the people that came back were white. This is how we know it's true. For the first time in forty years, we have a white mayor. Everything's been black in this city for at least forty-five years. Mayor, police chief." He goes on a rant about the former mayor, Ray Nagin, who grew up in Treme, the same neighborhood as Glen, the same neighborhood we're going to later tonight. "He won't even walk in that neighborhood right now. He's that uppity." Yes, Glen uses the U-word.

The politics are hardcore here at this pleasant jazz festival on the levees holding back the mighty Mississippi. The people wear their politics right on their sleeves, and I can see why. Their town knows the direct effects politics can have on people's lives. They know every day when they walk down those streets and see the water-marks. Glen's outrage seems to come from a poisonous gumbo of racial history, political corruption, and centuries of injustice. Right where we're standing is the site of New Orleans's first slave market. This is haunted ground. Bad gris-gris.

Soon the sun is gone and we are too. We board the ferry and cross back across the river. Glen leads us to Treme. It's one of New Orleans's oldest neighborhoods, lined with small one-story houses set back from buckled sidewalks and patchy lawns. This was where free blacks came to live early in the city's history. Now it's in danger of gentrification.

When we get out of the cab, Glen points up and down the streets, telling us there used to be bars everywhere where you could go and hear live music. Now there's just a couple left. We're standing in front of one of them. A few guys mill outside the door, including an ancient-looking gentleman whose head looks like it was shrunken down from a larger size. He is tall and thin as an oboe. Glen introduces us: "This is Benny, the second-oldest active musician in New Orleans. You playing tonight?"

"Yes, I am," says Benny.

"Benny's about to beat the shit out of that drum," says Glen. "You watch."

We walk inside. The place is tiny, packed with people of every age and hue. It is the first truly and fully integrated place we have been to the entire trip. Shoved into the corner are eight black musicians warming up, the Treme Brass Band. They only play here once a week, on Wednesdays. Benny shuffles over to join them and straps a big bass drum to his chest. Then they start and it's 1925. People are on their feet with the first trumpet notes: swinging, shaking, their arms flinging droplets of sweat into the thick air. It feels preposterously good, all of this thrilling music mixed with the booze and the pot. Couples fling their bodies around the cramped dance floor, their limbs blurring into the slinky music. In the back, as promised, Benny beats the shit out of his big bass drum.

Meghan: Treme is one of the oldest areas of New Orleans; it is an area known for its rich African American and Creole culture along with its brass and jazz music history.

As we walk through his neighborhood, I jokingly tell Glen he should run for mayor someday, and he sort of half laughs, which in my experience tells me the thought has crossed his mind. In reality, it is people like Glen who should run for higher office: people who know the ins and outs of their city and the people who live in it and maintain a palpable sense of pride for it.

Each house that Glen points out has a story and a person attached to it, and we barely go ten feet without running into someone he knows. I start to feel giddy and grateful to be able to have such an experience, meet such cool people, and absorb such an interesting side of New Orleans that I most likely never would have without this trip or Glen. I grab his arm and yell, "Take me to some Treme music!"

Glenn laughs and says, "Follow me, little lady."

Within a few minutes we are outside a small building that looks like a reconstructed house that is painted bright yellow, with the words THE CANDLELIGHT LOUNGE printed on the side. We walk inside and it is the way I imagine what walking into a speakeasy from the quiet outside world of Prohibition must have been like. Loud brass music is playing from a group of musicians surrounding a giant drum with the words TREME BRASS BAND stamped on it; people are dancing, sitting, tapping their feet, and drinking. There's a haze in the air and kinetic energy that is instantly appealing.

The entire place is filled wall to wall with people. Twinkling lights surround the bar and fall from the ceiling. Not one person looks like they aren't enjoying themselves. I grab Michael by the neck and yell over the music, "Goddamn it, I love this city!"

"I know!" he yells back. We push our way over to the incredibly crowded, sweaty bar where Glen is holding court. After we get our drinks, Michael and Stephie start dancing. A random elderly man dances with me, and we all start getting down. Someone hands Michael a colorful umbrella. Stephie is unleashed.

At some point a woman approaches me and says, "You're Meghan McCain, right?"

"Yep," I say. "I'm drunk, so please don't ask me anything too crazy because I'm painfully honest when I'm sober, let alone drunk."

"Oh, I just want to know why you're hanging out with the guy from *Kids in the Hall*," she yells over the music.

I smile and practically strain my voice, it's so loud in here. "Actually, he was on *The State,* which is by far a superior comedy show. Fuck *Kids in the Hall.*" I have never seen the show *Kids in the Hall,* but I feel the need to defend Michael and *The State.* I know enough about Michael at this point that asking Michael about his time on *Kids in the Hall* will illicit a similar reaction to asking me how I feel about my father choosing Sarah Palin as his running mate will do.

I realize that yelling "Fuck *Kids in the Hall!*" is probably a signal that I need a little air, so I politely excuse myself. I can outdrink most people, but I can really outdrink Michael and Stephie and I need to pace myself, as I am likely three or four drinks in the lead.

Michael: The band finally takes a break, and I step out with Stephie for some air, although the torpid night offers little relief from the heat. Meghan is already out there, sitting on the low concrete wall lining the sidewalk outside the bar. People are cooking food in big smokers in the open air: red beans, rice, chicken. A woman is standing in the middle of the road in a tight top and tight pants, yelling at somebody: Glen.

"I *am* Treme," she yells over and over at him. "Motherfucker, I AM TREME!" Glen waves his hand in her direction, unconcerned. Meghan says they've been going at it like this for several minutes. I notice that the yelling woman is not wearing shoes. She moves towards Glen, confronting him: "I ain't addicted to nuthin'. Never have been. And never will be. Not even Treme."

Meghan, Stephie, and I watch, mouths agape, as the woman unravels there in the middle of the street. Glen keeps his back to her.

"You ain't gonna fuck with me," she says.

Glen claps his hands together and keeps repeating, "We got this! We got THIS! Thanks to Trombone Shorty, we got this. All of this. And we gonna be here forever."

Glen tells us later he's been involved in a property dispute with this woman and her family. I don't understand the details but it seems to boil down to an accusation Glen made against them about their taking advantage of people living in the neighborhood with the purpose of using a city program to buy their homes at under-market values and then sell them to more well-heeled investors, white investors, who want to gentrify Treme. Trombone Shorty, who has become a worldwide sensation with his *Billboard*-topping jazz album, *Backatown*, has likewise been buying up properties in the area in an effort to slow down or stop gentrification. It's a conflict about money and the soul of the neighborhood.

"We got this," Glen keeps saying. "This" for him means more than a few crumbling houses in Treme. It's an entire history, a way of being he is fighting to preserve. He says, "The musicians that played in my neighborhood, they brought me out of the womb." I think he means it literally. This neighborhood, and the people in it, are his blood.

One of those people is Willis, a tall and gangly young guy in whose beat-up Buick we find ourselves a few minutes later. "His grandfather Charles Johnson was one of the greatest clarinetists that ever lived," Glen tells us by way of introduction.

It turns out Willis just got out of jail. It's unclear why, although it seems to have something to do with cocaine. His house is one of the ones that the screaming woman on the street "stole." The details are hazy to me, both because Willis's voice is quiet, his accent is almost impossible to understand, and because I am getting higher and higher from the cigar we keep passing around, which is, of course, stuffed with marijuana. There's something about a loan and forged signatures and going to city hall to get them to open up casework, and although I am trying to be sympathetic to Willis's unintelligible plight, I find the only thing I really want to do is lean my head against the car window and watch the streetlights zip by as we bump along.

At one point after we've been driving for what seems like a long time, Meghan leans over to me and whispers, "Is this a good idea?"

"Yes," I tell her. "It's a very good idea."

We start laughing and cannot stop.

Meghan: More drinking, more dancing, more talking about life with Glen, Willis, Michael, and Stephie. Another joint is lit outside the bar. More flirting . . . more, more, more, more. I am three sheets to the wind. My mind is foggy from the combination of partying, southern humidity, good company, and the intoxicating atmosphere that New Orleans just exudes. I thank Glen for the most amazing night of our trip, thank Michael for meeting me and coming up with the idea for a book, and thank Stephie for always being so sweet, because she is the sweetest girl in the world that ever lived.

"Seriously, Stephie," I tell her, "you must dream about rainbows, lollipops, and ponies. You're the nicest person I've ever met." She smiles and laughs, a tinkling sound like fairies make. Right as we are all saying goodbye to Glen and Willis I yell at everyone, "Let's do this every year! Promise, let's do this exact same thing again every summer until we die!"

Michael: The rest of the night is more of the same: music and dancing and then I am drinking a sugary glass of absinthe with Willis, who I love even though I cannot understand a word that comes out of his mouth. Stephie runs into a friend from college, and two law students corner Meghan for many minutes to talk about politics; she finally catches us up outside whatever bar we're at, pissed.

"I thought you had my back."

"I didn't know where you were."

"You didn't look."

That may be true but what does she expect? I barely know where *I* am. I give her a hug and she tells me that she loves me, her entire hard edge melting right off into the ocean of the night. Willis packs another cigar and lights up. We smoke some more and say our good-byes, Meghan's farewells topping all of us in their outlandishly sincere bonhomie.

"Quack, quack," says Willis, which means he sees police. Glen shields the cigar from view with his back and they roll right by us. There are hugs all around, then somehow I am back at the hotel in bed, my mouth feeling as if it's been stuffed with cotton balls and my ears still ringing from all that wonderful wild music.

Meghan: I wake up in the hotel the next morning and feel extremely hungover. I roll out of bed, turn the shower on, and attempt to pull myself together in any way possible. My head is throbbing with pain, but I feel like laughing.

For all the fun and excess that the night before has given us, the day ahead is going to be a lot more serious and somber. We are going to spend the day taking a tour of the Lower Ninth Ward.

It's incredible to think that Hurricane Katrina happened so recently. For a lot of people Hurricane Katrina and the handling of the disaster by the Bush administration was the end of trust, or at least support, of the Bush White House. No matter which way you spin the events, it's difficult to give President Bush any leeway. A lot of people died unnecessarily because of the lack of effort and outreach from Washington. Everything from "Heck of a job, Brownie" to "George Bush does not care about black people" will forever haunt my memory of watching the terrible images of people standing on rooftops, lined up at the Superdome, and the endless red X's and body bags.

I do not pretend to completely understand where things exactly failed, starting from what could have been done to strengthen the levees so they wouldn't break, to getting FEMA to New Orleans faster, to everything that made Hurricane Katrina the disaster and tragedy that it was. All I know is what I felt when it was happening, as I prepare to see how far the worst-affected part of the city has come.

At a café we meet up with Jacques Morial, an outreach and research director for Heath Law Advocates of Louisiana, and immediately start discussing what it was like for him during Hurricane Katrina. We talk about everything from President Bush to Mayor Ray Nagin and his infamous "Chocolate City" comments. A few years ago I happened to meet Nagin's cousin, who asked me what I thought of the mayor, and I said that I thought he did what he could during an almost impossible situation. I didn't think he was a saint or a criminal, but a politician put in a situation where he was given very little help from the federal government.

Jacques was born and raised in New Orleans, has lived there his entire life, loves it dearly, and never once considered leaving after Katrina, though he does understand why some people just couldn't bear to come back. I tell him about Willis, and how he'd been in jail during Katrina. He wasn't released from jail during the floods until the water had reached his chest. Just the mental image of men (and possibly women) thinking they might drown in a locked cell seems like something out of a horror movie, not something that happened in the United States a mere few years ago.

"Yeah, they eventually let all the prisoners out," Jacques says with a sad shake of his head. "That isn't even the beginning of the kinds of stories I have heard."

We drive out to the Lower Ninth Ward, and I realize that my words will never do justice to the physical landscape or the energy of the place, but I hope that I can somehow encourage other people to go on this journey to better feel for themselves its beautiful eeriness.

We pass a number of different houses that have been rebuilt in the architectural style they had before Katrina. There are also large areas of empty lots that sit vacant, some packed with garbage and debris covered in layers of uncut dead weeds and new grass. It looks like an archeological dig in reverse—the history of the people too recent, the fossils and potsherds in need of centuries of decomposition.

Other areas are spotless in their renewed perfection, the effort to erase the brutality of the storm outshining the ease with which the bougainvilleas bloom on their tumultuous vines. However, there is no sense of closure to the refurbished Lower Ninth Ward. Almost like a tattoo that has only been partially removed, there is still evidence of the devastation in the demarcations visible on many of the houses that haven't been restored.

We drive by house after house, and Jacques shows us how far the waterline had risen. He points out different houses where people had to be rescued from their roofs after using axes to break through the rafters and climb on top. Luckily, some people had kept axes in their attics because of lore about the levees flooding.

"If you saw it on the news," he tells us, "this is where people waited sometimes for days to be rescued. Just sitting up there out in the hot sun, not knowing if they were going to die or not."

For whatever reason, the image of my father's prison, the "Hanoi Hilton" in Vietnam, springs to mind. I visited the Hanoi Hilton when I was in college and we went on a family trip to Vietnam. I feel now as I did then, glad to witness what is left of the physicality of a place that held such horrific experiences, yet also angry that history has let such things happen. Human beings and politics can be so grotesque and barbaric, but hope can always be found somewhere, disguised, in that complicated kaleidoscope.

We get out of Jacques's car and walk around. In the midst of the old-style architecture of traditional wide-porched New Orleans houses are the startling eco-friendly "Brad Pitt houses," built by Pitt and his Make It Right Foundation. Make It Right has pledged to rebuild the parish, and has completed fourteen houses, with nineteen currently under construction. They are slowly moving families one by one back into their homes, which are affordable and environmentally sound. They are also putting money into community centers and gardens, doing their best to reestablish the Lower Ninth Ward as a place where middle-income families can thrive.

All that said, the houses visually stick out like a sore thumb. No one needs to point them out, as they look like futuristic *2001: A Space Odyssey* cubes, or like something we may one day build on Mars. They're not what I would call beautiful, nor do I completely understand why the foundation chose to go so far away from the traditional feeling of the place. I respect and appreciate the intent of Brad Pitt, and the nobility of his mission, but they seem weirdly . . . arrogant, as though a panel of experts handed down a decree to the people of Whoville saying, "Trust us, you'll *like* living on this dust speck."

We stand in front of one particularly unfortunate-looking house, towering over its historic neighbor on stilts that seem to say, *Next time I'm going to make it, but you aren't.* I try to see what the building will look like once the shrubs have grown and the trees come back, but honestly, it looks more like a jacked-up trailer than anything else.

I ask Jacques, "Would it have been really difficult to make environmentally friendly houses that also resembled the aesthetic that used to encompass the Ninth Ward?"

"Those eco-friendly homes are not without controversy," he says softly.

Maybe I am wrong, maybe the Lower Ninth Ward should be rebuilt not trying to recreate the past exactly as it was, but shaped with more consciousness of the kind of future the Lower Ninth Ward *should* have, which still seems like it's a complicated one.

We make our way over train tracks and empty lots where a makeshift deck has been built over the levee so that visitors can look out onto the barge of muddy water clotted with weeds, grass, tree branches, and assorted stumps.

"We built this because we never want people to forget and we want to show them where it happened," Jacques says as a small bike tour led by a young man from the neighborhood passes. "He does that for free," he explains. "He just wants to give people tours of the Lower Ninth—I mean, you could buy him lunch afterwards, but it doesn't cost anything to go on the bike tour."

"Hey, Jacques!" the young man yells. "Doing a tour, I see."

"Beautiful day for it!" Jacques greets the man back. As we watch the tiny tour weave into the Lower Ninth, I feel hope coming off the area in fresh waves. The guide didn't seem sad; he seemed happy to be sharing his town with a handful of strangers, just as Glen, Willis, and Jacques have been with us. The pride all these natives feel is contagious, and even as the Brad Pitt houses loom over the neighborhood, it's apparent that there are enough people in here and out there to bring the Lower Ninth Ward of New Orleans to a better place, even if it's taking too long to do so.

Little Rock, Arkansas

Lot Lizards

Meghan: This will not be my first visit to Little Rock. I traveled there during my father's campaign for an event and a fundraiser and I remember being, as terrible as this may sound, very bored. I'm hoping it was situational, given that I was traveling with my father's campaign staff, who were essentially adult babysitters— there to make sure I didn't get arrested or create some kind of media drama. The trip basically consisted of getting on and off a campaign plane, waiting outside a fundraiser talking to volunteers who had previously worked for Mike Huckabee (and seemed to prefer Mike Huckabee over my father), and watching *Sex and the City* reruns in my hotel room. Maybe this trip to Little Rock will prove a little more exciting.

Much to my relief, Michael, Stephie, and, dare I say, Cousin John and I seem to be getting into a rhythm with one another. The long RV rides and our constant meals together have slowly gone from feeling like the awkward first few weeks of school and started to evolve into the later free-wheeling weeks of summer camp. Before I left for this trip, I had dinner with friends and told them I hoped it was going to be exactly like camp, and I felt that Michael Ian Black would make a good camp counselor, or at least fellow camper. His hilarious work on the movie *Wet Hot American Summer* was clearly evidence to the yes side of the table, seeing as how it is set at a summer camp. The no side of the table depicted the two of us screaming at each other in the middle of the desert, with me hitchhiking my way home and calling the book off. Happily, we are nowhere near the desert.

I have very dear and close friends that I describe as "the inner circle." It's always been difficult for me to let new people in and it gets harder every year as I get older. So it's surprising to me, as we spend more time on the road and have more meaningful conversations, as the sweltering southern countryside passes outside the window, that Michael has actually, and possibly unintentionally, wormed his little way in. He's a terrific listener, and has even given me some great advice. I know I go all Rambo on him when we're talking politics, but with each passing mile marker, we grow that much closer.

I even half-joke with Michael this morning when we leave for Little Rock, "You know, if you're in, you're in for life now, and my drama is now your drama, right?"

Michael looks at me and deadpans, "I love your drama. I know. I'm in."

I can't help but produce a huge Cheshire Cat grin. It's a perfect answer, and pretty much at that point I let go of all my walls. I'm sure that doesn't mean we're going to stop fighting or debating our absolute world of differences and beliefs. It just means that the discussions are going to be more honest.

Michael: If I have any excuse for wanting to go to Little Rock, it's that there isn't much else on the way to Branson. Also, this trip has been a Republican freak fest from moment one and I need to get a little Democrat love. What better Democrat lover than Bill Clinton, whose hometown also houses his presidential library? We figure we'll make a daytrip to Little Rock, stop at the William J. Clinton Presidential Library & Museum, and then hit the fabulous Little Rock nightlife.

As we head up I-55 from Mayor Nagin's "Chocolate City," we do some research on what to do in The Rock. Yes, we know Little Rock nightlife is probably not going to compare to the goings-on in New Orleans, but we figure there has to be *something* to do. After researching the matter on Google, we determined that, in fact, no, there is nothing to do in Little Rock. The entire town disappears in a puff of smoke at five o'clock in the afternoon.

We then put the query out to our Twitter followers. Mostly we get the expected snarky comments, but a few people mention going to North Little Rock for strip clubs and danger. We've already done the strip club in Vegas, although "danger" holds some appeal. I'm not sure what kind of danger they're talking about, but I assume it's the kind of homogenous corporatized danger that occurs when heated words are exchanged at a Dave & Buster's.

As crazy a gun culture as we have in America, I almost never feel like I am in any actual danger. That's a good thing, but it seems at odds with the way the world views us. When I say "the world," I am talking specifically about a couple of the au pairs who have come to live with my family over the past few years. These are mostly French girls in their early twenties. My wife, having lived for a year in Paris, is an unabashed Francophile and wanted our kids to learn French. They didn't.

One of the reasons Martha was not worried about me going on this trip with Meghan was probably because she saw how I conducted myself around our series of barely legal French nannies. I always acted like a perfect gentleman. Because I am, in fact, a perfect gentleman. Anyway, all of these girls expressed the same fear when they came to America: that they would get shot. Around the world, or at least in high schools in France, the impression of America is that we are a trigger-happy, gun-crazed culture in which every day is likely to end with a bullet wound. There are some neighborhoods in America where that is no doubt more accurate than others, but it's not something I've witnessed. Meghan argues that carrying guns makes us *more* safe, not less, because people are less likely to get into violent confrontations when they believe there is a good chance their opponent is armed. I don't know if that's true or not, but I do know I am considerably less comfortable around cops and soldiers than I am around receptionists. (And, for the record, only one of our au pairs got shot. That's a joke.)

Also, if I had a gun, I'd want to use it. I mean, what's the point in going to all the trouble of getting a concealed-weapon permit if at some point you aren't going to whip it out and yell, "YOU GONNA

FUCK WITH ME, MOTHERFUCKER? YOU GONNA FUCK WITH ME???" I would probably do that every day.

So even though I know that there are millions of gun-carrying lunatics in America, and even though I know people get shot here all the time, because I have never experienced any of it, I tend to dismiss actual "danger." I mean, there are other kinds of danger certainly. There's drug danger and unforeseen danger and going-over-waterfalls-in-a-barrel danger and all the rest, but I have to come to view America as a relatively safe and peaceful place. On any given day, the greatest danger I face is the possibility that I have accidentally purchased "lightly salted" pretzels instead of the regular kind, a mistake that fills me with the same dread I might experience upon confronting an armed adversary on the mean streets of North Little Rock, Arkansas.

Meghan: Anyone who has been to Little Rock knows that the only tourist attraction worth visiting is the Clinton library. Now, this may surprise you, but I am not a huge Clinton fan.

When I first heard about the Lewinsky scandal, I was just fourteen, and my father was talking on a car speakerphone to his then right-hand man (and for the political junkies out there, my father's "alter ego"), Mark Salter. Mark obviously was not made aware that I was in the car with my father when he said, "Have you heard this shit about this intern fucking Clinton?"

My father immediately switched the phone off speaker and groaned "JEEZEEEE! I'll call you back when Meghan and I get back from the store."

Concerned, I said to Dad, "What was that all about? Did the president do something?"

"Don't worry about it, honey," he said. "Don't worry about it." And that was pretty much it.

Unfortunately for my parents, the Lewinsky blow job was widely discussed in my eighth-grade class. Up until that point I had no idea what a blow job was and couldn't really comprehend the discussions about "the blue dress," "the stains," and "depends on what your

In Jerome, Arizona, enjoying the view, if not the background singing.

We are family:
brother, sister, M16.

With Jimmy McCain: "Your hat is on backwards, sir."

With Mike, Cindy, Holly, Kyle, and Jimmy. Celebrating the 4th on Whiskey Row. *Not pictured:* rodeo (because there was no damned rodeo that night).

Nermal and friend.

Meghan posing as General Custer.

Michael looking incredibly virile astride his mount
(*caption written by Michael*).

We've just picked up the RV, which is why we look happy instead of nauseous.

"Are you kiddin' me?" Our Gumdrop, Cousin John.

Emperor of Zappos, Las Vegas.

With Cargill and Jessica and dog. *Not pictured:* 10,000 Warhammer figurines.

Home, sweet home. *Not pictured:* stench.

Lookin' for gators down on the bayou.

Our guide feeding a gator its natural prey: marshmallows.

Meghan bravely trying to hide how pissed she is with Michael down on the bayou.

We took him on the road with us. (The baby gator, not the guide.)

With Glen. If we all look a little f-ed up, we are.

Posing with giant floral butterfly because why is there a giant floral butterfly at the Dixie Stampede in Branson, Missouri?

Just chillin' on the steps of Graceland.

Ordering Jell-O shots like a champ.

With President Clinton's limo in Little Rock, Arkansas.

"What a country!" With Yakov's head.

Drunken, awful singing in Branson, Missouri.
Not pictured: the huge gash Michael just opened on his
leg after falling into the drum kit.

Inside the simulator at Ft. Campbell, Kentucky.

We stopped at a Pirates game. Five innings later,
Stephie was furious with us for refusing to leave.

Inside Senator McCain's office. Door to the private senatorial bathroom ajar to the right.

With Stephie, Senator McCain, and Senator Graham out on the town.

definition of sex is" that were happening all around me. Then during school lunchtime, in a bathroom with a bunch of other eighth-grade girls, one of them proceeded to describe "blow job" in somewhat graphic and accurate detail. Maybe my parents had sheltered me more than most, but I was shocked and confused, and mostly couldn't stop wondering, *Why would the president or Monica Lewinsky do such a thing?* Yes, ladies and gentlemen, Meghan McCain's first exposure to oral sex was also, sadly, political.

While I dislike President Clinton, and am actually one of those people who still think it was deplorable that he got an intern to blow him in the West Wing during business hours, I am a big fan of Hillary's. I disagree with many, many of her policies but have a respect for the fact that she pushed through many doors and shattered many glass ceilings for women in politics. I love women who don't put up with shit, and Hillary clearly doesn't.

Michael seems to have very little problem with the Clinton-Lewinsky affair, at least in terms of the presidency. I'm not a prude or a hypocrite. I have been very, very honest about the kind of lifestyle I lead, which in Republican circles, is actually considered by some to be controversial. I am pro-life and I don't believe in abortion, except in cases of rape and incest. I do believe life begins at conception and that abortion is morally wrong. I could never have an abortion. I believe in birth control in all forms and that condoms should be available everywhere. I also believe that people are born gay, which many say is a sin. But I have referred to myself as a "liberal Christian," in that my God and my Jesus do not make mistakes.

I have never cheated on a boyfriend, ever. I grew up with three rules from my parents: "Don't lie, cheat, or steal. Everything else is fair game." I think part of the reason why I never went through a "rebellious" phase is because my parents were very lenient and understanding with me—as long as there wasn't any lying, cheating, or stealing involved. This is why, for me, it is a completely black-and-white situation: President Clinton cheated and lied. You can argue all you want, but he cheated on his marriage vows, he cheated on his role as an employer, and he cheated the country from many months of what should have been personal-conflict-free governing. Don't even get me started on the lying. How anyone could argue that his misbehavior did not affect our position on the world stage is incomprehensible. The core actions—seducing a young woman and having her get you off—alone are deplorable, but then the way he went on to play the victim was ultimately worse. On top of everything else, this all took place in the Oval Office of the White House. Sure, I'll go to President Clinton's shrine, but don't ask me for a minute to say what he did was no big deal. To an impressionable, patriotic fourteen-year-old, it was—and still is—a *very* big deal.

Michael: The Clinton library looms up ahead of us. I don't know if I really love Bill Clinton or if my good feelings for him are based on the fact that Republicans hate him so much. Man, do they hate Bill Clinton. Now that he's been out of office for over a decade, it's easy to forget just how much vitriol was hurled in his direction when he was president. Okay, an intern blew him. I'm sure a lot of other women did too. That guy probably collected blow jobs the way I used to collect comic books. Outraged Republicans couldn't understand why Democrats didn't care. The answer is simple: because we didn't. Yes, given the choice of having our commander in chief getting hummers in the Oval Office or not getting hummers in the Oval Office, most of us would probably answer "not," but it's nothing to get too worked up about. I doubt W. ever got so much as a light ball cradling in there, yet I'll take the Clinton presidency over the W. presidency any day of the week. Peace and prosperity always trump faith and fidelity.

That's something social conservatives don't understand about the general voting population. For moralists, America's bedrock is biblical. They believe when you start hydrofracking that foundational stone, all sorts of terrible things happen. Men start kissing men, children start practicing wizardry, and soon we are all swimming in lakes of fire and wondering where it all went wrong. That's not how people like me see our country. For us, it pretty much comes down to a good economy and safety. That's it—lights on, bills paid, kids clothed and educated. Nobody blowing my shit up or breaking into my crib. Morality doesn't even really enter into the conversation except insomuch as we do not want our presidents to be actual crooks (see: Nixon, Richard M.). Or, even if they are crooks, at least be smart enough not to get caught. Clinton, for all his faults, is not a crook. He's not corrupt. He's just a guy who likes to get his dick sucked by ladies other than his wife. Not my business.

And say what you want about his sexual mores, the guy was a good-to-great president. One could argue about the truthfulness of the phrase "greatest peacetime economic expansion in American history," and one could argue about who is ultimately responsible for said economic expansion, but the fact that the argument even exists at all is a testament to the presidency of Slick Willy. Any way you slice it, America did well during his eight years in office. How much of that was his doing? I don't know and I don't care. When we look back at our history, we don't remember the Speaker of the House or the Majority Whip. We remember the president. Presidents, fairly or unfairly, receive the lion's share of credit and blame. Clinton was president during the nineties, and the nineties were pretty good. So I'm excited to go pay my respects to the man's administration as we turn off US 65 towards 1200 President Clinton Avenue.

Meghan: Ex-presidents are usually looked upon with much more admirable eyes out of office than in. President Clinton is no different. As Michael says, "peace and prosperity" trump "faith and fidelity." Among the reasons why the nineties were not entirely a peaceful and prosperous time, the actions of President Clinton and his subsequent impeachment trial are high up on the list. It was a very tumultuous, complicated, and embarrassing time for the country, and in many ways the final last days of the president having respect for the White House.

Michael may look back at the Clinton years with fond memories and nostalgia, but I look back on them with embarrassment and cringe. Maybe Clinton is to many Democrats what Reagan is to many Republicans. A somewhat glossed over and heightened icon of a time gone by where each party was in a sort of heyday—although Reagan never had a sexual affair in the Oval Office and was never impeached. I'm just saying. Also, Michael may be fond of the nineties because it was a great time for his career. Don't get mad, Michael, it's kind of true.

I don't know what I originally expected from the Clinton library, but it looks out of place in comparison to its surrounding landscape. That being said, I don't think the Clinton Foundation or the Clintons themselves would want to necessarily build a structure that looked like an old log cabin, but I wasn't expecting it to look so much like a structure from the future. It has all *The Jetson*'s stylings of what people in the 1960s imagined buildings would look like in 2040. Much like the Brad Pitt housing in the Lower Ninth Ward in New Orleans, the Clinton library is not cognizant enough of the surrounding landscape, and seems more interested in making an architectural statement. My personal aesthetic may lean more towards traditional styles, but even so, this place doesn't even look like a library.

Michael: The main building is almost a perfect architectural metaphor for Clinton. Like the man, the library (excuse me: "Presidential Center") is boxy and outsized and modern in a nineties sort of way, all steel and glass that gives the illusion of transparency. Upon closer inspection, however, you discover that the gleaming glass is tinted a milky white, obscuring the building's inner workings, and the views inside are actually quite limited. The building is part riverboat, part USS *Enterprise*. I heard somebody say it looks like a double-wide, which is true, but if so, it's the most grandiose double-wide in the history of white trash.

Cousin John drops us off at the front and retreats to the far reaches of the parking lot for a sweaty nap. Unbelievably, the center is featuring an Elvis exhibition. The comparisons between Clinton and Elvis are legion, and accurate. Both were poor white southern kids who came from nothing to achieve the greatest heights of their chosen professions. Both had enormous, insatiable appetites for things they knew to be bad for them. Both could bite a lip and tear an eye in a genuinely sympathetic way. Elvis was a gifted musician.

Clinton loves Elvis. How could he not? They're basically the same guy. The exhibition is called *Elvis at 21*, and the first thing I notice upon entering, apart from the air-conditioning, is the iconic white polyester Elvis jumpsuit bedazzled with American flag beadwork and topped with a huge double-American-eagle belt buckle. It is America in all its chintzy glamour. I can think of no better symbol for the nation or the man who used to run it.

To the right is Clinton's limo, an armored Cadillac. Up close, the trappings of presidential power don't look nearly as impressive as they do on TV. Basically the car is just a car. It's a big car, but there's no footbath or hot chocolate machine or anything. Honestly, I've been in Corollas that seemed almost as nice. At Reagan's library, they've got the actual *Air Force One* he used housed in a specially designed airplane hangar. You can tour the plane, and the thing that struck me about it was how normal it seemed. Yes, it's *Air Force One*, yes it's a magnificent symbol of American power, but inside it's just kind of an airplane.

One of the few things I've learned about wealth is that money can only buy so much. The food I eat doesn't taste all that much different from the food the richest man in the world eats. The chair in which I sit isn't so much different from any other chair. Houses are, ultimately, houses. Boats are boats. To me, the only reason to be president is for the toys, but seeing them up close I realize the toys are impressive but not *that* impressive. They don't blow me away. The fact that I could order a grilled cheese on *Air Force One* whenever I wanted one would be cool but not cool enough to take on being president. Being Elvis, on the other hand, would be awesome. You get around-the-clock grilled peanut butter, banana, and bacon sandwiches, for starters. The rest is gravy. Boatloads of beautiful sausage gravy.

Meghan: It is a little embarrassing to admit how excited I am that there is an Elvis exhibition going on. I am an Elvis fanatic. I love

Elvis! I love his music, I love his style, I love his legacy. I once got into a small scuffle over Elvis in London while studying abroad in college. A random Englishman said he thought Elvis was overrated and the real "King" was Mick Jagger. I'm told that I called the Rolling Stones pansies and firmly stated that Elvis was and always will be "The King!" For the record, I don't think the Rolling Stones are pansies at all, but I prefer Elvis any day of the week. Besides, Elvis was just one hunky guy—the Rolling Stones are four men, just saying. I'm delighted to know that while I'm not enjoying my tour of Clinton's shrine, I will at least be able to see some cool Elvis costumes and pictures.

Parked in the lobby is the limo Clinton used while president. Michael, Stephie, and I stand around it taking cheesy pictures, and then split up to tour the center. Listen, the center is well done. It is exactly what a presidential library should be: a complete and utter whitewash of the life of a guy lucky enough to have an affable alternative like Ross Perot chew at the Republican base enough for the other guy to be elected to lead the country. No disrespect to the highest office in the land; it's just that I get a little tired of all the revisionist history that happens the minute a flawed human being gets to be in control of his past misdeeds. I'm looking at you, WJC.

We watch a video about the life of President Clinton, we take a tour of giant pictures of the president throughout his life, we view political collectables on display such as bumper stickers, buttons, banners, bandstand-style hats with CLINTON written on them. I can't believe how young both Bill and Hillary look in all the pictures. The ridiculous displays of campaign memorabilia make me laugh a little, because our home looks a lot like this, without the giant cantilevered building to wrap it all in. The same type of stuff, buttons, hats, bumper stickers, bobbleheads, T-shirts. I guess it just comes with the territory.

Am I a changed person after walking through this place? Not really, but there are some points of interest: a display of beautiful gowns that Hillary Clinton wore as First Lady, a somewhat decent history lesson, and a catalyst for a debate with Michael over whether or not fidelity is an important factor in presidential politics. I still maintain that it is important and a large indicator of character. Michael doesn't care, which seems a bit ironic given how important marriage and family values are to Michael in his personal life.

Michael: It's not like I had really high hopes for this library to live up to some presidential standard, but I have to admit I'm disappointed that it's little more than a massive shrine to the forty-second president. It's got the replica Oval Office, the de rigueur NFL-style highlight film of the presidency, the timeline showing all his legislative accomplishments. But nowhere do I see the words "impeached," or "Whitewater." Nowhere do I see the names "Kenneth Starr" or "Monica Lewinsky." These are significant historical omissions in a place designed to remember history, not rewrite it. Of course, the thing about these presidential libraries is that they are funded by private donations. They can do whatever they want with that money, so if they choose to make the place into an exercise in hagiography, they can. Even so, I'm peeved. I'm a grown-up and can accept that one of my political heroes wasn't perfect. This place sucks.

Any self-delusion I harbor about the differences in Meghan's and my respective ages is shattered by the following conversation:

Her: "How old were you during the impeachment trial?"
Me: "Well, it was what? Ninety-eight? So I was twenty-seven."
Her: "I have very little memory of it. I was very young."

She wasn't *that* young, I remind her. She was thirteen or fourteen. But still, the idea that one of the most seminal political events of my lifetime barely registered on her teenage consciousness is a little disconcerting.

Her: "Do you think he should have been impeached?"
Me: "For getting blown in the West Wing? No. For this place? Hell yes."

Meghan: Between the depressing paving over of recent history and the oppressive slamming of the hot, moist day as we leave the library, all of us are depleted and I just want to shower all of it right off as soon as I can. We pull into the Red Roof Inn in North Little Rock, noting the less than quaint surroundings as we pass two gas stations and a Waffle House dotted by the kind of low-shouldered housing with burnt-grass front lawns that speak to a lean economy. One of the things Michael and I have in common is that we have very low standards when it comes to hotels. Sure, I love a five-star, super-fancy hotel as much as the next person, but I find that I always end up spending fifty dollars on a Coke from the minibar and the Internet service inevitably sucks. Cheaper chain hotels normally have great Internet access, a breakfast spread for free in the morning, more to offer when it comes to the kinds of characters lurking around and more opportunity for a more interesting experience or adventure. I have spent so much time on the road in my life at cheaper chain hotels, and the most memorable things that have happened to me were at a La Quinta Inn, not a Four Seasons.

After showering and taking a little rest inside, we decide to find some BBQ, Cousin John driving the giant RV to a restaurant in the middle of a strip mall. I'm feeling my second wind; good beer and good BBQ can do that to a person. We tried to figure out what the nightlife in Little Rock has to offer, once again checking our Twitter feeds for any new hints from the outside world. We come up completely empty-handed. Why is there no nightlife to be found in Little Rock? I had hoped for a good blues bar, at the very least.

Back at the hotel I present Michael with a fifth-grade challenge: "We're going to hang out here all night, you're going to call it." He's in. There's no bar, no restaurant, no gift shop, no minibar to raid. Had we known, we would have picked up some beers, but instead we sit in the cheap chairs in the lobby of the Red Roof Inn, looking at each other. I pick up a dog-eared brochure for Dolly Parton's Dixieland Stampede.

"Hey, Michael," I say. "Look, this is the 'most fun place to eat'!"

He raises an eyebrow over the same brochure in his hand. "Four courses of fun," he says without smiling. "Shame it's in Branson. Little Rock can't even advertise its own fun. Why? Because there isn't any fun to be had."

He goes back to updating his Twitter feed and I look around the lobby, noticing a heavily tattooed woman using the guest computer.

I nod in her direction. "I'm gonna go talk to her because I know you won't," I say to Michael.

"True."

I stroll over, noticing that the tattoos on her arms wrap under her sleeves and up her breasts up to her neck. There's even the word "misfit" in ink over her right eye.

"Hey, girl," I say. "Do you know if there's anything to do around here? Me and my friend Michael over there are on a road trip across country and we're looking to go out."

She looks up from her computer and smiles. "Not unless you're into dirty strip clubs," she says.

"Well, not tonight I'm not." I laugh. She tells me that she's a single mom, in Little Rock to attend trucker school. She wants to become a trucker to support her kid. I ask her if it's hard being one of the few females in a male-dominated industry.

She says, "Isn't everything run by men? Let me put it this way, I'm one of only two women taking this class."

"Men are intimidated by everything, I swear," I say. "Especially strong women with strong opinions." She agrees and we start chatting about being a woman, going to school, her tattoos, my tattoos, how she also takes pinup girl pictures in her free time, that she has a son named Phoenix who is staying with her parents while she's at trucker school. She's lovely, friendly, and funny, and seems really excited about becoming a trucker and the money it's going to bring in for her and her son. We talk about exes, and I'm having more fun talking to her than I was with Michael. I always have more in common with women than men, and it's nice to have a little girl talk with this complete stranger.

I introduce her to Michael.

"You guys are probably the only nontruckers in this hotel," she says. "Most of the people here are in trucker school with me." Michael tells her he wants to meet more truckers. More truckers unfortunately do not show up. Eventually she says good night after showing me pictures of her Suicide Girls–style pinup layouts on her Facebook page, explaining how she's found this very supportive online community of women who embrace alternative approaches to beauty, steeped in the retro-goth style of erotic models like Bettie Page.

The pictures are sultry and beautiful, much different than her sweatpants lobby look, but who doesn't look different in their sweats? She suddenly recognizes Michael and geeks out a little bit.

"Ohh my God, you were on VH1, right?" she asks.

"Yes, *I Love the*—"

"*Eighties!*" she shrieks. "I loved that!" And I love this conversation. I love that she recognizes Michael and seems simultaneously surprised and a little embarrassed that he is creeping around a hotel lobby with some random twenty-something blonde. I hug her goodbye as she leaves and says good night and I slide next to Michael on the lobby chair.

"Call it, bitch," I say.

"No, I'm not even tired. You call it," he says, stifling a yawn. That is a total lie; Michael gets tired like a baby girl, needing naps throughout the day. I know he's tired. It's just a matter of time now.

Michael: I will not call it. I have an endless capacity for indulging in boredom. Being bored is one of my favorite activities. Meghan, on the other hand, is borderline ADD. There's no way she can out lobby-sit me. I like my chances at this particular competition. Stephie caved at the onset of this game, refusing to participate. She thinks it's immature. Which it is. And stupid. Which it is. And pointless. WHICH IT IS NOT.

The point is, obviously, to win. Why don't people understand that the point of all things is to win? Politicians certainly do. That's why they do what they do. To all those people who bemoan the fact that politicians routinely put party above country, consider the nature of the people serving as politicians. Winning is their entire raison d'être. Our political system, and much of our notion about what it means to be American, is about winning. That's who we are. Americans are winners. To even get elected to office, a politician has to run an almost impossible gauntlet of fundraising, campaigning, and character assassinating. The only people who are going to bother doing all that are hypercompetitive by nature. Why do we expect them to lay that aside once they assume office? They can't, any more than Meghan can go outside without full makeup on. It's a genetic impossibility.

Their mandate is to win: to win, win again, and then win some more. Which is not to say that they do not *also* try to do the right thing; it's just not as important as winning. I once asked Jake Tapper, the senior White House correspondent for ABC News, what he thought is the ratio of a politician's decisions made for political expediency versus political conviction. He replied, "Two-one." Which is better than I would have guessed.

As for Meghan and me, we're just going to sit here in the lobby of a Red Roof Inn until one of us decides to call it quits. Is that any less immature, stupid, and pointless than what passes for our political system?

Five more minutes pass since the Suicide Girl went upstairs. It must be almost nine o'clock.

"You want to call it?" I ask Meghan.

"If you want to."

"I'm not calling it."

"Well you know *I'm* not calling it."

We sit like that for a little while longer. After half an hour or so, the sliding doors to the lobby open and two girls walk in. Well, "girls" might not be anatomically accurate. One of them is definitely a girl and one of them seems to be floating in some sort of genderless limbo. They approach us, giggling.

"We read your tweet," the girl says.

"We wanted to meet you," the other "girl" says.

Meghan shoots me a look. One of the main rules her father's office has given her is never to tweet your location. I guess they don't want the daughter of one of the most powerful senators in Washington to go around broadcasting her location. They are probably more worried about nefarious kidnappers than giggling pre-op transsexuals, but still, I feel somewhat abashed.

The girls introduce themselves: Sammy and her friend Ursula. I will let you guess which is which. They explain that they were sitting at home when Sammy saw the tweet. She called Ursula, who was by herself playing video games, and they decided to have an adventure. So they got in Sammy's car and came to find us. Which they did. And now that they're here, the conversation is pretty stilted. After about three minutes or so, they've run out of things to say to us and I gently encourage them to wrap things up by saying things like, "It was so nice to meet you" and "Thank you for coming all this way to say hello."

Finally they bid their good nights and head back to their car. My back is to them but Meghan watches them get into the car.

"They're just sitting there," she says to me.

"They're just sitting there?"

"Yeah, they're just sitting there staring at us."

Meghan admonishes me for tweeting. "My father's office will have a shit fit if they find out."

"Her father's office" has been a frequent subject on the trip. "The office" is like a third parent, or maybe a nanny, that keeps tabs on the McCain family and their various comings and goings, all in the name of serving the senator. Meghan hates it. She's twenty-seven years old, but finds herself constantly having to worry about what "her father's office" is going to say about her actions. Of course, it's easy to sit back and go, as I do, "Tell them to fuck off," but it's not that easy in practice.

"The office" is an extension of her father, and as such, everything she does, fairly or unfairly, can be used by his political opponents against him. If the daughter does something they don't like, it becomes ammunition against the father. As such, "the office" is constantly on guard, constantly monitoring what Meghan and her siblings do to make sure all of it is consistent with whatever the senator is out there saying and doing. It's not fair, of course, and Meghan pushes back as hard as she can, but she also loves her dad and doesn't want to screw things up for him by going out on the road for a month with a married, older comedian she doesn't know, for example.

In this regard, I feel bad for her and her family. It can't be easy to live your life under a microscope. I couldn't deal with it if it was me. As a parent, I can't imagine what it would be like to subject your kids to that kind of scrutiny either. Maybe the culture was different when Senator McCain was first elected to Congress in 1982. Maybe, but I don't know.

The thing I'm learning is that when one member of a family enters political office, the entire family enters with him or her. Every family member is subjected to scrutiny. When you run for office, it's not enough to think that you would be good in the job. You've got to consider every single person in your immediate family: their careers, their personal lives, any past indiscretions or financial mistakes. All of it becomes fair game. Any mistake one family member makes becomes a referendum on the entire clan. No wonder so many political kids get screwed up. It would be very hard to run for office with an Ursula in the family, at least as a Republican. As a Democrat, "she" might be an advantage.

After ten minutes sitting out in the parking lot staring out the windshield at us, Sammy and Ursula finally drive off.

Meghan: After they leave, I once again ask Michael, because we have been sitting in the lobby of a North Little Rock Red Roof Inn for over an hour at this point: "You want to call it?"

"Hell no," answers Michael, but I know for a fact that "Hell no" actually means "Yes, I'm old and exhausted and I want to go back to my room to troll Twitter." I know him, I know he wants to go to bed and tweet, or post a video blog about President Clinton and Little Rock, so I am going to stay up all night out of principle alone.

I am, however, sick of sitting in the lobby. I want to go out and explore, since there is really no other option.

I tell Michael I'm going to take a walk and he actually looks concerned.

"You can't take a walk out there," he says. "It's dangerous and the Suicide Girl just told us there are truck-stop hookers and meth heads."

"Don't be such a pansy," I reply. "I'll be fine." Michael insists on joining me, with his worried face sternly attached.

We walk outside into an area that, to put it mildly, looks more sketchy than when we drove past it earlier, high up in our air-cooled RV. The darkness doesn't help. We walk along the dead-grass edge of a utility road scattered with trash, broken bottles, and beer cans. We don't see another single person. After a nervous few minutes of vulnerability, we arrive at a gas station where, yes, we see a woman in a short, tight, pleather miniskirt, a tank top with no bra, and giant tottering heels. Our friend from the lobby was right: this apparently is a good place to pick up prostitutes.

I try not to stare or look shocked, and fear I'm doing both. Michael actually looks really surprised and a little concerned for the woman.

"How does that happen?" I whisper to him. "How does one get there?" I know I said I have conflicting feelings about strippers, earlier in the trip, and I do. Prostitution is a different story. I don't think there is a person on the planet who as a little girl dreamed of being a roadside hooker. This is not the first time I've seen a prostitute, but it is every bit as sad as the few times before. I think about the recession, people hitting hard times, and am awash with gratitude for all the opportunities I have been given. Hell, my problems are nothing compared to a significant portion of the rest of the population's. I feel terrible for women caught in this world, and wish there was a way to tell them there is a better way and a better life. I'm just not sure that is necessarily a true statement, nor do I think they want to hear it from a woman like me. The economic disconnect is striking at midnight outside this filthy gas station in North

Little Rock, but what worries me most is that this scenario is being repeated in too many places to count across the country.

Michael: We circle to the front of another gas station, but there are a couple of hoodlums inside so we decide not to go in. I mean, I don't know if they're hoodlums or not, but what are they doing hanging out at a gas station at midnight in North Little Rock? Of course, by that definition, we're hoodlums too.

More tantalizing than whatever offerings are for sale at the gas station, however, is the cheery yellow Waffle House sign we see a couple of hundred yards away. I love Waffle House. They seem to be mostly a southern chain, so I didn't know about them growing up in New Jersey. I have since become an ardent admirer because they make delicious waffles, and what could be better than that?

We make for it, dodging a couple more Lot Lizards on the way. I don't know why this area is teeming with meth-head hookers. I suppose it's the high population of bored truckers and easy access to the highway. The truckers pull off the road for the night, and right there are scraggly, wild-eyed whores ready to take their business. The women all have the same purposeful walk, like carpenter ants looking for crumbs of food.

It's kind of thrilling to be out in the wild Arkansas night among them, but it's also depressing. Who are they? How did they end up out here wandering around the asphalt at midnight doing this? Meghan and I don't say much to each other as we walk, but we're both goggle-eyed.

Considering the hour, the Waffle House is surprisingly crowded. Several tables are filled. The clientele is mostly young and male and mean looking. A group of boys lolls in a back booth. Two guys and a girl huddle over their food, talking quietly, their faces hard. The waitresses, none of them younger than fifty, shuttle coffee pots among the patrons. They look like ladies who say things like, "I'm not gonna take any of your guff."

The windows are all encased in fog, giving the place the look of a steam room in a seedy massage parlor. We're both kind of appalled and delighted to find ourselves in these circumstances. A few minutes after we order our waffles, the door opens and a portly Asian guy, easily three hundred pounds, struts into the restaurant. On his arm is a woman stilting precariously on stripper heels, her face smeared with cheap makeup. They're arm in arm and the guy has a shit-eating grin on his face, as if he can't believe his luck at finding himself in such grand circumstances, as if he is about to sit down at the captain's table on the *Queen Elizabeth*. He seems to possess not a shred of embarrassment at parading his low-rent hooker through a Waffle House in North Little Rock. For her part, she holds her head high, even haughtily, as if daring anybody to give her a second look: minor nobility surveying her duchy.

Another girl darts into the restaurant to use the bathroom. The waitresses pretend not to notice her. A few minutes later, she darts back out into the night. The threesome catty-corner to us get up and stumble outside. I watch them have an intense conversation outside their car, half expecting somebody to pull a switchblade. To my disappointment, nobody does, and they eventually squeeze side-by-side into the front seat and roar away, the car belching exhaust fumes.

Some more people come and go. The Asian guy and his friend eat in silence, his hand occasionally finding the small of her back. We have to clear away the steam on the windows to look outside, but there's nothing out there to see.

The sadness of the place soaks into us like syrup. Watching these waitresses, none of them wearing wedding bands, knowing they have to come here night after night to serve this ghoulish parade of humanity. To see these cracked-out Lot Lizards in their miniskirts, to see these truckers who pay them. The whole thing is miserable. It is the dank underbelly of Little Rock, exactly what we were hoping to find when we tweeted out our request this morning. What's sadder, though, is contemplating all the Waffle Houses and truck stops and lonely titty bars out in the middle of nowhere, scattered out across the country like forgotten cards in a game of fifty-two-card pickup.

As open-minded as I am about legalizing drugs and prostitution, seeing this mess is a very cogent argument against. Besides the servers, I think Meghan and I are the only ones in here who aren't on something.

I don't think this scene was what Meghan had in mind back in Prescott when she kept yelling at me that "freedom doesn't come free," but the setting here is just as apt as the Green Zone in Baghdad, or indeed, anyplace we've been to so far. Freedom really isn't free, and this is the price we pay. Ideally, America gives you the freedom to be anything you can be. The flip side is that it also gives you the freedom to completely fuck up your life.

When we are finished with our waffles, we pay the check, leaving the waitress a big tip.

"You want to call it?" I ask Meghan.

"Yeah," she says.

"Me too," I agree.

So we call it, walking back to the hotel over broken bottles and chewed-up asphalt. All the fun has gone out of the evening. I'm super-depressed as I close my hotel room door behind me and get into bed. I lie there for a few minutes. Then I do something I almost never do: I get back out of bed and lock the deadbolt.

Branson, Missouri

What a Country!

Michael: About forty miles outside of Branson, Meghan asks Cousin John to pull over so she doesn't puke. The ride has been wicked hot and bumpy and Meghan is now telling us that she is "famous" for puking. That must have been a delight on her dad's presidential campaign. Cousin John finds a roadside liquor store that promises air-conditioning. The first thing we notice for sale at the liquor store is blue jeans, which is odd. They've got a rack of the things right when you walk in. Perhaps it's for people who are so drunk they've pissed themselves and need a change of dungarees. Also on sale: the Bongzilla Beer Bong, a height-adjustable pole capped with a giant funnel into which beer is poured. Six plastic tubes snake from the bottom, allowing half a dozen girls in bikinis to enjoy maximum beer guzzling. I know it is meant specifically for girls in bikinis because that's what the box shows. While I am no expert on the world of retail, I can say this with certainty: this is an excellent store.

We spend close to an hour among the booze and beer bongs and snacks, waiting for Meghan's head to clear. I purchase my wife a small plastic keychain that reads "Silly rabbit, tricks are for whores." (When I present it to her after the trip, she does not laugh.) I purchase similar keychains for Meghan and Stephie. They feign delight, but I notice neither of them attaches any keys. Cousin John and I wander around the store a bit, chatting while Meghan settles her stomach with a soft drink. After a while she declares herself ready to go, having not puked. I am disappointed.

We clamber back into our stifling, and increasingly stinky, RV for the final push to Branson, Missouri. I am probably more excited about Branson than any other stop on our trip. Mostly because I can't wait to make fun of it.

Meghan: So here's a little confession: I had never heard of Branson, Missouri, before we started planning our road trip. When Stephie first brought up Branson as a suggestion, I asked her what it was like and she said, "It's kind of like the Vegas of the Bible Belt, except I'm not sure if it's a dry county or not." Out of sheer curiosity alone, I thought it sounded like a great idea. Pretty much compare anything to Vegas and I'm in.

After a few quick Google searches while on the RV, I see an advertisement for Dolly Parton's Dixie Stampede, and I shout out to Michael that our Red Roof lobby research will not have been in vain after all. Vegas of the Midwest with a Dolly Parton attraction?! I worship at the altar of Dolly Parton. She is a woman who can do no wrong in my eyes and I am obsessed with everything about her. Her music, her hair, her cleavage, her movies, everything! If it's cool with Dolly, I'm more than sure it is going to be cool with me. We are so there that it makes me grin.

The more research I do, the more interesting Branson becomes. Surprisingly it is a relatively old tourist destination targeted towards wholesome family fun. For whatever reason I kept having flashes of Clark Griswold and the Griswold family from *National Lampoon's Vacation*. I tell Michael that we have turned into the Griswolds.

"I'm totally Russ, the smart-ass son," I say. "And you are *totally* Chevy Chase's character, Clark."

Michael barely looks up from his laptop. "Only if I get to sleep with Christie Brinkley," he says without stopping his typing.

"Christie then, or Christie now?" I say, trying to egg him out of his Twitter trance.

"Either," he says, not missing a beat. The RV takes a wicked, everlasting curve, and I start to feel like I might vomit again. Branson can't get here soon enough.

Michael: Branson has been a resort community almost from its founding in the 1880s. The first actual tourist destination was the Marvel Cave ("America's third largest cave"), bought in 1894, then leased by the Herschend family in the 1950s for, of all things, square dances. The Herschend family then opened Silver Dollar City, an amusement park based on a frontier theme, still in operation today. In fact, it's a major draw in Branson. The original cave is on-site and available for tours. No square dances.

In the 1960s, performers started moving their live shows to Branson. More and more followed: Roy Clark, Andy Williams, Yakov Smirnoff, the Oak Ridge Boys. With the shows came restaurants and other tourist attractions. Now the entire city is devoted to wholesome family entertainment and goofy golf. I first became aware of Branson's existence in the early nineties, when people suddenly started talking about the place as a family-friendly, affordable tourist destination. Branson seemed like Las Vegas's goody-two-shoes baby sister.

To me, it sounds indelibly hokey, one of those folksy "aw shucks" kind of places where people call you "sir" and "ma'am" as they extract every possible dollar they can from your wallet. No thanks. If I'm going to get ripped off, I want to at least do it someplace where the entertainment wears nipple tassels.

In all my travels across America, I've never had occasion to go to Branson and see what it's really like until now. So I'm excited. I'm going to mock this place with all the snarkiness I can muster. Hopefully I will not cross the line into outright cruelty, but if I do, Branson will have nobody but itself to blame.

Stephie has booked us in someplace called Chateau on the Lake, a name so pompous it cannot help but be a letdown. And yet, as we drive up to the hotel, there is the lake and there is a giant building that looks less like a chateau and more like a mid-level Indian casino, but I'm not complaining. Not after our night in the demilitarized zone known as North Little Rock. Here in Branson, there are no meth heads anywhere within sight. Unless the hotel has a rack of blue jeans in the lobby, I'm sure I will be pleased.

For Cousin John, it's got to seem like a huge step up. Sure he's still sleeping in the RV, but now he's got a view of Table Rock Lake. It's a little slice of Ozark heaven up here. For the record, I am not a completely heartless overlord, requiring my chauffer to sleep over the garage. In fact, just last night I suggested he sleep under the Red Roof, my treat.

"Can I offer you a nice hotel room?" I asked him. "Air-conditioning?"

"Are you kiddin' me? I used to live in a van in a hundred and twenty-eight degrees in Southwest Texas," he said. "I think I can deal with this. Thanks, though."

"Offer stands."

"Maybe another time."

I think for Cousin John, this whole trip is a kind of vision quest, an opportunity to get out of his cozy Aspen existence, see the country, and test his endurance. What he hopes to find I don't know, but I get the sense from him that he is a man on some kind of spiritual mission. He often says as much. His dad died last year and I think it had a profound effect on him. All of the bluster, the constant stories, teasing Meghan, all of it operates in parallel with what I think is a deep confusion about his purpose. Of all the jobs he's had—tow truck driver, hotel porter, bouncer—the one that I think had the biggest effect on him was river guide. For a couple of seasons, he led whitewater rafts down the Rio Grande. When he talks about those days, he gets kind of misty eyed.

"Were there girls?" Meghan asks him.

"Are you kiddin' me, Gumdrop?" he answers. Yes there were girls. And booze. And camaraderie with the other guides. But there was something else, I think. There was the responsibility he had of getting his clients down the river in safety. And I think that responsibility meant a lot to him. It was a pure expression of how I think he views himself. As a guide, but also as a passenger on the trip. He's doing the same thing for us, guiding our little RV down the river. I don't think he's as happy with us as he was out on the Rio Grande, but he's playing a role he knows, and I think it suits him. Hopefully it won't be so hot out for him up in the mountains. I don't know how he's been able to sleep in that thing. It's been so miserably hot, and yet he does it without complaint. He's a strong dude.

Meghan: As much as I like being on the road, and don't mind riding in an RV, it has begun to get really smelly inside, and my nausea keeps coming and going in unexpected tsunami waves. I already get motion sickness pretty quickly, but add in an RV toilet that doesn't seem to be draining properly, random trash and dirt that's kicking around on the floor, and a completely worthless air-conditioning system, and I am more than shocked I don't vomit all over Michael Ian Black's linen pants and Crocs, which really would not be a tragedy.

The drive to Branson is really windy, and I applaud Cousin John for doing such a good job maneuvering it because if I were driving, we would have already ended up like an accidental *Thelma and Louise*.

When I see on the horizon the Lake of the Ozarks and the gorgeous mountain views, I feel relieved. Stephie tipped us off that the hotel we will be staying at, the Chateau on the Lake, is a really nice hotel. I am running out of clean bras and T-shirts and just can't bring myself to sink to the Michael Ian Black level of rewearing dirty clothes. The fact that we are going to a hotel that has a laundry room and a decent restaurant makes me as happy as if we were pulling up to the Four Seasons.

As we approach the Chateau I feel more and more guilty that we have not booked a room for Cousin John. He's become a real trooper. Like everyone else, I am finally getting into a rhythm with Cousin John and beginning to understand his sense of humor. I don't always do well with laid-back "hippies," if you will (although "hippie" isn't really an accurate description of Cousin John), but Cousin

John is sweet and mellow, and really just wants everyone to live and let live. Plus, he makes the peace sign anytime I get a little too aggressive with an opinion, which actually works well at disarming me. If only my parents and Michael had known this trick earlier, we'd all have been saved a lot of heartache. It's weirdly effective.

The Chateau is gorgeous, in an Epcot Alps kind of way, and my guilt at not offering Cousin John a room in its homey interior spikes. I ask Michael if we should combine resources and make an exception to our tightly orchestrated budget, and he tells me that he tried last night to no avail. This makes me feel a little bit better, and I can look forward to washing my tank tops somewhat guilt-free.

Michael: I practically run into the hotel to get out of this stifling air, bringing up the rear behind Meghan and Stephie, who are already chatting with the check-in girl, who is *really* cute. One thing I did not expect to find in Branson was attractive people of a healthy weight, yet the very first person I meet is somebody I would consider leaving my wife for. She's doing an internship here while studying for her hotel management degree at the University of Kansas. Meghan is up in her grill asking inappropriate personal questions: Does she like it here? What's the dating scene like? How long does she have to stay here? The girl and Meghan chat for a bit. I hang back, not saying anything because pretty young women make me nervous, as evidenced by my experience having Phoenix rub her tits all over my face in Vegas. So I just kind of wait for her to go, "Hey, you're that dude from VH1!" and then ask me to stick my tongue down her throat. This does not happen.

The hotel itself is fairly upscale, including a "glorious ten-story atrium lobby with a setting that mimics the beauty of the Branson outdoors." And glorious it is! Lots of greenery and burbling water features. I love it. This has to be Branson's finest hotel. ("Four Diamonds," as rated by the AAA.)

First order of business: laundry. My linen pants and T-shirts are starting to get a little raggedy, even for me. I throw some stuff in the machine and walk around the hotel a bit with Stephie. We amble over to the in-hotel candy and ice cream bar, saunter outside to the fancy swimming pool, and then decide to stroll down to Table Rock Lake. Unfortunately, there is no direct walking route to get there, which means we have to clamber down the winding drive for about a half mile or so, which is not easy to do in heat and Crocs. But it's worth it. The lake is lovely, and its shoreline is filled with happy families doing waterfront activities. I guess that's called "swimming" or something. I don't know because I avoid it as much as possible, but we do roll up our pant legs and wade into the warm water. Mmmm. It feels great.

All around us are well-behaved people having outdoor fun on a sweltering July afternoon in Missouri. Despite my best efforts, I can find no fault with any of them. Everybody's getting along, and unlike in Vegas, it doesn't seem to be a competition for "fakest-looking human being." The people here are unselfconsciously flabby. They look, dare I say, like people. The first tendrils of shame start to crawl up my spine; why is my first instinct always to make fun of everything? These are just regular people on vacation. Why do I have to bring them down? Why do I have to be such an asshole all the time? I have no good answers. Sometimes I find myself to be such a caricature of an elitist East Coast liberal that it's embarrassing. Standing in the shallow water with my pants rolled up to my knees while looking around at all these pasty white families is one of those times. Right now, *I'm* what's wrong with this country.

Meghan: When we walk into the hotel, it really is quite nice. It has a real concierge, glass elevators, and a giant waterfall and river/pond with drawbridges going over it in the main lobby area, and most important, a laundry room.

After we check in, I immediately open up my self-admittedly way too large suitcase, and my clothes nearly explode out of the bag because it is packed so tight. I am woman enough to admit that I really did bring too much crap on the trip, but as of yet I am the only one not reusing shorts and underwear, so that has to count for something. I pack all my dirty clothes in my computer bag and purse, and carry the rest in my arms down to the laundry room.

Naturally, between the time I cruised the empty machines, gauged how much laundry I could get done, sorted it, and brought it back downstairs, someone has already taken up two of the three machines. I'm pretty sure I can see a pair of linen pants swirling around, and seriously consider stopping Michael's machines and taking his wet clothes out until mine are washed. But then I consider the greater good for humanity of letting his clothes finally get what they deserve, and push my whites into the open machine, hauling my darks back to my room. I'm thrilled to see the huge stone-tiled shower and put myself through a thorough wash cycle, exfoliating, shaving, and conditioning the hell out my body. Not since my Vegas sex shower have I felt so squeaky clean. I already love Branson. Branson is the Mecca of the Midwest.

Michael: We are going to see the comedian Yakov Smirnoff tonight. Yakov has been a Branson staple since 1992, when he opened his own theater here. For those, like Meghan, who have no idea who he is, a brief history: Smirnoff is a Russian émigré who came to America in 1977 and, very quickly, became one of the nation's most popular comedians. His schtick was to point out the differences between America and the Soviet Union, always wrapping a joke with the catchphrase "What a country!" He even had his own short-lived sitcom, creatively called *What a Country*. When the Soviet Union collapsed, so did his career. He moved his act to Branson a couple of years later, and twenty years on he's still going strong here.

When we mapped out our itinerary, I thought it would be great to interview Yakov. He's a true American success story, a guy who came with nothing and ended up making his American Dream come true. Plus, I figured he'd want to talk to us. I do standup, Meghan is a professional talking head; we're not just a couple of fans looking to get an autograph. We are practically comrades. The good kind.

Stephie wrote him a lovely email in advance of our arrival asking if we could interview him. He blew us off:

Dear Stephie,
Thank you so much for your interest, but I do not have the time
right now as I am booked with other commitments. I do wish you
the best success with the book!
    Love and Laughter,
    Yakov

It is a somewhat gracious blow-off but I am still irritated. Yakov, don't even give me this shit about how you "do not have the time" to meet with us. We both know you live in Branson; you definitely have the time.

Also, it would have been good for him to sit down with us. Our book is a love letter to America. He is the recipient of American love. Plus, we have so much in common: I too am of Russian Jewish heritage. I too am a comedian. I too am an American patriot. And Meghan's dad IS America.

Irritating.

But I will not allow my annoyance with the man ruin the show for me. I am determined to love Yakov even if he doesn't love me back.

Meghan: I was born in 1984, which I have come to learn was right around the time of Yakov's career heyday, so I had never heard of the man before our trip.

I google him and discover that he's in one of my favorite movies, *The Money Pit,* which makes me think it's going to be a family-friendly fun night. I like family-friendly humor, and Yakov is in fact living the American Dream. I love any stories of success about immigrants who ended up making it big in this country, so I figure we are probably in for a pretty good show.

There is, however, one little dent in our plan. Before we head out to see Yakov at his theater, Stephie tells us that Yakov has blown off our emailed request for a meet and greet. Of course there have been times in my life when I myself have been guilty of doing the same thing, so I shouldn't be annoyed that Yakov blew us off, but I am. Even though Yakov's email is a nice enough blow-off, I think it's a little shot to Michael's and my egos. Nothing like a "celebrity" who's been off the radar for twenty years not knowing who the hell you are—or worse, not caring who the hell you are—to make you feel insignificant. To be fair, an hour ago I didn't know who the hell he was either.

"Total blow-off," Michael repeats, clearly a bit wounded that a fellow comedian wouldn't want to trade tales. "He's not even trying."

"But he signed it 'love and laughter' and he wishes you guys success," Stephie says, ever the sweetheart.

"Yeah," I say, my excitement over going to the show a little deflated. "It's still a blow-off."

Michael: The first thing I notice about the Yakov Smirnoff Theater is its size. The place is bigger than the Sapphire Club back in Vegas. As you drive in, there's a huge Yakov billboard featuring a giant sculpted Yakov head and, in case you didn't know, a banner that reads "Famous Russian Comedian." I feel a pang of fear.

The entrance to the theater also has an oversized Yakov head, maybe seven feet tall, and wearing a bright-red clown's nose. It's a great place to pose for pictures, which we do.

As showtime approaches, we venture inside. The theater's walls are lined with grotesquely patriotic paintings, all signed "*Yakov.*" I did not know that Yakov is also a painter, and in fact was an art professor before coming to the United States. You can buy his paintings in the Yakov gift shop, which also features Yakov CDs, DVDs, T-shirts, books, and all manner of Yakov Smirnoff ephemera. I do not purchase anything nor, as far as I can tell, does anybody else in the building. Nobody wants to take a little piece of Yakov home with them.

Not that there are a lot of people here. There are not. Showtime is only minutes away and the place is deserted. There was more bustling activity going on in the Lower Ninth Ward.

An usher shows us our seats, which are close to the front. Third or fourth row. Behind us is a vast and largely empty theater. I'm guessing the place holds over a thousand people. If it's 15 percent full, I'd be amazed. It's a legitimate bummer. But the show must go on, and soon we are enveloped in the irritating strains of traditional Russian music. A troupe of four "Russian" dancers comes out, kicking and clapping and occasionally yelling, "Hey!"

Meghan: I pretty much want to visit every single attraction possible in Branson; it all sounds like fun. I cannot help but be a little pumped about this place, as Branson really is stunning: the trees, the lake, its sunset, and even the Yakov Smirnoff Theater. When we arrive, Stephie's future in-laws, Ken and Cathy, and their friends Burt and Nancy are already there, waiting for us. They all live in Lee's Summit, which is within driving distance of Branson.

I love Ken and Cathy almost immediately. They are an absolutely adorable, warm, friendly couple, exactly what one imagines "the sweet couple down the street" in Middle America to be. They have been married thirty years.

Cathy co-owns a hair salon in Lee's Summit, and Ken is a battalion chief in the Lee's Summit Fire Department. When Stephie double-checks these basic facts with Ken and Cathy over email after our trip, Cathy says, "And, we just got back from square dancing, Meghan. You can put that in the book too."

We make small talk about Branson, their work, their son's and Stephie's upcoming wedding in the fall, and voting for my father. I speed-dial my dad so he can thank Ken personally, something I love to do when people seem to be particularly big fans of his. The look on Ken's face makes it totally worth it. Who doesn't want everyone to love their dad? After all the strippers, hipsters, bohemians, and Suicide Girls, Ken and Cathy are a nice change of pace and I welcome the dynamic they bring to our group. Even snarky Michael seems charmed by their easy ways, and of course, Stephie is clearly excited to see them. It's just nice to meet nice people sometimes.

Michael, Stephie, and I pose for pictures in front of a giant sculpture of Yakov Smirnoff's head, just as the Griswolds certainly would have done. The mouth on the Yakov sculpture slowly opens and closes and we all ham it up, trying to make a sculpture of a come-

dian's head look interesting. I tweet one of the pictures and immediately there is a flurry of "What a country" and "In communist
Russia" tweets, including one from Joel Stein, the *Time* magazine
columnist. I feel like I've been missing out on the Yakov party, and
think the show is probably going to be especially entertaining because it will all be new for me.

Apart from the Yakov gift shop, the lobby also features a ton of
paintings, all of which are "America-inspired" in some way. There
are American flag hearts, pictures of the Statue of Liberty, paintings
of eagles and stars, and so forth. All of these paintings were painted
by Yakov because he is also an artist. I love American flag anything.
Put an American flag on a beach towel or expensive art, it doesn't
matter. I will buy it. I actually really like this art; Yakov is a talented
painter, and I would have bought a piece if I didn't have to haul it
the rest of the trip in the RV.

I sit down with everyone in the only-maybe-quarter-full theater
and the show begins. Before Yakov comes on there is a reel of all his
highlights: Yakov on Johnny Carson, Yakov hosting a talk show of
some kind that looks particularly eighties, Yakov meeting President
and Nancy Reagan, a clip of Yakov acting with a very young-
looking Tom Hanks in *The Money Pit*. I go from not having a clue
about him to feeling as though I grew up with him living next door.

For whatever reason, the clip of him shaking hands with President Reagan sticks out. I love President Reagan, as all good Republicans do. I think at this point, not loving him in the Republican
Party is equivalent to not loving Jesus. It's incredibly poignant for
me to see Yakov with one of my idols while both were still so vital.

But then the show starts and Yakov spends half the time telling
cheesy, but in a good way, jokes. Not really my type of humor—I
mean, look at the comedian I picked to write a book with—but
harmless, G-rated, family-friendly humor nonetheless. A lot of it
feels dated. Like Yakov maybe hasn't written any new material since
he met President Reagan. Before long I can't quite tell if the joke
he's just told was in one of the clips, or if he already told it at the
top of the show. It all starts to blur and I clench my jaw, anxious,

and I start to get fidgety. Yakov makes jokes and people in the audience sort of half laugh. I try to laugh and feign interest in his humor, but it all starts to feel very uncomfortable.

Michael: Yakov spends the next ninety minutes alternating between jokes and trying to sell us Yakov stuff. No exaggeration: he spends a solid ten minutes of his show giving us the hard sell for his *other* show, *Yakov's Dinner Adventure*. There's a video advertisement for it, and then Yakov attempts to induce us to purchase tickets by talking about how great the food is, pointing out that our seat backs have collapsible trays on them like airplanes so we can watch the dinner adventure while eating, and then lowering the price again and again like we're all in a late-night television commercial for Ginsu knives.

"Would you come see the show if I told you it was twenty dollars?" he asks. Someone in the crowd yells back, "What about ten dollars?"

"Sure!" Yakov grins, as though he's made the deal of the century.

He grins all the time, regardless of the joke or the sales pitch. It starts to look like it hurts. Then, out of nowhere, he tells a long story about how he painted a huge mural for the city of New York for the one-year anniversary of September 11, but did not want his identity revealed, preferring it to be an anonymous gift. The mural was enormous, hung by cranes, and unfurled at the beginning of the memorial that year. It stayed at Ground Zero for fourteen months, before it was tattered by high winds and poor weather and had to be removed. It's a lovely gesture, but if he wanted the gift to be anonymous, if he wanted it to be a pure expression of his love of country, why is he telling us about it now? And why is he offering pieces of the original mural for sale in the gift shop?

Because we're so close to the stage, within Yakov's field of vision, I feel obligated to smile and laugh as much as possible, grinning right along with him (and yes, it does hurt), but Meghan feels no such compunction. She sits beside me, arms crossed, sneering. This show is really pissing her off.

Meghan: There is nothing wrong per se with Yakov's comedy; it just feels like someone retelling his stories about a better time in his career. Yakov, for whatever reason, has not exactly evolved with the times, and every time he cracks "What a country!" the laughs around me are fewer and die faster. I absolutely hate the term "has-been" because I think it is often a cruel and unfair generalization, but that is how the majority of people would probably describe Yakov and his show in this moment.

I spend a lot of time giving speeches, mostly at college campuses. Giving speeches and entertaining an audience is one of the best and most flattering things I am asked to do, but at the same time it is also indescribably difficult and draining. Engaging a roomful of college students about the future of the Republican Party and trying to make it funny and edgy at the same time is truly one of the hardest things I have tried to master. "Tried" meaning that although I think I am good, I don't think I'm done evolving as a speaker. Either way, it is something I take extremely seriously and consider one of the greatest honors in my life. Like Yakov, I stand in front of a roomful of people telling my story.

Not that long ago, I was a college student who didn't care about politics and felt disengaged from the process. My speeches encompass basically all of my life's experiences up to this point. It's about my time growing up as a senator's daughter, my life on the road during the 2008 campaign with my father and Sarah Palin, my time as a columnist, "pundit," and commentator, being a woman in the media and having my looks and weight scrutinized publicly, my experience in the world of Republican politics, and where I want the Republican Party and the world of politics to go. The speech continues to evolve as I do. When the 2008 election ended, I realized how profoundly changed I was as a person and that I felt like I could speak for a certain new breed of young Republicans who are evolving and don't fit into the old-school mold.

I also felt compelled to fight for the party that I love, and worry that the way the media has come to depict the party is off-putting and one-noted—as though every Republican holds the same beliefs, to the same degree. I've been on a one-woman mission to break that stifling mold and show people of all ages and backgrounds that there is room for them in the party.

I love what I do. I love the world of Republican politics and I would never want to do anything else. I am proud of the fact that there are people out there who do not just simply see me as "John McCain's daughter," but as someone who speaks for a side of the party that too often gets neglected and overlooked.

That being said, it's unbelievably difficult and hard. I worry I am not evolving fast enough to keep pace with all the facets emerging from the far-right side of the party. Not to say that I am far left, but it seems that the only time the party grows a new branch lately, it's out the crazy conservative side instead of anything that might look appealing to people under thirty—my target audience.

I pull my attention back to the show, where Yakov now stands behind a podium pretending to be "President Yakov," and for whatever reason, I have a flash of me standing behind a podium, telling the exact same story at forty-seven that I do at twenty-seven. Good God, what if I never have any other stories than the ones I have now? What if in twenty years I am standing on a stage in Branson, telling people about my dad's campaign for president and how it inspired me to get other people involved in the Republican Party? What if I stop evolving? What if this is as good as it is going to get with my life, my role in politics, and my career? What if I have already peaked?

As the show goes on—and on—Yakov tells stories of immigrating to the United States and becoming a citizen. To my great and uncomfortable shock, he tears up. Now, I believe that Yakov had a moving experience when he moved to this country, and that he is grateful for the help of strangers who gave him food and clothing when he didn't have any. Still, he has been doing this show every night for twenty years. Can his tears be at all genuine? Maybe they are. Maybe I'm cynical. I don't know. But when he ramps his touching story up into a video of the mural he "anonymously" donated to Ground Zero, and the audience comes to their feet in unified, patriotic togetherness, I feel more than a little uncomfortable. This group togetherness ends with an exclusive offer to own a piece of the mural—a "piece of history"—conveniently available in the gift shop, along with any number of DVDs, tickets to the dinner show, and copies of his book. As I watch the worlds of patriotism and commerce collide in front of me, I am speechless. I'm a little pissed off. I also start to have a internal panic attack.

Michael: Afterwards Ken and Cathy ask us what we thought. I've just met these people and I don't want to say, "I thought it was one of the worst things I've ever seen" because maybe they loved it. Instead, I make some noncommittal noises about his considerable enthusiasm and ask them how they enjoyed it.

"We thought it was terrible," Cathy says.

I heave a sigh a relief.

"And we've seen it before," she adds.

She says Yakov has been doing the same show for the past nineteen years. I don't know that I've ever heard a more dispiriting statement.

"He's been doing that same, crappy show for almost two decades?"

"Yes."

I ask Meghan what she thought.

"It was one of the worst things I have ever seen," she laments. "And I saw my father concede the presidency." That's pretty bad.

For some reason, her mood is totally sour. She's barely talking. When I ask her what's wrong, she says she doesn't want to talk about it. Did I do something to piss her off again?

Meghan: I leave the theater in a daze, stroll back through the lobby with my happily chatting clan up ahead of me. All my preshow exuberance is gone, my admiration for the patriotic paintings vanished. When we get outside, Michael and Stephie can tell something is up. They can both read me pretty well. It is not exactly that I didn't like the show, which I didn't really. I have been to not-so-great shows and speeches before. I think there was something about the desperation and dated feeling of Yakov's show that made me get down. It was sad. I wanted to know what happened to his career. I wanted to know how one has such a large following and then ends up desperately hawking swag to small audiences in Branson, Missouri. Yakov once appeared on Johnny Carson and made him laugh, and now he's stuck wringing laughs and money out of people's nostalgia and patriotism. He's flogging the same story of his American Dream that he made his name on. What if that's me? What if I am Yakov Smirnoff?

Going on this road trip has come at a very serendipitous time in my life. When I met Michael I was living in Los Angeles, trying to develop my own talk show, something I have not yet talked about publically. I uprooted my life and moved to Los Angeles thinking that this deal was going to be something amazing, the next step in my life and career. What could be better for me than a talk show with political undertones for young women? I thought it was something that had a ton of potential and could show a different, dare I say, less fluffy side to women and daytime television.

I went through an incredibly long series of testing and tryouts that ultimately ended in me not being what the producers had in mind. Still, they put me through a million paces and intense scrutiny, from the way I talk, the way I sit in a chair, which side of my face looks better to the camera, etc. It was an emotionally draining experience, and I spent more than a few days leaving the studio crying on my drive home. It felt different than the scrutiny of politics, because at least in politics people will tell you they don't like you and your point of view to your face. In my experience, in Los Angeles everything is very foggy and clouded. I was very bad at pretending to be anything other than what I am and there was a lot of emphasis put on "faking interest"—not a huge strength of mine.

I found the business to be filled with people who were scared of hurting feelings in business settings, to the point where it seemed ridiculous. I'm not asking for sympathy; I'm in the industry I am in and I love politics and political media. I did not love what small glimpse I had into the talk show world. The entire thing ended with me spending a month trying to get a straight answer from my collaborators. I eventually had to confront them with the fact that it was obviously not happening. It was a draining experience and the first event in a very long time that made me seriously question myself. Once again I think that maybe things in my life would go easier if I could just chill out a little bit. Stop being so direct, stop having such strong opinions, etc. It gave me a hard dose of reality about the kind of person I am and the kind of person I am not.

Also, I hated living in Los Angeles. I never quite clicked with the people I met there. I am a terrible driver and I hated driving. I had a hard time meeting people that I felt were actually interested in having an honest conversation or maintaining any type of real relationship. Pretty much all of the stereotypes about Los Angeles I found to be true. Maybe it was just my experience at that particular time with that particular group of people, but I was unhappy there. There is a quote, by Jack Kerouac from his book *The Road*, about Los Angeles that pretty much sums up how I felt about living there: "LA is the loneliest and most brutal of American cities; New York gets god-awful cold in the winter but there's a feeling of wacky comradeship somewhere in the streets. LA is a jungle."

The truth is that, as hard as I work and as much determination as I have, which is fed from a very real and raw place, I could become irrelevant. I could fail in the world of politics and not ever evolve or experience anything new. I could end up in Branson.

Michael: When we get back to the hotel, the adorable check-in girl is gone and Meghan remains in a shitty mood. Branson is about wholesome family celebration, and neither of these occurrences are anything to celebrate. As Meghan's mood goes, so goes the trip. I ask her again what is wrong and finally, over drinks at the hotel bar, she opens up.

The Yakov show *really* upset her. For one thing, she was angry at the exploitation of patriotism that ran rampant through the show's nine-hour running length. (Actually, I think the show was closer to two hours, but it felt like nine.) She and I have had several conversations about the way patriotism is used as a weapon in politics, the way public officials (Republicans) wield the flag like a sword. As a result, the word has taken on an ideological bent that it never had before. She hates when love of country is used like this or, as in Yakov's case, when it is exploited as cheap sentimentalism. But that's not what *really* upset her about the show.

What really upset her was that she worried that she was looking at her own future when she saw Yakov. I laugh when she says this. How can she possibly compare herself to him? But she's serious.

"You don't understand," she says. "Women in my profession have a very small window to make an impact. I've got to do something *now* if I want to survive."

The Yakov show has unwittingly created an existential crisis for her. Say what you want, but that is some *powerful* theater.

I tell her she's crazy: she's only twenty-seven. Plus she's already done so much. But she doesn't want to hear it. Seeing Yakov Smirnoff, a wildly successful comedian twenty-something years ago, reduced to these pandering and groveling circumstances is too much for her. She worries she will end up exactly like him, middle-aged and irrelevant. I tell her I'm middle-aged and irrelevant and it's not so bad.

She finally laughs. "It's different for men," she says. And she's right.

Meghan: Things are not equal for women in America, not even a little bit, and not at all for women in politics. It is why women are so turned off from the process. On my birthday this year, I tweeted that I was enjoying turning twenty-seven, and I was surprised by how many people remarked on how I was in my late twenties and I had better start doing what I needed to do because my biological clock was ticking and wrinkles were coming soon. I got one tweet that said, "Wow, you're in your late twenties, that sucks!" As if entering my late twenties and beyond is a death sentence. We live in a youth-obsessed culture and it permeates every single industry, and politics is no different. In fact, politics may be a little worse than most.

People have written things about me that range from questioning why I am not married and have not started having babies—because if I don't I am going to end up barren and alone—to an unbelievable grotesque obsession with my weight fluctuations that have been a source of much talk in the media for years. I'm looking at your less-than-Atkins ass, Glenn Beck. I have already had people make comments about the time coming soon for Botox and plastic surgery.

If the world of politics is crazy, then the world of media and politics is crazier. I am not an actress or a model. Yet the same beauty standards are applied to women in politics, and the sterotypes are more extreme. One gets to be Sarah Palin, the gorgeous, stupid airhead. Or Hillary Clinton, the aging, mercenary bitch. I do not think nor believe those should be the only options for women in politics. I want to do everything; I want to help break glass ceilings that have already started cracking before me. I want to fight for what I believe in, use my voice, speak out, help make change, and be allowed to wear clothes that make me feel like a sexy woman.

Over our first drink of the day, I spill to Michael and Stephie. I spill all of the failures, the paranoias and fears I think most people have on some level or another. That I'm not going to make an impact. That, after Los Angeles, I'm going to freeze up from fear of failure. Michael and Stephie sit across from me wide-eyed and listen to my melodrama. They both share different fears they have about the future, which makes me feel better. We keep drinking and talking and slowly we all get tired. I hug both of them before we head off to bed. As I get undressed and get into bed, my mind is a bit more at ease, and I think about how amazing it is just to be doing this sort of project with both of them and being in Branson on such a beautiful summer night—and that from here on out the end goal in my life is to not end up like Yakov Smirnoff.

Michael: When we go to bed, I think Meghan's feeling a little better for having unburdened herself. Tomorrow's going to be a fun day, I remind her. An amusement park in the morning, and then

Dolly Parton's Dixie Stampede at night. Dolly Parton is older than Yakov and still relevant, I remind her. If I was a betting man, and I am, I would say Meghan McCain is probably more likely to end up like her. We bid our good nights and head off to our rooms. I go to bed and try to sleep, but the same thought keeps occurring to me: *Jesus, what if I end up like Yakov Smirnoff?*

My hopes for Silver Dollar City are pretty slight. Even the name itself sounds so 1950s gee-willikers corny that I can't muster much enthusiasm for the morning's activity. Plus, I have now reached an age where I no longer enjoy rides. If I turn my body more than forty-five degrees too quickly, I throw up. I went on the Tilt-A-Whirl with my son the summer before and had to lay down on the asphalt afterwards for twenty minutes to recover.

The website certainly doesn't get me any more excited. It invites visitors to "Step back in time to an 1880s craft village." I can't imagine a place I would like to step back into time less; maybe a medieval village ravaged by plague. A "crafts village"? Holy shit, that sounds boring. What sorts of rides would an 1880s craft village even have? "Come ride The Loom!" "Prepare yourself . . . for the Butter Churner!!!" It sounds awful.

Listen to me and listen good: Silver Dollar City is great. I'm not being sarcastic. SDC is a ripping good time. The place is clean, well maintained, the roller coaster I rode was speedy and didn't make me vomit or pass out, there were no scary tattooed, shirtless teenage boys making out with their slutty, tattooed teenage girlfriends, the food was reasonably priced, and—get this—the crafts portion of it was *awesome!*

We spend a good half an hour hanging out with a retired couple, Jim and Pat Summers, watching them whittle wood into sculptures. We talk a bit about New York. Pat wants to go but Jim refuses: "I'm a hillbilly boy. That's too many people for me."

I mention that we saw Yakov the previous night.

"He's a good man," says Jim. "Not only is it a good show, he's a good man. He treats his people so well that they just don't leave. The only way they leave is through retirement."

Great: now I feel bad about bashing the guy.

He recommends we save our appetite for the Dixie Stampede later that night, going through the entire menu with me: "You get a full Cornish hen."

"Uh-huh," I say.

"And they give you a slab of tenderloin that's half or three-quarter-inch thick."

"Wow."

"They give you wedge potatoes, corn on the cob, biscuit. They'll start you out with a bowl of soup."

"Mm-hm."

"The creamy soup is really wonderful."

"Huh." He really seems determined to tell me every single item of food they serve at the Dixie Stampede.

"They have apple fritters for dessert . . . let's see if I can think what else."

"That's a lot already."

"But they don't give you any silverware."

I start laughing.

"No that's true. It's all finger food."

Next to me, I overhear Pat telling Stephie, "The food's excellent."

Jim moves off the topic of food and onto the topic of Silver Dollar City. He tells me they work really hard on keeping "this a good, Christian park. It's the only park I know of where I could bring my grandkids and tell them 'Okay kids, meet me for lunch at one o'clock,' let 'em go, and I wouldn't worry about them for a second. For a second."

"We need places like that," I say. "We were in Vegas last week and it wasn't like that."

I mean it when I tell Jim we need places like Silver Dollar City. As much as the word "Christian" makes me instinctively recoil because of its occasional sanctimoniousness, I do think there's something valuable about places like Silver Dollar City where families can come and not hear bad language or see fights or drunkenness, where there are no jangly slot machines or wet T-shirt contests. This place is squeaky clean, and I can feel my cynicism sloughing off like dead skin.

Of course, it's also a totally artificial environment. As much as I enjoy being here, there's no denying that it's nothing more than a utopian mirage. As much as the Republicans try to paint Democrats as desiring some Marxist utopia, this place is basically that. Just replace the word "comrade" with "Christian." There's nothing wrong with either dream, I suppose, but that's all they are. Utopias don't exist in real life, regardless of their political or religious leanings, no matter how many roller coasters.

Why an 1880s craft village? Because it's far enough back in time that we can romanticize it and make ourselves believe that America was something other than it was. We can pretend it was a simpler (i.e., better) time. I'm happy to indulge in the fantasy, but I suspect the 1880s had fewer strolling banjo players and more babies contracting scarlet fever. Fewer hand-blown glassmakers and more sharecroppers.

My problem is that fantasies like this sometimes become the basis for manipulative, oversimplified political platforms. When I hear conservatives talking about "real America," I imagine they're talking about Silver Dollar City, a made-up American fantasyland. Or maybe they're talking about Branson as a whole, a city whose entire image is built on good old-fashioned, family-oriented American fun. But Branson is no different than anyplace else. There's crime here. And drugs. And poverty. Also, Branson is almost 95 percent white, which doesn't reflect "real America." I never know what they mean when they say real America, but I always feel like, wherever it is, I would not be welcome.

Meghan: After a good night's sleep, and a good day's recreation spent at the charming Silver Dollar City, I feel the need to write Yakov Smirnoff an open letter of apology. I have nothing against Yakov Smirnoff. After seeing his show and his blow-off email, I still have nothing against this man. People have to do what they have to do to make a living and make themselves happy, and I genuinely do not want Yakov Smirnoff's feelings to be hurt due to my self-admittedly strange and unusual reaction to his show and watching him perform. So here goes:

Dear Mr. Smirnoff,

Hi, this is Meghan McCain. You may not have heard of me, or care, but I saw your show in Branson and tried to meet you this summer. If for some reason you end up hearing about this book, or reading it, I want to apologize if it ends up making you feel bad, as that is not my intention. I know what it feels like to have random people say negative and possibly unwarranted things about you publicly and I am sorry if this ends up having a negative impact in any way. You look like you have a nice life in Branson, Missouri, and seem content and happy from everything I could observe. I mean no ill will towards you and I apologize if anything in this book in any way hurts your feelings. I do believe you are living the American Dream and have made a great life for yourself, which is very admirable. I just didn't love everything in your entire show, and for whatever reason had a strange reaction afterwards that says more about me and my life, than you and yours. I still would love to meet at some point and maybe my writing partner, Michael, could join you sometime on stage in Branson, Missouri, to update your standup a little bit? I would still love to hear your opinions on making it big in America and your life leading up to Branson. Please forgive me if this book in any way ends up making you feel bad in any way. Like I said, it is more a reflection on me than you.

All the best,
Meghan McCain

Michael: Having had the entire Dixie Stampede dinner menu enumerated to me by Jim, I am more than open to Meghan's suggestion that we eat dinner before the show. I mean, as tempting as eating Cornish game hen and tenderloin with my hands is, I also would be okay with something a little less disgusting sounding.

We find the only Thai place in Branson because we're in the mood for some of that famous Missouri Thai food. It's nice to throw some vegetables down my gullet after a steady diet of gas station goodies and road crap.

Then it's off to the Stampede, housed in an enormous theater on Branson's main drag, a riot of theaters, restaurants, souvenir shops, and, of course, goofy golf. Unlike at Yakov's theater, this place is hoppin'. The theater is bigger than Yakov's, and in the round, so it surrounds the "stage," which is a large oval earthen floor piled with dirt. This is for all the horses that will soon be galloping around doing their horsy tricks. I can't say I am necessarily looking forward to the combination of dirt, livestock, and finger foods, but here we go.

The show's premise is slightly weird: a friendly re-creation of the Civil War. In the words of the emcee: "Tonight we're going to take you on a journey back to a rivalry that forever changed our great United States."

I'm squirming a little bit when he says that just because I feel like our nation's deadliest war was slightly worse than a "rivalry."

He continues: "Now, it all began on April 12, 1861, in Charleston Harbor, South Carolina, bringing us a great civil war that taught us to become a stronger nation."

That's the end of the history lesson. The date that he's referring to is the Battle of Fort Sumter, when Confederate forces opened fire on the fort, barraging it with gunfire and artillery for thirty-four straight hours, until the fort finally surrendered, miraculously only suffering one fatality. Four years of bloody war followed, claiming over six hundred thousand lives. This fact is understandably glossed over as we are assigned our "teams." One half of the theater is "the North," and one half "the South." I am relieved to find us on the North, as I do not think I could fully commit to clapping and cheering for the side of slavery, although I do notice at least one African American family on the Southern side during the show, and they seem to have no problem waving the flag of Dixie.

The show itself is a series of songs, comedy, acrobatics, and horse-related challenges. There is also a herd of buffalo, which don't have much of a reason to be there but which look extremely cool nonetheless.

For all of its hokum and twisted historical contrivances, I have to say, I *love* the Dixie Stampede. It is just an unapologetic, foot-stomping, old-fashioned good time. Honestly, it's just hard to argue with the entertainment value of attractive young people singing patriotic songs on horseback. By the end of the evening, I am thrilled when the North defeats the South, just like in real life. Do I whoop? I do. Do I holler? I do. Do I eat every single one of my delicious apple fritters with my fingers? Yes. I. Do.

After a musical video send-off from the one, the only, Dolly Parton, we all file out through the packed gift shop. People are snapping up all sorts of souvenirs: dish towels, plates, candies. There are no Yakov paintings for sale here, which I'm sure is a disappointment to everybody.

Outside, as we wait for the cab, we stand beside a family of Southerners. One of them, a boy around fifteen, stares at something on the sidewalk. It's sort of long and black and thin. And it's writhing. The boy pokes at it with his foot.

"What is it?" a family member asks.

"I think it's a worm."

"That's not a worm. It's a snake."

"It's a worm."

"It's a snake."

Within a couple minutes, there are probably half a dozen people staring at this poor thing debating its worminess.

"It's a worm."

"Ah don't think so, Marcus. Look, it's trappin' at her." (I don't know what "trappin'" means.)

"Get away from there, stupid. I'm not takin' you to the hospital!"

The conversation with Marcus continues for several minutes. Grandma waddles over and says definitively: "That is a snake."

Meghan is now standing beside everybody else staring at the thing and interjects, "I think it's a baby snake."

Marcus pokes at it with his finger and his mother screams, "Don't, stupid!"

Whether it's a snake or a worm is never determined, but I have to say, the whole conversation with the family and Stupid Marcus is just as entertaining as the show we just saw, which is to say *very* entertaining. For the record: I think it was a worm. I don't know if this is Real America or not, but tonight, a little buzzed, a little bloody, it's *my* America, and I love it.

Meghan: Ultimately, Branson has given me more than I ever bargained for. My first legitimate quarter-life crisis at Yakov Smirnoff's is more than any woman could bargain for. I am pleased that Michael thinks I am going to end up more like Dolly Parton than Yakov as I get older. I mean, if Yakov is the worst-case scenario, Dolly is best. And let's be fair here, it is probably a lot more fun being Yakov Smirnoff than I am giving him credit for.

When people describe the "happy, content, Middle America," Branson is the first place I will think of from now on. It's clean, it's family friendly, it's a really great time and a fun vacation destination. Seriously, I mean it. I ended up having just as interesting an experience in Branson as I did in Las Vegas.

As we finish up our last night in Branson and end up drinking yet more Bud Lights and singing random songs yet once again, it all starts feeling like a little family. This book, these people— Michael, Stephie, and Cousin John—we are all on this weird, crazy trip together in the dead of summer and none of it feels accidental. I think we are all starting to feel like we are on a mission together. At the end of the night, Michael bashes his knee into a snare drum as he steps onstage to join the band and sing. Stephie and I laugh so hard tears start rolling down my cheeks. Just good clean fun. Good clean fun in Branson, Missouri.

What a country.

Memphis, Tennessee

Black and Blues

Meghan: If you do not believe in climate change, or that our planet is in any way having extreme weather issues at all, I suggest you take a road trip in an RV without substantial air-conditioning across the South next summer. This summer isn't just hot, it is steamy. It is muggy. I am sweaty to the point where the underwire of my bra is soaked with sweat by midmorning. I am from Arizona and have a high tolerance for heat; however, the heat is so oppressive this summer it is bordering on tragically funny.

Michael, Stephie, and I are all constantly perspiring—many days Michael has visible sweat stains everywhere on his T-shirts. Makeup seems more and more pointless because it just comes off halfway through the day. Stephie's cheeks are an adorable rosy red pretty much the entire time. And Cousin John, forget it. That boy is just glistening from morning to night, are ya' kidding me? It is absurd. Any decorum regarding any of us attempting to look presentable has officially gone out the window as we crawl deeper into the South.

Though let's be honest, Michael doesn't care about looking presentable when he goes on late-night television shows, let alone while cross-country touring in an RV. But I am now following his slovenly lead, rewearing my clothes, or more specifically, the same pair of jean shorts with rotating tank tops. Part of me likes it. There's something liberating about giving up on caring about one's personal appearance. I resisted as long as I could but it is absolutely egregiously, *gnarly* hot. Memphis in July may just be the peak point of heat saturation.

Michael: We arrive in Memphis after about a six-hour drive from Branson. Meghan's big idea was to stay at the Heartbreak Hotel, right across the street from Graceland. For weeks, she's been after Stephie to make sure we're booked there. Yes, yes, Stephie assures her. Meghan insists it's going to be amazing. As we get close, though, she is having second thoughts.

"It might be a dump," she says. "Sorry."

And it kind of is. Not North-Little-Rock-Red-Roof-Inn dumpy, but not that much better. The small lobby is all purple and gold, and a couple of blown-out TVs play old Elvis movies. Cousin John seems particularly transfixed by *Blue Hawaii,* in which the King sings and surfs while sixties hottie Joan Blackman shakes her coconuts at him. There's Elvis stuff everywhere. There's an Elvis gift shop, Elvis music plays nonstop, and the hotel bar is called, of course, the Jungle Room. It's almost as bad as Yakov's gift shop. Despite their best efforts to disguise it with memorabilia, the whole place is dingy and beat up, more Fat Elvis than Thin. I can deal with it for a night if it makes Meggy Mac happy.

She looks around and says, "Gross."

So nobody's going to be happy. Whatevs.

We're visiting two Tennessee towns, the black one and the white one. Memphis and Nashville. Memphis is the blues. Nashville is country. Yes, Elvis lived in Memphis, but he was more of a black performer than a white one. That's why so many black people hate him: he stole his whole act from them. To quote the great Chuck D.: "Elvis was a hero to most but he never meant shit to me."

Black-white racial tension is an impossible, unbridgeable fact of being American. It just is, and pretending otherwise is delusional. There's nothing mysterious about its cause: white people enslaved black people for a few hundred years. That's a difficult speed bump to cross on the road to racial harmony.

Most Americans like to think of themselves as open-minded, tolerant, and free of bigotry. I think most Americans are full of shit. I include myself in that statement.

First of all, I always have racial awareness. If I meet an African American, my first conscious thought of that person is his/her race. The thought is unbidden and unwelcome, but it's there. I notice a person's race before I notice anything else, even before their boobs! Second, I tense up when I meet black people. The tension is due, I think, to a special social phobia, the fear of doing or saying the wrong thing. Which, of course, I have done.

A perfect example: I once hung out at a restaurant with the former New York Knick Charles Smith. Smith was a six-foot-ten power forward during the Knicks' 1990s heyday. At that time, I zealously followed the team and was thrilled to meet the guy. I had a vague memory of Smith being involved in the NBA Player's Association and asked him about his time there. He told me that, yes, he had been a regional representative, which led to me ask if he'd ever considered getting into broadcasting because during those times when I'd seen him speaking for the Player's Association, I'd found him to be very "articulate."

As soon as the word fell out of my mouth, I wanted to run. "Articulate" is one of those loaded words white people patronizingly deploy as backhanded compliments to blacks, as if a person's skin color would make them less likely to be able to string together a thoughtful sentence. Charles graciously ignored the remark and continued to engage me for a few more minutes, after which I ran into the public restroom and gave myself a swirly.

Of course I didn't mean anything: he *was* articulate. But my fear of falling into those sorts of rhetorical potholes feed that tension I have, the fear of doing something wrong or insensitive, and, underneath it all, the fear that I might be an actual bigot.

As a result of this tension, I find myself overcompensating around African Americans, being deliberately kinder and more giving of my time than I would with whites. If a black dude wants to hang out with me after a show, for example, I am far more likely to do that than I would be with a white dude. Honestly, I'm not that friendly: I don't want to hang out with *anybody* after a show, but when a black guy shows me some approval, my heart does joyous backflips. Isn't that just as racist as feeling the opposite?

Call it "white guilt," call it whatever, but it's there and I hate it. I suspect African Americans experience this tension too, although I have never spoken with any about it. Race is the most difficult topic for us to discuss as Americans, harder to talk about than politics, money, or religion, because it cuts to the core of who we are, the foundational, unkept promise of America: that all men are created equal. No they're not. Not here.

White guilt is maddening because I feel implicated for crimes I had nothing to do with. None of my ancestors even arrived in America before the twentieth century. Yet I still feel lingering guilt for slavery. Hell, I feel guilt for Columbus! Why is that? Why do we drag the sins of our forefathers around with us like Marley's chains? At least I'm not German. I have no idea how they deal with that.

Meghan: It was my bright idea to stay at the Heartbreak Hotel right across the street from Graceland in Memphis. My good friend Piper recommended it. She's an Elvis superfan to the point where she paid five thousand dollars for a lifelike Elvis ceramic statue that now sits in her living room. On different holidays she dresses Elvis in matching festive décor. She also has a line from an Elvis song, "I Can't Help Falling in Love with You," and the date of her wedding anniversary tattooed on her forearm.

I have been to Graceland numerous times throughout my life, but I have never stayed at the Heartbreak Hotel. It was Piper's excitement over the heart-shaped pool that made me insist we stay there. I mean, a heart-shaped pool; who wouldn't want that?

To put it nicely, the Heartbreak Hotel could use a facelift. It's pretty run-down. I was expecting more of a Disneyland Hotel experience: sparkly and clean with shiny gold ceramic floors shaped like a gold album and Elvis impersonators greeting you in the lobby. No such luck. The Heartbreak Hotel is basically your average motel with a cool purple-velvet couch in the lobby, Elvis movies playing on an old television, and, yes, a heart-shaped pool.

My room is a little run-down as well, but there are pictures of Elvis hanging above my bed and working air-conditioning, so I'm not going to complain. I guess I had just gotten spoiled staying at the Chateau in Branson.

We all check in and go into our routines—shower, check email, possibly tweet, change clothes (which at this point means a non-sweaty tank top); Michael puts on his Crocs, Stephie calls her fi-ancé, and we all meet back in the lobby. There is rarely any time for anything else. It's like taking a break in your bunk at camp, with no chance to actually wind down.

There's been a lot of talk from Michael about Memphis being "the black" city we're visiting in Tennessee. Yes, from my experi-ence, Memphis is more culturally diverse than a lot of cities we have visited and, yes, there are a lot of black people here, but I'm surprised that it's something Michael keeps talking about and ob-sessing over.

That said, it's crazy to think that it's only in the last sixty years that the civil rights movement took place, resulting in the election of the first black president in 2008. This is the thing: talking about race makes me uncomfortable. I don't mean in the "I want to turn the other cheek and pretend racism doesn't exist" way. I mean in the "I think it is still, even today, an incredibly loaded and sensitive subject."

Have I had any real experience with racism? The only thing I can claim fully is that my little sister, Bridget, was adopted from Bangladesh in 1991, and her skin color is a lot darker than mine. I barely have any memories that come before Bridget's arrival. As clichéd as this may sound, I truly have never seen her skin color as any kind of barrier or even really that much of an issue. In fact, the only time I can recall being specifically aware of it was when we went shopping for baby dolls as little girls and my mother bought Bridget several dolls of different skin colors to play with. And there was a time once when we were at a hair salon and I asked someone to get my sister and they came back saying they didn't see her, and I had to clarify that we do not look alike and that she has black hair. Stuff like that, but nothing that was ever a hugely large incident growing up.

I don't even know how to properly explain this other than my mother says that when she brought Bridget home we just accepted her as our sister. The only questions seemed to deal with Mom's stomach not getting bigger. Bridget and I shared a room growing up, and we loved and fought as all sisters do. We used to play tricks on my brothers and fight over who had to get up earlier to use the shower first because we also shared a bathroom. I would tease her for having such tiny hands and she'd tease me about being so short. We would have dance-offs in our room and sing along to the Cranberries. Normal sister stuff.

There is no way to explain it other than Bridget is my sister, she's always been my sister, and I believe God brought her to my mother and us as the final missing piece in our family. I love my sister in every way, and I simply cannot imagine my life without her. She is my partner in crime, the equalizer against my two brothers. She is a piece of me and I of her. I always get angry when anyone makes her race an issue and, of course, from time to time people have.

The one time that really mattered, that left an everlasting painful mark on my and my family's lives, though, was during the 2000 presidential race, when Karl Rove started an underground whisper campaign about my father, alleging that Bridget was "his illegitimate black love child." Yes, sick, fucked up, a disgusting and embarrassing scar that will forever remain on presidential politics and South Carolina history. I was furious, upset, and heartbroken when it happened, and even now if I think about it, it makes me want to vomit. Karl Rove is a pathetic excuse for a human being and has never publicly apologized for his cowardice and culpability for what was said about my little sister in South Carolina during the 2000 race. So am I aware of and have I had experiences with racism and race baiting? Yes, I can honestly say that I have. That incident will forever be a part of my family's narrative and my little sister's life. It is a permanent reminder to me about the dark and evil side that politics can sometimes have and that, unfortunately, our country can sometimes feed into.

Michael: Memphis sports a modest strip of bars and restaurants running about five blocks along Beale Street. It's got a festive look, lots of neon signs, and wailing harmonicas blasting from bars, but the area is pretty dead. One of the bars is offering walk-up Jell-O shots, so I order one for everybody. Stephie doesn't want hers so I take it. I've never had a Jell-O shot before because it seemed like something only sorority girls did, but I knock mine back and then gulp Stephie's. I think about ordering a third but Meghan seems to think I'll collapse.

"That's some serious shit," she warns me, and I think I detect in her tone the barest trace of awe. Yes, friends, I double-fisted strawberry Jell-O shots because that's the kind of hard-living man I am.

Across the street, a blues band is playing a set outside. It's not a formal concert space, just a concrete area between two bars. The audience comes and goes and is fifty-fifty white tourists and black locals. The two groups self-segregate, with the whites closer to the sidewalk, the blacks closer to the band. I don't know if they're aware that they're doing it; it just sort of happens like that, the way salad dressing separates if left alone too long.

There are a lot of Republicans, and at least one prominent Democrat (Geraldine Ferraro), who argued during the 2008 election that the primary reason Obama was gaining so much traction was because of his race. It was a strange argument to make: that a black man was succeeding in his quest for the presidency precisely *because* of his race and not in spite of it. Furthermore, it's an argument I happen to agree with.

I don't think Barack Obama, freshman senator from Illinois, two years removed from being a state representative, would have been elected to the presidency if he were not a black man. A similarly qualified white man would not have gotten the nomination. My question: is that a bad thing? Americans wanted so much to put our troubled racial history behind us that we were willing to hand the presidency of the United States to a guy who, no matter how smart and—I'm going to say it, ARTICULATE—was probably not ready for the job.

That said, I don't think we would have elected him if we did not feel him capable, or had he not spoken to our deepest desires about who we wanted to become as a nation and how we wanted to portray ourselves to the world after eight years of a Brooks Brothers cowboy in the Oval Office.

For the record, I voted for Obama both in the general election and the primaries, and I would be lying if I said my vote didn't have anything to do with race. It did. Electing Barack Obama was an important step for the country, an affirmation of our hope (and change) for ourselves. It was something we needed to do, and I'm glad we did it even when he acts like a total wuss.

Meghan has wandered off by herself so she's missing the band, who are great. The singer is one of those classic bluesmen, growling and shouting and mopping his head with a white rag. The band behind him churns away, the white people keep time vertically, the black people horizontally, swaying instead of bopping. It's a small thing, I guess, but I can't help but I notice. When the band passes the hat I put in ten bucks, then Stephie and I wander off to meet Meghan for dinner. (I would like to point out that Stephie doesn't put any money in the hat because she is obviously a racist.)

Meghan: Downtown Memphis or "Beale Street" is kind of like a weird hybrid of Bourbon Street in New Orleans and the Broadway strip in Nashville, except smaller and with blues bars instead of country bars. We have been doing our fair share of drinking on the trip, or more accurately, I have been doing a fair share of the drinking on the trip, and eating pretty much total crap the entire time. The best it seems to get is pulled-pork BBQ and pretzels, so I am starting to feel really bloated. That combined with the heat, and I don't know how I am going to brave another night hitting the Jack Daniels. Michael kicks off the evening by buying Jell-O shots, and slamming two.

"You should be careful they aren't filled with Everclear, because that stuff will knock you on your ass," I sort of half-yell at Michael as we slowly start walking away from the outdoor stand selling the shots.

"They aren't filled with Everclear," Michael answers without even turning around, then looking at me dismissively. I secretly hope they are, as I have yet to see Michael really wasted, and I'm getting sick of him and Stephie just watching me get tipsy by myself. It's starting to make me feel self-conscious, and besides, it isn't that fun to get my buzz on alone.

As we make our way farther and farther down Beale Street, we stop to watch a blues band playing on a small bandstand in an open concrete area. We are not the only tourists there; in fact, there are quite a few standing around listening to the music, bobbing their heads, and sort of half dancing. The band is really good. They display the sort of raw, entrancing talent that may be common to places like Memphis, but a rarity everywhere else. The three of us stand around, also half dancing, clapping a little, and listening to the music.

At some point Michael wanders off to the other end of the area and dances by himself, completely fixated on the lead singer of the band. I wonder what is going through Michael's mind. Don't get me wrong, the lead singer is extremely talented, but Michael looks so fixated, I wonder if he's never seen a live blues musician before. This is the thing about Michael: traveling with him is kind of like traveling with a kid at Disneyland who wanders off if you don't watch him or keep him entertained. He complains about me texting too much, but most of the time I'm just killing time, waiting for him to wander back around to find me. He also lacks a little bit of chivalry. I am incredibly spoiled; my father, my brothers, my grandfather, ex-boyfriends, agents, friends, friends' boyfriends, they are all pretty much chivalrous men. I love men who treat me like a lady: opening doors, ordering drinks, offering me an arm when I'm wearing high heels. Michael isn't really like that. It's neither here nor there, but I have a tendency to get very nervous in large crowds. I chalk it up to spending an entire childhood at political rallies and encountering a few too many crazy people at them. When Michael wanders, my anxiety spikes, especially if we're someplace I've never been. I'm sure he doesn't do it on purpose, but it drives me absolutely crazy. I'm not saying I need looking after like a child, but if I'm going to go on the road with a full-grown man, I prefer he be a little more considerate of the two ladies traveling with him.

So while we're watching the band, I am getting overheated and standing alone to the side, and I tell Stephie I'm going to go find us dinner. I wander back up the Memphis strip—neon signs for different blues bars, different restaurants, some of them looking extremely cheesy in a Señor Frog's sort of way.

We end up at a restaurant next to BB King's bar. I am happy to be inside, out of the humidity. I am happy that a beefsteak tomato salad is on the menu, and I am happy that I'm in Memphis with Stephie and Michael, right at this moment. As much as Michael drives me crazy at times, wandering off, saying things that I sometimes perceive to be insensitive, we have all definitely reached a genuine comfort level with each other. Stephie never bugs me. She is an anomaly among human beings: sweet, understanding, open, and with a dark, dirty sense of humor underneath that innocent layer. Stephie is salt of the earth, and she is invited to anything I ever do or anywhere I ever go for the rest of my life.

I order an extremely dirty martini with blue-cheese-stuffed olives, the tomato salad, and a big, fat New York strip steak. Michael finally asks a question that I can tell he has been curious about for a while.

"What exactly does your family do?" he asks. "I mean, like, how do you guys make the bulk of your income?" Translation: Meghan, I've been to your house, your family has a lot of dough. Where does it come from? I almost spit out my Grey Goose on him, look up, and sort of half sing, "Lord have mercy, ahhh! Okay. Okay."

Whatever else is going on in America, one cannot deny that the demagoguing of success and wealth has been a somewhat more recent trend. I am not embarrassed by the success my family, and my grandfather in particular, built. I think it's incredible and I am very proud of all the accomplishments in my family. I think my late grandfather Jim Hensley is exactly what the American Dream is all about. He started out as a bellman in Phoenix, Arizona, and went on to build an incredibly successful and lucrative beer distributorship. I am proud of all of that and painfully, painfully aware of all the opportunities I have been handed because of his hard work, and the hard work and success of my mother and father. I only have to wake up and read my Twitter feed every morning if I want to be told that I'm a spoiled rich bitch who has been handed everything. My hope is that as Americans we stop judging and ridiculing those who have achieved great success, especially through hard work and perseverance.

After I explain my grandfather's business to Michael, he moves along quite quickly, wanting me to tell him a bad relationship or dating story. That has become a weird game with the three of us, me sharing my rocky and colorful past relationship stories, which always make everyone laugh, and then Stephie and I make fun of Michael for getting married as a teenager.

Michael: Our stay at the Heartbreak Hotel that night is uneventful. Thank goodness they do not pipe Elvis music into the rooms. Mine is bland and featureless, except for the black-and-white photo of midcareer King wailing into a microphone. Something about the photo is itching at me. The way his face is scrunched up, the flamboyant way he splays his hand, the intensity with which he's singing—all of it reminds me of somebody, but it takes me a minute to figure out who. Then it hits me: the singer from the band we saw on the street. Elvis looks just like that guy, plus a rhinestone-studded jumpsuit.

Whether it was cultural pilferage or just the natural and inevitable next step in America's evolution, Elvis was the first white guy to transport black music fully into the mainstream. He was James Dean and Little Richard and Eminem all rolled into one, the first true white rock 'n' roll rebel. I bet white America would have eventually embraced rock 'n' roll even without him, but Elvis introduced black and white America to each other in a new way, embodying all of America's cross currents of race and sex, piousness and excess. He was a contrarian even to himself, a drug addict who volunteered to become an "Agent at Large" for Nixon's war on drugs. He was, in the end, the perfect expression of the American Dream, self-made, brilliant but flawed. All the similarities between Elvis and Bill Clinton I thought about back in Little Rock come bubbling back at me, but I also think you could draw a (less obvious) line from Elvis to Obama.

Just as Elvis was probably inevitable, so was Obama. Eventually somebody other than a white guy was going to be elected president. It might have happened earlier if Colin Powell had decided to run in 2000, but he didn't, so the job fell to Obama. Both Elvis and Obama represent the collision of cultures, which is how America has always marked its own progress, from 1492 on. In Elvis's case, the collision was musical, in Obama's case biological. Both men were charismatic, inspirational figures who energized America and, then, the world. Both won Nobel Peace Prizes (except Elvis). Both were scorned and both did a lot to earn that scorn; hopefully Obama never makes any movies like *Blue Hawaii*.

It scares me that there aren't more Obamas in Congress. Why doesn't our legislative branch represent more of who we are as a nation? Congress is something like 85 percent white. As I write this, there are only two African American Republican congressmen. Before that, an entire decade went by when there were none. If the stereotypical image of Republicans is as smug, old white guys it's because, for the most part, they are. Democrats are better on this front. They've got their fair share of smug old white guys too, but they've also got some smug black guys, ladies, and Latinos. They've got an entire smug rainbow.

A fair question would be to ask if it matters. Should congressmen physically resemble their constituents? What about financially? Does that affect their ability to govern fairly? Although I have no empirical data to support my conclusion, the answer is yes. I take that back. The actual answer is, *fuck* yes. If we really have government "of the people, by the people, for the people," then that's what it should be. Not "of the people, by some of the people, for the people." Our government should be as diverse as its citizenry. Which is why I would like to be the first to nominate my North Little Rock transsexual friend, Ursula, to run for Congress.

I turn off the light and think that our trip to Graceland in the morning is bound to disappoint. People expect the King to live in a castle, but by all accounts Graceland is architecturally unexceptional, a grand but normal house built on a human scale. Personally, I'm kind of excited to tour the grounds and house, to see the actual toilet where Elvis took his final, drugged-out dump.

Meghan: Graceland! I love Graceland and, yes, I insisted that we visit, and, yes, I have been quite a few times and know exactly what to expect. I am excited Stephie and Michael haven't been because it is fun to see the King's house through new eyes.

"I'm really not much of an Elvis fan," Michael snips as we pass Elvis's plane *Lisa Marie* on our way to the entrance.

"Really, Michael?" I shoot back. "Really? I guess you're not really much of a fan of apple pie, hot dogs, or freedom either." Seriously, who isn't an Elvis fan?!? We buy our tickets, sign in, get on the Graceland bus, and make the drive across the street to Graceland.

As we get out and make our way through the front door of Graceland, I get a little butterfly in my stomach. There is just something about visiting such an American legend's house. The man has had just as much impact on American culture as our founding fathers—and, yes, you can quote me on that. Graceland has a very Tara-esque feeling from *Gone with the Wind*, but more retro and '70s. If you haven't been, schedule your trip as soon as possible.

We make our way through and I notice Michael is smiling. I point out my favorite chair in the jungle room, the tear on the pool table from where one of his friends missed a pool ball. I tell Michael my favorite Elvis songs. We walk past Priscilla's wedding dress and the photos of her on her wedding day to Elvis. I swear to God if I ever get married, I will do my hair *exactly* like Priscilla did on her wedding day; that woman is nothing if not stylish. Also if I ever have a daughter, I'm naming her Priscilla. If I have a son, I'm naming him Waylon. Swear to God. I'm in hog heaven. I like seeing all of Elvis's costumes. I like seeing the leather jumpsuit he wore on his "comeback" concert from Hawaii.

I don't know exactly what it is about Elvis, other than he was the first of his kind and changed music and American culture forever, but there's something about him that appeals to every generation. I think the latter part of his life, when he went through hardships with prescription drugs and weight gain, is obviously sad but it doesn't make him any less of a legend or an icon; it just makes the lengths that support people go to enable celebrities egregiously tragic. And why do they do it? I guess to be around famous people and steal some of their wealth. As I stand in the middle of gold-leaf heaven, I find it ironic that the people on tour are here in their T-shirts and flip-flops, as much to worship the excesses of a very wealthy man as they are his talents. Given a choice, they'd probably take the money over the music.

This hypocrisy hits hard the day after my dinner-conversation defense last night. The anti-wealth trend is on the uptick, evident everywhere you turn. Look at Occupy Wall Street. Look at the way Mitt Romney has been treated during this election cycle, with his wealth perceived by many on the Left as a liability. Being wealthy, or coming from substantial means, is not lauded in America today like it was in Elvis's day.

There is obviously a wealth disconnect in this country, and, yes, Wall Street has screwed a lot of people in Middle America, but what concerns me is the new edict that you should be embarrassed by personal wealth and success. That is what continues to worry me about the Obama administration. The "spread the wealth around" feeling will always be one of the biggest alerts about what kind of political ideology our president adheres to. We should encourage hard work and success and not publicly scorn people once they get there. Even some of those who grew up without wealth can too easily forget where they came from. I do not flaunt my family's money because, well, only a spoiled asshole would do that, but I also don't like feeling like it's something I need to hide or be embarrassed about.

I do agree that the tax code is out of control, but I also believe in a free market system where checks and balances come into play. I apparently was one of the few people *not* offended by Mitt Romney's comments that he enjoyed firing people who didn't do a good job working for him. I do not understand why that was perceived as such a shocking thing to say. America is a capitalistic society; if you do a bad job, you should not be able to keep it. Alternatively, if you do a good job, you should be promoted. None of this seems particularly controversial to me, but to a lot of people it is.

Michael: There are four different gift shops on the premises: Good Rockin' Tonight, Elvis Threads, Elvis Kids, and Gallery Elvis, which sells "upscale art pieces and collectibles." If you are purchasing your artworks at Graceland, I would be surprised if "upscale" was a priority, but that might just be my innate, elitist liberal snobbery talking.

We queue up for the shuttle bus line with our tickets in hand, then take the short ride across the street to Graceland. As previously described, it looks like a house. The grounds are thirteen acres, and there is a surprising dearth of Christmas lights. I just sort of assumed that, even in July, Graceland would be festooned with Christmas lights and cars jacked up on cement blocks. But no.

Our tour guide is almost comically bad. She speaks in the sing-songy cadence of a community theater performer. Also, her name is Crystal, which seems like the perfect name for a Graceland shuttle bus tour guide. What I learn from Crystal is that Elvis purchased the home when he was "ONLY twenty-TWO and ALREADY an international STAR." If you're wondering if there is any eating, drinking, smoking, video, or flash photography allowed within Graceland, Crystal also provides the answer to that question. No.

The shuttle bus releases us at the front door to begin our self-guided tour. From the outside, Graceland has a low-rent *Gone with the Wind* kind of vibe. The house is brick clad, and there's a large portico supporting four large white pillars. It's not quite elegant, but if somebody you knew owned it, you'd think it was a pretty sweet place.

Inside is a whole other story. It looks like 1977 threw up all over everything. Every room is different. It's a crazy quilt of draperies, leather, stained glass, mirrored ceilings, wood paneling, and ceramic monkeys. The whole, dizzying effect is enough to induce epileptic seizure. I love it. I really do. As off kilter as it is, it feels like an honest expression of the man who lived here. Unlike so many other homes of dead Americans now serving as museums, Graceland feels like a place where an actual human being lived, a human being with terrible, terrible taste.

We visit the old smokehouse he used for shooting, the racquetball court he built in 1975. (Judging by his later physique, I'm not sure how often he played.) We see the long gallery of gold and platinum records, which used to hold a slot-car track. There's the pool area, the playground, and, at the end of the tour, Elvis's grave. I visited George Washington's home at Mount Vernon a year before with Martha and the kids. It was a similar experience, actually: long lines of people waiting to pay tribute to an American icon, a tour of the impressive, but not incredible, house featuring all the amenities of the day, and concluding with a stop by the great man's grave. I bet Elvis would be tickled by the comparison. I bet George Washington would not.

Meghan: When we get to Elvis's grave, I point out that his middle name is spelled wrong. Michael seems surprised.

"Yeah, a lot of people have conspiracy theories about that," I say. "As if it's proof that he's still alive, but I think that he passed on a long time ago."

At the end of our tour I drag Michael to take a picture outside of Graceland. In the picture we are sitting in front of the steps, both of us leaning back on our elbows. Michael has a snarky, confused look on his face. I am beaming with a grin from ear to ear across my face. I tweet the picture with the caption MICHAEL AND I HAVE RELOCATED TO GRACELAND, although, let's face it, Graceland is much more a house that I would live in than he would.

As we are leaving, I am carrying two giant bags from the Elvis gift shops, and I'm glad to hear that Michael has enjoyed Graceland.

"See, I told you!" I chide him. "He was the King! Every American should pay homage and a little respect."

Michael: When we're done looking at Elvis's famous misspelled grave, we take the shuttle back across the street. Meghan asks me what I thought about Graceland. I tell her I loved it. Which is true.

I love it for the way it reduces an icon to human size. I love it for what it represents, the perpetual American mythology of the self-made man, and the reminder of how easy it is to fall from great heights. I am not an Elvis fan and probably never will be, but I love his story. And, like Elvis, I also love peanut butter, banana, and bacon sandwiches.

Cousin John picks us up in front of the Heartbreak Hotel. We're off to Nashville, the white half of our black and white tour of Tennessee. As we roll out of town, past old brick warehouses and empty storefronts, I keep flashing back to the band from the night before, the singer howling the blues on a sweaty night in Memphis. It's true that the crowd self-segregated, but it's also true that everybody was clapping along, dancing, and having a good time. All of us out there, together, swaying and bopping along to the same great American music.

Nashville, Tennessee

Honky-tonkin'

Michael: Meghan is making a shit-ton of promises about Nashville: we're going honky-tonkin', we're hanging out with her famous country music star buddy, we're gonna eat crazy southern food, blah blah blah. She's so excited you'd think we were going shoe shopping. I don't get it. I've been to Nashville before and I don't know why she's freaking out so much. So they make country music there, so what? Country music sucks.

It's a misnomer to think that all elitist liberal jerk-offs like me *only* listen to Brooklyn-based indie bands with names like Thundernuts. Meghan buys into the stereotype too. Whenever we talk about music, Meghan says things like, "I'm *sorry* I don't find Radiohead as *incredible* as you do." Just snarky little comments to get under my skin. But, I have to say, I think I am far more tolerant of different music than she is, with taste that ranges from "Sweet Home Alabama" to Kid Rock's cover of "Sweet Home Alabama."

So, yes, I am open-minded and tolerant. That said, country music really does kind of suck. At least the glop they're pumping out of Music Row in Nashville these days. Not because it's country, but because it's not country *enough*. Modern country is what used to be called "pop rock," an uninspired mélange of broken hearts, bad puns, and inoffensive guitar solos. It is the low-sodium chicken noodle soup of musical genres.

My guess is this happened after hip-hop and R&B began dominating the charts, leaving a certain segment of the population (conservative white people) feeling alienated. Unable to find anything else to listen to, they just kept hitting the "scan" button on their radios before stumbling onto country music. Once Nashville discovered that they were gaining new audiences from disillusioned pop listeners, they moved further and further in that direction. The end result: Rascal Flatts.

Traditionalists like me miss country outlaws like Merle Haggard and Waylon Jennings. When Loretta Lynn came out with a new album produced by Jack White a couple years ago, I bought (illegally downloaded) it, because I love the old-school stuff. But the bland crap that people call country today mostly just leaves me wishing Johnny Cash would come by and punch whoever is making that shit in the face.

Meghan: Nashville, the southern city of which all other southern cities are envious. It's not just the country music capital of the world, but also a place that combines the nostalgia of all things classically southern with the contemporary edge of a modern city where dreams get made. I love Nashville. The food, the people, Broadway—the street that is a country music lover's mecca—my friends who live there, the experiences I've had, the food, the energy; there are too many things to list. I have always had a good time visiting here.

I love most American cities, but Nashville really is one of the greats. Michael, on the other hand, well, Michael doesn't really like country music, and seems to have pretty lukewarm feelings about going to Nashville; he keeps calling it the white Tennessee. The only country music he likes is Johnny Cash. Saying you're a fan of Johnny Cash is kind of like saying you're a fan of peanut butter; everyone in their right mind likes peanut butter *and* Johnny Cash. It would raise an alarm to me if Michael didn't like Johnny Cash, although he didn't like Elvis, so I guess it wouldn't have been such a huge surprise if he didn't like the Man in Black.

Michael, however, doesn't like any modern country whatsoever. He hates it to the point that it caused a long argument in the RV on our drive to Nashville, which ended with me forcing him to listen to Jason Aldean on blast. I attempted to show him recent music videos of my favorite country artists to emerge in the last five years. The only sign of life I got from Michael was from Kellie Pickler's music video *Best Days of Your Life*.

"I think that girl is hot, does that count?" he asked. No, Michael, it doesn't.

We have extremely different tastes in music. He likes Radiohead, and the kind of whiney hipster music that I don't think Republicans are even allowed to listen to. And if we dare like it even a little, the band will be really insulted that any Republican is a fan and issue a statement that said Republican needs to stop listening and or using their music immediately. Michael also likes songs that were really big in the mid- to late nineties, which makes me laugh, because that was probably the last time he was out and about listening to music in bars.

I'm pretty easy to please when it comes to music, and I am not a music snob. I like a little bit of everything. I am aware of the fact that artists like Taylor Swift may not be considered classic stone-cold country, but I do like her. I like it all. I like Loretta Lynn, Dolly Parton, Hank Williams, Woody Guthrie, Miranda Lambert, Jason Aldean, Willie Nelson, and pretty much everything in between. There's just something about country music that speaks to me.

Michael: At the moment, Meghan is high on a new band called Steel Magnolia, a cute boyfriend-girlfriend duo from Louisiana that is performing tonight at the Grand Ole Opry.

"They're *amazing*," she says.

I doubt it. But we've got tickets for the show, so I guess I'll find out for myself. My one other time at the Grand Ole Opry was on a family vacation when I was a kid. Surprisingly, my lesbian mother from Chicago is a big country music fan. One summer, she and her partner took us kids to Nashville for a week. I have three memories from the trip: riding a roller coaster called the Wabash Cannonball, eating GooGoo Clusters, and going to the Grand Ole Opry. Of those three activities, I would rank the Grand Ole Opry third. To me, it just seemed like a hokey, live performance of *Hee Haw*.

In May of 2010, the Opry and much of Nashville flooded after two days of torrential rains caused the Cumberland River to overflow. The flooding did not receive the kind of national attention that other floods of recent years got, possibly because the BP oil spill was occurring at the same time, as well as a plot to bomb Times Square. Plus, now that major flooding has become a common occurrence, it just didn't get the national airtime it might have in years past.

Which brings me to global warming and Republican orthodoxy. It is endlessly fascinating to me that a political party has decided, en masse, to reject a conclusion reached by nearly the entirety of the scientific community. Many Republicans will not even acknowledge that the Earth's surface temperature is warming, which as far as I can tell is indisputable.

Doesn't whatever is causing melting ice caps, rising ocean levels, coastal flooding, increasing precipitation, and encroaching deserts deserve a more careful consideration by one of the major political parties of the most powerful country on the planet? Doesn't that seem logical? Doesn't it seem like at least some members of that party would stand up in front of the C-Span cameras and say, "Guys, our shit is fucked up here"?

The answer is obviously yes, unless that political party is unwilling to concede that any of these things are occurring. But to do *that,* a political party would have to be willing to ignore reams of scientific evidence to the contrary, which no political party would do because it would make them look foolish. It would be like disputing even basic, settled science like evolution. And no political party would do that.

One of the brilliant side effects of the Republican establishment aligning themselves so closely with the Christian conservative movement is that it allows their rank-and-file to dismiss reason. Religion, by its definition, is an act of faith. Faith requires no evidence. On the contrary, if there *were* evidence, it would no longer be faith. Republicans have figured out a way to blur the lines between faith and reason in such a way that the two become indistinct. The "theory" of evolution is a perfect example. Mainstream Republicans, including nearly all recent Republican presidential candidates, are on record as saying they do not believe in evolution, which at this point is like saying they believe the moon is made of cheese.

In September 2011, a Protestant Religion Research Institute poll showed only 32 percent of white evangelicals believe in evolution. The same poll showed that 31 percent of Tea Partiers "were significantly more likely than other religious or political groups to believe that humans were created within the last 10,000 years." Sorry to use statistics here, especially because statistics are science, and science is stupid.

When Republicans talk about "the war on Christianity," this is what they're talking about. It is a war that they themselves have launched, in an effort to make their evangelical constituents feel besieged and marginalized. If they feel their value system is under attack, they will grow more insular, and they will reject more of what they are being told is a "liberal mainstream media bias" against them, forcing them to turn to "alternative media" like Fox News and talk radio, which will continue to feed them this not only alternate news but alternate reality.

If you want to find at least one significant reason why America is polarized, this is it: because Republicans are lying to their base about science.

I don't know whether the Nashville floods were caused by global warming or not, but I know that climate change predicts increased precipitation, and I know that climatologists are saying that's exactly what's happening. So the question is, who are you going to believe: climatologists or Rush Limbaugh?

Meghan: For all of the reasons that I'm happy to get to Nashville, I'm even more so because it's Cousin John's hometown. He is so excited to visit his grandmother that he is practically jumping out of his driver's seat. I can't help but feel a little sentimental at how excited Cousin John is to see his "nana."

She is an elderly woman living in a house her husband built for her that sits on top of a large hill surrounded by grass, trees, and a small river with a bridge. It pretty much looks like any ideal, average American setting. We sit around in her living room as Cousin John catches her up on his life, and eventually we all watch *Dr. Oz* together.

There is something really sweet and endearing about how much Cousin John loves his grandmother. I already like Cousin John, but now I can add to my growing admiration that he is a really genuine guy who looks after his family.

While we're watching *Dr. Oz*, Michael and I pick up our spat over global warming, a frequent topic of ours in the sweltering heat of the tin can on wheels that we're slowly cooking ourselves in. Much to Michael's chagrin, I happen to be that rare Republican who actually believes in climate change, and I agree that there is enough scientific evidence to support the facts that explain just how badly our planet is being damaged by humans. We are on the cusp of dangerously altering our earth's climate.

All that said, Michael's fondness for saying, "Republicans are lying to their base about science" is complete liberal hogwash. That statement is also utterly absurd and simplistic, and quite frankly I expect more from Michael than that. Let me tell you something, Michael and Democrats everywhere, you are the ones who have completely screwed up the way the dangers of climate change have been communicated to the rest of the country; and by "the rest of the country" I mean pretty much everywhere that is not Los Angeles or New York City. I believe in climate change, but I'm sick of hearing about it from Leonardo DiCaprio and Al Gore.

First of all, the people who don't believe in climate change don't believe it because as far as they are concerned it is a liberal, elite, yes, Hollywood-manifested problem, that may or may not have enough scientific evidence to back it up. I am scared of what is going on with our country and the environment, but the idea of being lectured about it by Hollywood actors and directors who have never left Malibu, and whose idea of "helping the environment" is buying a Prius while yelling at everyone else, makes me want to vomit. Right now, America and Americans are really hurting. People cannot afford to buy their families dinner, let alone worry about buying an expensive hybrid car, going green, or shopping at Whole Foods for eco-conscious foods. Let me tell you something: going green is difficult and expensive and Hollywood is not doing anything to make it easier or more accessible for the rest of the country. Can you blame Americans for not wanting to be lectured to by multimillionaire celebrities who go on and on about saving the environment, yet spend a majority of their time on private planes that leave a carbon footprint larger than many towns people live in?

Laurie David is the ex-wife of Larry David (the creator of *Seinfeld* and *Curb Your Enthusiasm*). She is a big, big environmentalist, dedicating pretty much her entire life to the green movement and trying to educate Americans on what they can do to help reduce their carbon footprint. She also produced the Al Gore documentary *An Inconvenient Truth* and wrote a book for children, *The Down-to-Earth Guide to Global Warming*. Laurie David also has come under fire because she demolished seventy-five acres of undeveloped wetlands and replaced them with swimming pools during a six-year construction project for her house on Martha's Vineyard. She was later fined for illegal wetland abuse and publicly ridiculed for her hypocrisy. She also openly admitted to flying private planes and the extra damage to the environment she is doing. I don't want to hear anything from this woman regarding the state of the hole in our ozone layer. She is a walking, talking cliché, and even I tune out when someone like this is preaching, no matter what their intentions.

This is the problem with the way the green movement is executed by many celebrities. There is even a term for it called "greenwashing," where a celebrity or company publicly touts being green and having a green lifestyle but actually doesn't always practice what they preach. Climate change should be something that is openly discussed and dealt with, but a big problem is that the entire thing seems so ominous and scary, for myself included. There is this idea that you have to be a huge multimillionaire celebrity in order to "green" your life. If there is one thing Republicans don't cotton to, it's liberals in Hollywood.

I do not want environmental issues to be taboo within Republican politics. I do not want it to be a "liberal" issue because, at the end of the day, it is a human issue. I think both sides are unreasonable and painfully unaware of the damage they are doing. Republicans cannot ignore the problems we are facing with the environment just because it goes off the general litmus talking points, and liberals need to start being more cognizant of the real issues facing average Americans. For better or worse, carbon footprints are not going to be one of their main focuses or concerns.

I wish we could meet someplace in the middle, but I don't have the highest of hopes. Environmental issues are still rarely talked about in Republican politics, and Democrats act as if Republicans are stupid and ignorant to not make it their number one issue. Both are wrong and doing damage. Let it be said that I am woman enough to admit that my ears start tuning out anytime I hear a self-righteous liberal going on a tangent about climate change and going green. It's a very clear example of the inability both sides have in not only not communicating with one another, but not even understanding the extreme worlds and perspectives they are both coming from.

Liberals, make it easier and simpler to go green and stop approaching the subject like it's doomsday and a giant tidal wave is seconds away from drowning the entire country. The dialogue about climate change is apocalyptic. If people feel like something is too scary, they tune out. Take baby steps and don't approach the situation like everyone has the access and opportunity to go green. Liberals need to start approaching this issue from the perspective of a Wal-Mart shopper in Dubuque, Iowa, and not Malibu, California. Please stop talking to Republicans like they are ignorant because they do not want to be lectured to by disconnected celebrities in Los Angeles who have all the access and financial means in the world to "go green." Most Americans are worried about their families and their jobs and they simply don't have the time, energy, or income to give to the movement. Everyone needs to come together to make this issue much simpler and much more accessible. For the love of God, Democrats, please use someone as a spokesperson to do this who is not such a cliché. Send Al Gore and Leonardo DiCaprio to lecture in Beverly Hills, and someone more relatable and less pretentious to speak to the rest of the country.

Republicans, you're not getting off easy either. This is the deal, guys: climate change is happening. This crazy-hot summer we're having on this road trip? Climate change is probably a big part of the cause. Haven't you noticed the weird hurricanes in New York City? The flooding in Nashville? I'm no scientist, but I know enough to know all of these things are related and that our weather patterns keep getting stranger and stranger each passing year. On top of everything else, pretty much every scientist in the world confirms that climate change is in fact happening and a large cause of it is due to human impact on the planet. We have to start evolving with the times and coming to the realization that this is something that is actually happening. The one thing I will give Michael in this argument is that it does look dated not to at least be open to the idea of climate change. Just because it has historically been a liberal issue does not mean it isn't also a Republican one, and can't be an American one in the future.

Michael: Let me get off my soapbox and back to the RV. We're rolling through some beautiful country just outside of Nashville. This is Pegram, Cousin John's hometown. He grew up here and we're paying a surprise visit to his grandmother before we continue into town. As we get close, he tells me about the area and some of the people who live here. I am particularly interested in Chicken Willy, who raises chickens for underground cockfights. I ask him to tell me when we pass Chicken Willy's house.

Cousin John points out the wooded estates of a few country stars, although you can't see much from the road. We're up and down hills, driving along narrow leafy roads. As we get close to his grandmother's house, his arm sweeps across the front windshield.

"My grandfather owned all this. Eight hundred eighty-seven acres. This hill, they actually named Haley Hill after my grandfather." He tells us his grandfather used to share his plumbing shop with Bill Monroe, the bluegrass legend.

He taps the horn as we pass a guy in front of his house.

"Was that Chicken Willy?" I ask.

"Nah. You'll see Chicken Willy. You can't mistake his house. He's got fifty fuckin' chickens in the front yard."

His grandmother's house is on top of a small hill, high enough to be spared the floodwaters from last year, although one of the bridges on her property got washed away. The place is modest, built by Cousin John's dad from the frame up. A big old Cadillac is under a tarp out front.

"Your grandmother doesn't know you're coming?"

"No. This is a total freaking surprise."

He's excited to be here, excited to show us where he grew up. He points out a bridge he fell off when he was a kid and the scar on his arm from the accident. Cousin John maneuvers the RV beside the Caddy and jumps out. The rest of us hang back, giving him time to go into the house and surprise his grandma.

After a respectful interval, we circle to the front of the house, where his aunt invites us in. Grandma is sitting on a La-Z-Boy watching *Dr. Oz*. She looks to be in her late eighties. Cousin John beams as he makes the introductions to "Nana."

Nana offers us lunch, which we decline. We make small talk for a bit before the subject turns to her husband, long deceased.

"He was in politics," she says.

"What did he do?" I ask.

"Everything!" she exclaims. Her family is all Democrats "from Bedford County!" she says with pride. We talk about her family and what all of the various members are doing. She gets a little befuddled as we talk.

"They tell me stuff, but I can't remember everything."

"Nobody can," I say. "I can't."

"Well, you're a lot younger than I am."

"I know. And I can't remember anything."

Meghan and Nana talk about Dr. Oz for a few minutes, agreeing that he's a smart man and it's a good show.

On the way out, Cousin John points out a picture of the uncle he said I reminded him of, the one with the glass eye. Meghan and Stephie start laughing hysterically. I look at the picture. He looks like a guy who would have gotten rejected as an extra from *Deliverance* for looking *too* inbred.

"*That's* who I remind you of?" I scream.

"Minus the glasses," Cousin John says.

Nana has allowed us to take the Caddy into town. We pile into the big old car and head out. A few miles down the road, we pass a small house. About fifty small wooden structures are scattered across the front yard. A mean-looking wiry old guy is just getting out of his pickup as we pass. Cousin John doesn't have to say a word.

"CHICKEN WILLY!" we all yell.

Cousin John is smiling from ear to ear.

Meghan: Eventually we leave Nana's and head into downtown Nashville, but not before finally seeing a picture of Cousin John's cousin that apparently is Michael's doppelgänger. There is a faded family picture hanging on the wall and Cousin John points and says, "See, aren't they the spitting image of each other." I can't stop laughing. The man looks nothing like Michael except for the fact that they both have black hair. The guy in the picture looks a little rough to put it mildly, has a glass eye, and is wearing overalls.

"He is the spitting goddamn image of Black, Cousin John!" I squeal, and Stephie and I proceed to take pictures of the picture of

Michael's twin with our camera phones. Michael looks pretty annoyed, which just makes me laugh even more.

We head outside into the climate-changed oppressive heat and
drive to another glamorous motel. Like every other time we check
in, it takes about an hour for me to shower, get cleaned up, change
clothes, and attempt to put on mascara, and for Michael to go to his
room and tweet.

We meet in the lobby an hour later and head to "Cascades, an
American Eatery" in the Gaylord Opryland Resort and Convention
Center, which is kind of like the Atlantis Resort without the casino
or waterslides. All I really care about is that we are about to eat a
real dinner, at a restaurant, sushi and everything. We each order a
ton of food and start to feast. We also order more than a few drinks.
I can't tell if we're punch-drunk from the long drive, or actually
drunk from the alcohol, but we soon realize that we are running
late on time and rush out to find the Grand Ole Opry.

You know how this is like *National Lampoon's Vacation*? Well,
this is the part where we are wandering around Wally World's
parking lot, except we're not running to "Chariots of Fire," and
we're all tipsy and overheated. Michael is really irritated. We are
wandering around, completely incapable of finding the giant theater. It sounds like it should be easy, but in actuality it is not. I
can't stop laughing and there is nothing else to do except to make
fun of Michael.

"We should just stay here forever. Actually we should go get more
beer. Actually I really want to see Steel Magnolia perform." It's a little bit of a shit show. I can't stop giggling, making light of the situation, and teasing Michael, who only gets more annoyed. Stephie
looks concerned and proceeds to try and figure out the directions.

I am giddy. There is something about country music that feels
like home. It's a whole genre of music that celebrates brassy women
who don't put up with crap. When a man cheats on you in a country song, you take a "Louisville slugger to both headlights" of the
guy's car. I like male country singers who loudly cry out in giant

sold-out arenas anthems about how much they like women who pray, wear cowboy boots, and are "hell raising sugars when the sun goes down." It's an industry where women are never too blond, allowed to be curvy and have extra meat on their bones, drink longneck beers, and wear cowboy hats. If men screw them over, they're gonna fight back.

I have always felt like there are two types of people in the world: country music fans and country music haters. I have a friend in the music industry who once asked me about my love of country music; he told me that he didn't get it but he was obviously missing something, because the only areas of music that continue to really grow in a faltering industry are country music and Christian rock. If that doesn't say something about America, I do not know what does.

Country music has always celebrated individualism, rebellion, freedom, our military, and being an American. I know there are other genres of music and musicians that also celebrate these themes, but it's all front and center in the country music world. As much as I think the Dixie Chicks are entitled to have their opinion and exercise their right to free speech, there's something I find liberating about the fact that speaking ill of America in a foreign country is something neither the country music industry nor their fans would stand for.

Country music is also traditionally an industry where being a Republican and conservative is celebrated and it won't hurt someone's career if they choose to be publicly vocal about their love for Jesus, America, or Republican politicians. It is actually probably the only area in the entertainment industry where you can get away with being so open. Throughout the years I have met many closeted Republicans. People who are in the entertainment industry in some way, some more famous than others, who are too scared to be open about their politics, fearing that the stigma attached to being a Republican might be detrimental to their life or careers.

My good friend Barret Swatek is an actress with a long Hollywood career. She was on the show *Seventh Heaven* and was "outed" as being a Republican when an entertainment reporter asked her a question on a red carpet about the last book she read. She answered without thinking that it was Sean Hannity's recent book. Now, I won't speak for my friend, but being outed as a Republican in Hollywood can become a thing. There is fear that people will not represent you or cast you because of your political beliefs. My friend Barret has felt the repercussions of her politics, but ironically that is how we originally met, because we were both loud, proud, young Republican women.

I guess Hollywood and entertainment people are liberal and open-minded as long as it means thinking exactly the same way as they do. When I first moved to Los Angeles, I was randomly invited to a very swanky Oscar party celebrating the director of a movie that had been nominated that year. I knew no one and felt extremely out of place and stupid for even going. However, I spotted a well-known television actor I had met at one of my father's fundraisers two years before, where he had been very engaging. I had been impressed that he would even show up and give money to a Republican, and told him so. He answered, "Of course, your father's an American hero." After spotting him across the room at this party, I walked over to him and his wife. He seemed really uncomfortable, and before I could barely get five words out of my mouth, he literally turned his back and walked away from me, saying, "You take care, Meghan." It caught me off guard and pretty much brought me right back to middle school again. This actor was clearly worried about having some kind of political conversation with me around all of his Hollywood friends.

I admire anyone who is open and honest about what they believe. I'm not an actor, I don't live in Hollywood, I don't know what it's like but I cannot imagine what it is like to believe one thing privately and be scared to address it publicly. I simply can't fathom reconciling that kind of life.

On the contrary, the country singers I met during the campaign were always out, loud, proud, and publicly playing songs for the cause. They didn't elect to hide out at fancy fundraisers, shielded by the privacy of a closed-press event. Of course, not all country music artists are Republicans, but the ones who are will tell you proudly to your face that they are.

When we get in to sit down, we have trouble finding our seats and I am informed that Steel Magnolia have just finished their set. Now I'm annoyed.

"For fuck's sake, Black!" It's Michael's fault; we're just making it all Michael's fault.

Michael: A few hours later, we're stumbling around the parking lot of the immense Gaylord Opryland Resort and Convention Center, drunk, trying to find the goddamned Grand Ole Opry. I'm lit off of two "John Dalys," which is vodka and peach, garnished with mint. It seemed like a southern summertime drink at the time; now it feels like an assassination attempt.

We wander through the parking lot, Meghan tottering on heels, Stephie in her jazzy "on the town" skirt, me in my linen pants and Crocs. Maybe John Dalys and sushi weren't a good idea. I don't know. I just need to go sit down somewhere before I puke.

Even though the parking lot is full, there's not even anybody around to ask where to go because the show has already started. Finally, we flag down a security guy in a golf cart, who gives us a lift to the Grand Ole Opry House. We weren't anywhere near it. It's not *our* fault we couldn't find the stupid theater. Honestly, I don't know how they expect drunk people to find their giant forty-five-hundred-seat theater, which is located exactly where the signs say it is. If the signs had been written in blurry letters, I would have been able to read them better.

After some confusion with the ticket takers, any of whom made Grandma Cousin John look like a sprightly colt, we finally take our seats well into the show. We sit down just as Steel Magnolia is finishing their set.

Ha-ha.

First impression of the Opry: this place is incredible. I don't know what I was expecting, but my memory of the Opry is way different from *this*. In my memory, we sat on apple crates and hay bales. It was like the barn from *Charlotte's Web*. But this place is nothing like that. It's modern, huge, and *packed*. Every one of the four and a half thousand seats is filled. On a Wednesday night. Not a bushel or a peck in sight.

The crowd is warm and polite and soon I am awash in steel guitar and fiddle. I don't even know who's performing. Some good-looking band in tight jeans and pressed Western shirts. Whoever it is, they're fantastic. I'm just waiting for Meghan to hurl her bra at the stage.

One thing I particularly like is the obvious reverence all the performers have for the stage on which they are standing. The Grand Ole Opry's been around since 1925, so the place is soaked in history and, very recently, forty-six inches of water. During the flood, a particular concern was rescuing a six-foot circle of oak flooring taken from the stage of the Ryman Auditorium, the sometimes home of the Opry since 1974. I can only imagine all the cowboy boots that have scuffed that floor.

The highlight for me is the end of the show when Little Jimmy Dickens comes out. He's ninety years old, a Grand Ole Opry staple for sixty years. Although he lacks the name recognition of a Minnie Pearl, he does have one thing she does not: he is alive. I know Little Jimmy from a novelty song he had in the sixties called "May the Bird of Paradise Fly Up Your Nose." Knowing this says more about my childhood than it does his choice of music.

He moves well for ninety, walking unaccompanied to the center of the stage, guitar slung around his neck, bedazzled in his old-timey Western dress outfit. A white cowboy hat probably adds half a foot to his four-foot-eleven-inch frame. Jimmy tells a few corny jokes and plays a couple of songs on that guitar. He sounds confident and full of life, and every eye in the house is rooted to him. When he's done, the whole crowd rises to give him a standing ovation. With a wave of his hat and an "aw shucks" grin, Little Jimmy exits stage right.

It's a great show. Meghan asks me what I thought. I tell her it was pretty good because I'll be damned if I'm going to admit to her how much I loved it.

"You loved it," she says. "Admit it, Black."

"I admit nothing."

As we wait for our cab outside the Opry, I realize I may have to revise my opinion about country music. After all, I had a great time, the musicians were unbelievable, the music itself felt authentic and heartfelt. But as we pile into the cab for the drive back to the hotel, I remember something important: country music sucks.

Meghan: The Grand Ole Opry, for those who don't know, is Mecca in Nashville. It is the stage where anyone who is anyone in country music performs and has performed. Pretty much every country legend in the history of country music has played there. What's legendary about it is that the stage is wooden, so it makes the acoustics that much warmer. When I have a car, or when I have access to satellite radio, I can listen to live radio broadcasts throughout the week from the Opry, and my favorite is the one on *Willie's Roadhouse* on SiriusXM.

We all eventually find our seats amidst a packed house and sit down. I attempt to explain who some of the acts are, but it seems to go over Michael's head, until Little Jimmy Dickens comes out. He is the oldest living member of the Opry, a country music legend (he's a member of the country music hall of fame), and stands barely five feet tall. He truly is a living legend and I explain all of this to Michael; in fact I make him rise to his feet out of respect when Jimmy comes onstage. Michael seems genuinely entertained by Jimmy's show. I mean, who wouldn't be? Jimmy proceeds to sing songs and make jokes about how he "looks like Mighty Mouse flying by" in his traditional rhinestone outfit. He's pretty much the perfect person for us to be watching that evening. It's really an honor to be there, especially because the place was entirely flooded less than a year ago. Nashville really does have a strong community and the place looks as good as new.

For whatever reason, I had not been informed that DIERKS BENTLEY was the final performer of the evening. I love Dierks Bentley and begin to scream when he and his band take the stage.

"Who is that?" Michael yells over the screams.

"I'll explain it later, but he's huge!" I yell back.

Dierks comes onstage, looking very sexy with his country swagger, and begins to sing a variety of his hits, every word of which I know. I stand up and sing along to them, including my favorite, "What Was I Thinkin'." He is fantastic on that stage and I can't believe we are so close. After Dierks sings his last song and takes a bow, Stephie leans over and asks me what I thought of his act.

"Stephie," I say, "your new mission as our tour manager is to find out the name of Dierks Bentley's scruffy, long-haired bass player. He looks like my future ex-husband." I'm half serious. Dierks Bentley is a sexy man with a sexy bass player. Country musicians are typically really sexy. It's just how it is.

Fort Campbell, Kentucky/Tennessee

Shoot/Don't Shoot

Michael: One of our original ideas when mapping our itinerary was visiting a military base. Obviously, Meghan's family has a long and distinguished history of service, but my father and grandfather both served too. They weren't la-dee-da *admirals* like Meghan's grandfather or whoop-de-doo *fighter pilots* and *war heroes* like her dad, but both did their parts. In fact, one of my treasured mementos is a photograph of my father's basic-training graduation: Second Brigade, Eighth Battalion, B Company, Fourth Platoon. He's standing in the second row of five, arms straight at his sides, looking hard-eyed just off camera. He's twenty-one years old. It's March of 1967, seven months before Meghan's dad would be shot down and captured over North Vietnam.

My dad never saw combat. He never even went overseas. In fact, he enlisted in the Indiana Army Reserves specifically to minimize his chances of being sent into harm's way. It worked. His reserve unit remained in Indiana throughout the war. Dad died when I was twelve, so I never got the chance to talk to him about his service, but I suspect his attitude was more or less that he did what he had to do to avoid getting shipped to Vietnam; I'm glad he felt that way.

Growing up, my mom's attitude about the military was pretty well defined. She used to say to my brother and me, "If there's a war, I'm sending you two to Canada."

When I ask about my grandfather and his time in the navy during World War II, she tells me she thinks he enlisted. "Everybody did. It was a very popular war." I ask her where he served and she laughs. "Rio. Can you believe that?"

I was wondering if her attitude about the military had changed at all over the years, so I asked her about it in a recent phone conversation. I reminded her that she used to talk about sending us to Canada. She said, "I still feel that way. I'll drive you there myself. And my grandchildren too. I just think this country invents too many wars."

I hate to say it, but I agree.

The military base we chose to visit is Fort Campbell, sixty miles from Nashville. It's a sprawling 106,700 acres on the Kentucky/Tennessee border, home of the famous 101st Airborne Division. Fort Campbell bills itself as "the nation's premier power projection platform," which "possesses a unique capability to deploy mission-ready contingency forces by air, rail, highway, and inland waterway." It's also where that photo of my father was taken, forty-five years ago.

Meghan: If you know one thing about my family's history, the first thing that comes to mind is probably their extremely long and distinguished history of military service to the country. My grandfather and great-grandfather on my father's side were both decorated four-star admirals in the navy, and my father is a famous war hero. Entire books and movies have been dedicated to their pivotal and historic roles in our nation's wars: My great-grandfather who was in World War II, my grandfather and father both of whom were in the Vietnam War.

My brother Jack is currently a lieutenant in the navy and graduated from the US Naval Academy in 2009. My other brother Jimmy is a former marine who enlisted while in high school. My family history of serving this country goes as far back as the American Revolution, when my ancestor John Young served on General George Washington's staff.

A naval air station in Meridian, Mississippi, is named in my great-grandfather's honor: McCain Field. Also named after my great-grandfather was a guided-missile destroyer, the USS *John S. McCain* (DL-3), which was later decommissioned. Another destroyer, the USS *John S. McCain* (DDG-56), was named after both my great-grandfather and grandfather; when I was a child in 1992, my mother christened it with a champagne bottle in Bath, Maine. My entire family was there and celebrated.

The McCain men are all known for being of a smaller build, using profane language, and liking to drink and gamble. They are also all known for being natural leaders. All the men in my family love and serve their country. You know that part in *Forrest Gump* where Lieutenant Dan has his family history explained and it shows the flashbacks of each of his ancestors fighting in every American war? That's kind of like the men in my family. I am most proud of this long legacy of service, and although I never served, if in some way I was called to, in a draft or a crisis, I would be the first one in line. I thank God for the men and women who serve this country to keep me safe. I get to go on road trips with crazy comedians and wax poetic about the future of American politics in gorgeous television studios for one reason alone—because men and women fight for my freedom to do so. The men and women who elect to fight for and serve our country are truly the best of the best of the best. We don't celebrate their service enough these days, and they all sacrifice so much.

Michael: I'm a little apprehensive as we drive onto the base. I just don't have much experience with soldiers or military culture. Spending time with Jimmy and his friends in Prescott helped, but that was on civilian turf. This is where soldiers come to learn how to jump out of airplanes and rappel from helicopters. This is where people learn to kill other people. I'm afraid they're going to make me crawl under barbed wire or yell at me to polish my Crocs or make me peel potatoes. God forbid I'm asked to do a single push-up. Because I will cry.

We're met at the Public Affairs Office by a trio of minders: two civilians and a staff sergeant. They ask that our visit be "off the record," meaning they do not want us to quote anybody directly. Nor are we allowed to videotape or make audio recordings of anything we see. They don't explain why and we don't press the issue. It sucks, but okay.

The thing I'm about to learn over the next six hours about the military is how good they are at being the military. These people, and everybody we meet, are so adept at promoting their own culture and ethos that it's kind of amazing. Every soldier we meet is working from the same playbook, all marching in perfect metaphorical lockstep. The experience is so scripted, so spit-shined and perfect, that it's impossible to believe, the way a reality show is impossible to believe. Yes, both undeniably have moments of reality, but the entirety is so heavily edited that it's difficult for me to fully buy any of it.

The experience reminds me of our Zappos tour in Las Vegas. In the case of Zappos, the weird corporate culture was an enforced cheeriness. Here at Fort Campbell, it's a steely, strident professionalism. They seem to be attempting to project an aura of invincibility, which I guess is what you want in an army. Both environments have an artificiality to them that I find difficult to reconcile with the way people actually conduct themselves in the real world.

But maybe that's the point. Maybe an army needs to believe itself to be superior in order to survive. What unnerves me about being among these guys, though, is the sense of otherness that I feel: a feeling of detachment among the soldiers, as if they are somehow removed from the society they are sworn to defend.

Or maybe it's just my own boyish insecurity among these men that's making me feel that way, a quiet shame that I haven't done my own part in protecting America. Maybe it's just an inborn suspicion of the military left over from my upbringing. Whatever the cause, I'm unable to ever fully relax for the duration of our visit.

Meghan, of course, is right at home among these guys. She's twittering at them about this and that, asking questions, flirting a little bit. They seem to like her a lot more than they like me. I don't blame them. As we make our way across the base, *I* like her more than me too.

Meghan: I talk with everyone, ask them about their time in the military, tell them about my brothers; just lots and lots of small talk trying to make them feel at ease. They're all extremely friendly and accommodating. It feels a little second nature; I am around men in the military all the time.

The first place we are taken is the ELS training simulator, where soldiers prepare for combat. After making pleasantries, we are ushered into a giant simulator screen with a bunch of guns connected. It's pretty crazy. Stephie, Michael, and I go in and watch the men train for a few minutes. The simulator is extremely loud and lifelike. As weird as that sounds, because it is a screen and fake guns, the soldiers are all lying on their stomachs with another guy touching them to signal when someone should shoot and where. The entire room is filled with screaming and blasts of rounds going off. It even takes me aback a little.

After they're done, their kill scores and reaction scores are tallied and they are told the results. When the lights go on, I can't help but notice all the men look like versions of Captain America. They are all built, handsome, and looking good in their camo. I have to force myself to concentrate on the task at hand; I had almost forgotten how hot men in the military look in fatigues. They ask us if we want to give the simulator a try. All of us want to. So me, Stephie, and Michael pick up fake M4s and the instructors show us how to shoot. Except that the simulator guns are a little lighter, it's pretty much like shooting an actual M4, which I have done a few times.

We all take the same positions that the soldiers did and start going through the same scenario that was just on-screen. We are in a desert town filled with insurgents and it is our job to shoot at anyone who opens fire on us. Everything starts happening really quickly—a man jumps out and starts shooting at us and I make an attempt to shoot back at him. The instructors start yelling at us where to aim and who is coming out and my heart starts racing. One of the insurgents falls to the ground, my gun jams; I am doing all of this wrong and it is freaking me out. This does not feel like a video game; it feels like the actual thing. The simulation ends, the lights go on, and I can see that Michael's brow is damp with sweat. My heart is still racing. Stephie looks like she might pass out. Michael looks more freaked out than me; in fact, Michael looks like something might be wrong. So I do all the talking.

"Hot shit!" I say. "And that is why America has the greatest military in the history of the world, baby!" All the guys like this. I tell them how amazing this training is, and I mean it. I can't imagine doing this in real life.

Whenever Michael laughs at me when I say that freedom doesn't come free, this scenario right here is what I am talking about, soldiers in situations where they are forced to kill.

Michael: This simulator is crazy. It can transpose any conceivable environment onto a large video wall. Soldiers then monitor the environment for hostilities and take appropriate action. In other words, the simulator teaches them when to shoot, who to shoot, and most important, if to shoot. To my ears, it sounded like a high-tech video game, which it is. Except that it's not. For one thing, the M4 weighs about as much as a Great Dane, and is about as easy to lift and shoot. For another, when the lights go down and Iraq comes up, no video game has ever freaked me out like this. Not even Super Mario Bros.

When the first simulation ends, I am out of breath and close to tears. There's an unexpected weight in the middle of my chest, a kind of adrenalized dread, as if I've just narrowly avoided a bad traffic accident. I am completely unprepared for this reaction. After all, I've spent countless hours in front of television screens shooting burglars and aliens and killer robots and never felt anything more upsetting than annoyance at having to repeat a level. But something about this experience is different—some combination of the huge, immersive wall, the barely modified weapon in my hand, the concussive popping of the gun, the soldiers yelling beside me. Something about it leaves me disoriented and upset. Neither Meghan nor Stephie seem to be having the same reaction as me, and I don't say anything because I don't want anybody making fun of me.

We walk over to the workstation to gauge our shooting. Surprisingly, nonviolent, spinach-chomping Nermal was the most effective shooter. She killed three or four bad guys. Meghan was next. I brought up the rear. They ask if we want to go again. No.

"Hell yes!" says Meghan.

We run through the simulation several more times, repeating the desert scene before moving on to jungle terrain. Each time we do it, I feel my emotional reaction lessening. I guess this is what desensitization feels like. Our last exercise is something called Shoot/Don't Shoot. This is a scenario in which, unlike the others, we are shown actual video of a potentially hostile situation. We're in tight quarters, a walled hut. Three angry-seeming actors are yelling at us in a language we don't speak—in this case, Pashtun. One of the actors waves a pistol in our direction. Do we shoot? I feel myself tense. What are we supposed to do here? What if he turns the gun towards us? We stand there, guns raised, our fingers on our triggers, unsure what to do. Then Meghan creates an international incident. She shoots the guy. Wrong move.

"You weren't supposed to shoot," our instructor says. He plays the videotape forward and, within a moment, the guy puts his pistol on a table and raises his arms.

"Shit," says Meghan.

We run through the same scenario again, but we do not know what the outcome is going to be, and when our instructor whispers in my ear, "Shoot him in the head," I do not hesitate.

POP!

The guy goes down. Oh wow, I just took that fucker out. To my surprise, I feel pretty good about it. I just killed a guy and it feels awesome. To my further surprise and annoyance, it turns out it was

Meghan who fired the kill shot, not me.

By the end of our half hour in the simulator, I feel almost numb to the experience, which troubles me almost as much as my initial emotional reaction; I mean, I'm legitimately annoyed that I wasn't the one who shot that guy in the head.

I also gain a profound respect for what these soldiers go through in a combat zone. We were in the most controlled, artificial environment imaginable and yet I still experienced incredible tension. What if I were weighed down with eighty pounds of gear in 120 degree heat? What if I'd been out on patrol for five hours in those conditions? What if I'd had to deal with those conditions every day for a year or more? What if it was my second or third tour of duty? What if I'd had friends who'd been injured or killed doing exactly what I'm doing now?

Fuck me, what if it was real?

Meghan: When we leave the simulation and head back into the waiting room, we see all the soldiers from inside again. They are all very polite and friendly but I know we are probably not going to get anywhere with them. First of all, seniors are in the room, as is PR for the base. In my experience, the only real way to talk to a soldier is over whiskey—lots of whiskey.

We talk to them about our book and what they are doing there and they are not really responding. I get it: they have better things to do than entertain Michael and me. I try flirting with them a little and it kind of works. Then I switch gears and tell them about our trip to Vegas and how Michael doesn't like strip clubs. This, they find entertaining.

The ugly truth is we are not going to be able to talk politics with these guys; it's just not going to happen. This is not the right setting and at the end of the day, soldiers are supposed to be apolitical; they are not really supposed to have an opinion and are only supposed to support our president. At the end of the day, these soldiers are not here to be political, or talk politics, they are here to do their job.

Looking at all these handsome, shiny faces makes me think of my brothers, and what Jimmy must have gone through. Easily the worst day of my life was when he deployed to Iraq in 2007. My brother was so determined to enlist that when he was seventeen my parents finally gave in and signed the underage permission letter. When you go into military service in this fashion, you are nothing more than a grunt, with no officer status. He went to basic training like every other man who joins the Marines and was sent off to war.

In the spring of 2007 when I was a senior at Columbia University, I got up at five o'clock in the morning, drove an hour and a half to Camp Pendleton with my mother, sister, and two brothers, and stood in a parking lot for a few hours waiting to say goodbye to my brother Jimmy for what might have been the last time. My family waited in a giant parking lot with probably a hundred other families, all of us in the same grim boat. We watched everyone give last wishes before leaving. I watched as men and women with baby faces put giant packs on their backs, picked up semi-assault rifles, boarded a Greyhound bus, and left to possibly go die in the Middle East.

That is what the cold reality of a deployment looks like: standing around a barren parking lot, waiting with bagpipes playing as you contemplate never seeing the person you love again. I stood there, that day, in that parking lot, hating my brother, hating the military, hating wars, hating that my family and my brother were being called to serve while so many others did not, and worse, did not seem to care or really understand our sacrifices.

I remember standing there with my boyfriend at the time, a good friend of Jimmy's who is also in the military, and screaming at him that none of this was fair. I couldn't lean on my mother because she was also a mess, so my boyfriend was the only option. He had to hold on to me because I could not stop myself from crying. He grabbed my hands and made me pray with him. I remember hot tears pouring down my face and feeling like I hated God. I remember feeling like I was watching this happen to someone else, that it was some sad movie about the Iraq War that a girl who looked a lot like me had a role in. I remember feeling angry at every other person in this country who would never have to go through what I was going through at that very moment.

When it was finally time for my brother to board the Greyhound, we walked across the giant parking lot to say goodbye to him in a sea of other soldiers. I hugged him really tightly. At the time I think I weighed more than him; he still has such a small frame but was waiflike as a teenager. I could barely get out of my mouth that I loved him and to be safe. I stood there and thought I would never see Jimmy again. I was angry at myself for not coming up with something more inspiring to tell him as we said goodbye.

I'm not enough of a poet to eloquently explain what something like this is like. Any of you reading this who has sent a loved one to war, you understand. A piece of you dies. A part of your heart just falls out of you and evaporates and if you had any innocence to begin with it will quickly evaporate as well. It was the worst day of my life. I wish that day and those moments on no one. That is why no one gets to lecture me, or my family, about war unless they've experienced it as well. I am a gray person, but on this subject, it's black and white. You've experienced it or you haven't. And those of you who haven't, you couldn't even begin to understand what it feels like, thinking that you are giving your brother's life for the good of the United States of America. That this country and freedom are important enough to you and your family; that all of you would give so large a sacrifice. Feeling like maybe you would die for it as well. And I do. I believe America and freedom are worth dying and fighting for. As painful as that is, I do.

Michael: To wind down the visit, we take some pictures with the guys and drive over to the Sabalauski Air Assault School, in which "the course of instruction is focused on Combat Assault Operations involving US Army rotary-wing aircraft." My understanding is that this means "doing shit with helicopters."

A pleasant guy with two inconspicuous silver bars on his cap greets us at Air Assault School. He's probably in his mid-thirties, a little round-faced but fit. He leads us through the school, taking us into classrooms, telling us a little bit about their mission, then leading us into the stifling heat where rows of soaking wet soldiers in full uniform are learning to fasten and unfasten payload nets.

After a while I ask the guy what his job is at Air Assault School.

"I run it," he says, and not for the first time today, I feel like an idiot.

On our way over, Meghan asked what percentage of soldiers are female. Nobody in the van knew, which was fine. I don't think anybody expected them to know things like that off the top of their heads, but I am very surprised when we return from our tour of Air Assault School to see three female soldiers lined up waiting to greet us. Somebody clearly plucked them from their duties to speak with us in response to Meghan's question. They seem less prepared than the guys we spoke with at the simulator, less gung-ho.

Two of them are sergeants, one an adorable twenty-one-year-old specialist. They are more willing to talk about their time in the service than their male counterparts we'd spoken to earlier. "I didn't get to do what I wanted," says one. "I studied forensics in college."

"What are you doing here?"

"Human resources."

Another says she is an engineer. She describes her job as "digging holes and blowing stuff up." She's been in for nine years, has a kid, and wants to get out. She's only got four months left. I ask her if she'll continue what she's doing when she leaves the service.

"No. I'm going to cosmetology school in Miami."

Meghan asks if they experience any sexism.

"No more than in the civilian world," one says. The specialist, twenty-one, the lowest-ranking soldier there, doesn't meet our eyes and doesn't offer any information about anything. I get it: there's no upside in talking to us, and a lot of potential downside. One military expression that has found its way into the popular lexicon is CYA: cover your ass.

After a few more minutes, our minder announces it's picture time again. I guess this is their standard "move it along" call. We take some more pictures and head out, this time to a change of command ceremony. One colonel is leaving, another one is replacing him.

We drive over to some hot parade grounds and sit in half-filled bleachers to watch the procession. Out on the grounds are three formations of solders lined up at attention in perfect rows. Beyond them is a tree line. Occasionally I notice people running from the tree line towards the groups, and then, a few minutes later, walking back out. I can't figure out why they are doing that.

We sit through a lengthy ceremony. A welcome, followed by an invocation, followed by several speeches and a presentation. Even under shade, it's uncomfortably hot, and out of the corner of my eye I notice somebody in formation toppling over. One of the soldiers just collapses onto the field. Another soldier dashes from the tree line to help him up, and walks him off the field as yet another soldier runs in to take his place. So that's why they're running back and forth: people are passing out!

The whole thing seems crazy to me, that these officers are standing up there speechifying while their troops are forced to stand stock still at attention for an hour in full uniform in 100 degree heat. Meghan and Stephie both look as shocked as I feel, but nobody else in the bleachers even seems to notice the bodies collapsing one after the other.

In civilian life, if I even see *one* person faint, that's a pretty big deal. During the ceremony, I must see about fifteen of them go down.

After the ceremony, Meghan brings up the fact that people were fainting all over the place, but our minder doesn't seem to have a lot of sympathy for them. He tells us they're trained to not lock their knees while standing at attention. Locking the knees restricts blood flow. That's why they passed out. In other words, it's their own damned fault.

It's getting late and I can tell that everybody's kind of itching to wrap up our tour. They bring us to the PX, where I pick up some army T-shirts for my wife and kids. Then we go back to the parking lot, where Cousin John is waiting.

They've got one more surprise for us. Our choice of MREs: meals ready to eat. They come in big cardboard boxes. We choose spaghetti and meatballs, pot roast, and chicken with noodles. Then we shake hands all around and thank them profusely for the tour.

I leave Fort Campbell blown away by the professionalism we experienced, the dedication, the discipline. There's a real sense of purpose here, which is something I think a lot of people (myself included, at times) lack in the civilian world. Here, people are training for specific missions. They understand exactly what is expected of them and are given the tools and resources to succeed. The trade-off is the loss of freedom that accompanies mission-specific assignments. Here you are told where to go, when to be there, how to dress. So many decisions are taken out of the individual's hands. That's great for a military organization, I suppose, but I don't know how well that translates to the larger experience of what it means to be an American.

"Freedom doesn't come free," is Meghan's catchphrase, the one she kept yelling at me at that bar in Prescott. I still don't know what that means exactly, but I feel like today gave me a sense of the cost.

When we get into the RV, Meghan instructs us not to eat the MREs. She's had them before. "They're disgusting and they give you constipation," she says. "Throw them away."

We do.

Meghan: As I watch the changeover ceremony, I feel an odd mixture of pride, honor, and reflection, which gets me to thinking about Michael's point at the beginning of Tennessee: how there's a black and a white city. There is no doubt that our military is comprised in part of lower-income personnel, particularly in the junior ranks. I'd like to think that this is a result of my generation not seeing color lines, but I'm not naive. We see them; we just don't make a big deal about it.

I do believe that in a lot of ways race really isn't an issue for my generation—at least not the way it was for our parents, or the generation in between. It doesn't feel as intense to me as it does for

Michael. I do not feel entirely comfortable speaking on the issue of segregation and racism in the same way that I do not feel comfortable having a man lecture me about sexism and being a woman in a man's world. Men cannot ever really understand what it's like to be a woman in America, and I have no idea what it is like to be a racial minority in America.

I have great compassion for the obstacles that still exist for all minorities in America, and I don't believe that we have reached full equality by any means. When you look at the representation of black men, Hispanics, and any shade of woman in Congress, it's pretty sad. I have a lot more hope for my generation when we reach the age when we get to power than I do for the last. I don't see color, I see character. I look around at the fainting soldiers on the parade ground and I see a generation unafraid to prove itself through war. Shoulder to shoulder, the races mix out there, and it becomes about brotherhood and sisterhood, not about individuals. Never about skin color. In some ways, the military has become the perfect racial melting pot.

Interlude

A Passionate Night in Cincinnati, Ohio

Michael: We spend a night in Cincinnati on our way to Detroit. Our dinner is at some local hoity-toity locavore joint where they slaughter the pig at your table and serve you the entrails cooked in butter you churn yourself; that kind of place. Anyway, as pretentious as it is, it is also delicious and we spend a couple hours lingering. Towards the end of our meal, we start talking with our waiter about politics. I guess I'm expecting him to be a Democrat because he's a waiter and works at the kind of elitist restaurant me and other jerk-off liberals like to congratulate ourselves for visiting.

As it happens, our waiter Joe is an Independent/Libertarian. He's a young guy, maybe twenty-seven, who believes in free markets and gay marriage. He also ardently opposes Obamacare. Like a lot of people we've spoken to on our trip, he talks about how he feels it's unconstitutional for the government to mandate that people purchase health insurance. I ask him if the restaurant gives him health insurance.

No.

Does he have health insurance?

No, but he's aware of the risk he's taking by not purchasing health insurance, so the onus is on him. He's young and healthy so it's worth the risk.

What if his appendix bursts?

That's a good point, he says.

Who's going to pay for that?

He doesn't know. The public, he guesses, because he can't afford it. He's a waiter.

So is it fair that he won't buy health insurance but the public should pay for his appendectomy?

No. But it's not fair that the government should tell him what he has to buy, either.

Maybe not, I concede, but he's asking all of us to subsidize his health care for his principles.

The argument doesn't resolve because these arguments never do. I've never met anybody opposed to mandated health care who walks away from an argument with a changed opinion, and vice versa. Ditto for every single issue. I don't think I've ever met anybody who has ever changed their mind about any political issue. Once formed, opinions affix themselves like squid tentacles. The more you wriggle, the more they seem to tighten. It's a curious thing. For all of our talk about civil discourse, for all of our high-minded optimism going into this adventure, I don't think either Meghan or I have convinced each other of anything.

That night, we have a long conversation in her hotel room about President Obama. Her feelings for him are, to put it delicately, complicated.

There's something I sometimes forget when talking to her about Obama. Her father lost the presidency of the United States of America to that guy. That's got to be a tough pill to swallow. Think about it: if one of your parents was that close to being president, it might stick in your craw a little too. So it's no surprise that she's not the guy's biggest fan.

But here's one of the things I love about Meghan McCain: even though her dad lost the election to Barack Obama, even though she has every reason to buy into the whole "Marxist/Kenyan/Socialist/Saul Alinsky/terrorist-loving crap," she does not. Meghan McCain is committed to finding the good in her president.

It wasn't always like that. After the election, she says she spent months in a haze, unable to do much of anything, afraid for the future of the country, and worried like a lot of conservatives that men in black suits would soon be coming for her guns.

Then she started looking around and realized the country was still going. No, she doesn't like Obama's policies and, no, she doesn't think he's a good president, but Meghan McCain is open-minded enough to say this: "I want to love my president. I wish I felt about him the way I feel about my father. I want him to succeed because I want America to succeed."

In other words, Meghan is a bigger man than I think I could ever be in her situation. Politicians talk about loyalty to country above party all the time. How many of them live it? How many of them are able to set aside personal grievances for the sake of the greater good? How many of them actively seek out the best parts of their political opponents instead of the worst? Not many. Meghan does.

It's not easy for her, just as it wouldn't be easy for me to seek out the best parts of the kid who beat the shit out of me in high school.

That's why it drives me crazy when people knock her; she's one of the few people I've met in politics who isn't absolutely certain of her convictions. People in her position are generally nothing if not sure of themselves, positive of their own rightness. And why not? They are usually surrounded by people who tell them they are right, who lobby them, who cajole and sweet-talk them. They rely on think tanks dedicated to reinforcing their vision. They watch television networks that do nothing but echo their message back at them. It feels good when people tell you you're right all the time; of course I wouldn't know what that feels like because I'm married, but Meghan probably does. She could easily live in the political positive-reinforcement bubble, but she does not.

I see her searching, I see her listening, I see her questioning her own assumptions about things. About guns, about health care, even about her own spiritual faith, about everything except the military. We Democrats like to believe we are the open-minded ones, but we're not. We're usually just as doctrinaire as the other guys; the only real difference between us and them is that we've got more vegans. I'm pretty sure they don't have any.

When people talk about the country being polarized, I think a lot of times what they are talking about is their frustration that the other side is unwilling to listen to them. Unfortunately, what most of them fail to realize is that, oftentimes, they are equally unwilling to listen. If this trip has taught me anything so far, it's that most people just need to shut the hell up and pay attention to what their neighbors and waiters and fellow Americans are trying to say.

And, by the way, I'm just as guilty of ignoring that advice as everybody else.

Dearborn, Michigan

Motor City Mosque 'n' Roll

Michael: It's weird that one small American city in Michigan is both the worldwide headquarters of one of the most famous American industrial success stories and the city with the highest concentration of Muslims in the nation. It almost sounds like the setting for a high-concept Hollywood romantic comedy.

Maybe Ashton Kutcher plays an ambitious young vice president at Ford who falls in love with a beautiful but hilarious Muslim assembly line worker played by . . . actually, I don't know who would play the young Muslim woman. When I google "funny Muslim actress" I get exactly zero results. To prove how odd that is, when I google the made-up phrase "porky little booger" I get one result, which means that "porky little booger" is a more commonly used term than "funny Muslim actress." In any case, they meet, fall in love, then have to navigate the treacherous rapids of each other's lives and disapproving families. In the end, they conquer their differences and live happily ever after. Possible title: *Guess Who's Coming to Ramadan?*

Dearborn embodies the contradictions of modern American life. This is where the First Amendment is currently being put through its paces, as well as being the hoped-for epicenter of an American manufacturing renaissance. It's a topsy-turvy kind of place, yet driving through, Dearborn strikes me as surprisingly normal. It could be any American city. Except that a lot of the women wear head scarves. And a lot of the signs are in Arabic. And Bob Seger lives here.

Our first stop is the Ford Rouge Factory Tour, billed as "Detroit's #1 Automotive Attraction." (No word on which automotive attraction is number two.) The tour starts at the Henry Ford, a large campus combining various Ford buildings, exhibits, and Greenfield Village, one of those immersive historic towns where people stroll around in period costume and engage in authentic old-timey activities, except nobody here is doing anything because it's so damned hot. It's like a half-assed Walt Disney project whose theme is "The World of Boring."

Shuttle buses drive visitors from the Henry Ford to the Rouge Factory complex about ten minutes away. As we enter the factory grounds, I am stunned at its size. The thing is massive, spread out over hundreds of acres, holding ninety-three buildings and containing 15 million square feet of floor area. Just to give you an idea of how big that is, it's almost twice as big as my house!

The self-guided tour starts at the Epcot-like Legacy Gallery, where a line of gleaming, historic Fords are displayed, all of them made here at the Rouge. I love looking at old cars, even though my automotive knowledge extends no further than an ability to identify steering wheels and cup holders. The last vehicle on display is a new F-150 pickup, the same vehicle currently in production here. It's a hulking, gorgeous thing, the Tom Brady of trucks.

Ford F-Series pickup trucks have been the top-selling vehicle in the United States for something like thirty-five years in a row. The pickup is a curious symbol of American individualism and ruggedness. In a nation where a third of the adult population is obese, it seems likely that the heaviest thing many of those drivers are hauling around is themselves.

Meghan: This wasn't my first trip to a car manufacturing plant. Ready for it, kids? Yes, I went to one during a campaign stop with my father, although it was with a huge crowd and the entire traveling press corps around, so I didn't really get to fully absorb the experience. I felt like this stop was an important one for Michael and me, given the intensity of focus on the auto industry that has come into play in politics in the last four years.

Our first stop before observing the production line is the Art of Manufacturing Theater, which is kind of like a Ford Imax theater with special effects built in. Michael, Stephie, and I sit down in chairs that lean back and take in the film experience (complete with heat and water misters for an added 3-D effect of what an auto plant is really like). The video goes through the history of the Ford company up to the present, when they are looking forward to the future of hybrid and green technology.

I cannot help it. I really like the Ford Motor Company because of its refusal to take the bailouts, and because it seems like a family-owned company with a real moral investment in America and the automaker's future. Of course, the film we watched wanted me to get that impression, but there's something about giant trucks and "Built Ford Tough" that tugs at my love of all things having to do with American individualism, ruggedness, and a refusal to be pushed around or made to believe that America and our companies are anything but strong, built to last, and the best of the best.

As you may have noticed, I like people and companies that are unabashedly all American and proud of it. It's not that I think people who do not choose to fly American flags and drive American-made trucks aren't patriotic or don't love America; I just like people who proudly display it like I do. Granted, I have a tendency to take it to the extreme at times—I came very close to tattooing a heart with an American flag on my ankle after we killed bin Laden.

Dearborn is a curious place, populated by all the people who work in this plant. Sadly, the cities of Dearborn and Detroit no longer have the Rock City and Motor City connotations they once had. Instead of images of the high-flying times of rock 'n' roll and auto production, now the images that come to mind are more associated with the recession, in particular the downfall of the American auto industry and the housing market crash.

During the campaign I once heard the city of Detroit described as "America's canary in the coal mine." Describing anything as a canary in a coal mine is in and of itself a warning. It's a reference to the caged canaries miners kept in the tunnels as they mined. If the canary died, it was a warning that poisonous gas had leaked into the mine and they needed to evacuate as soon as possible. It does seem as though Detroit has gone from being a symbol of the triumph of American industrialism to a grave warning sign about the direction in which the entire country could be headed.

For example, the last time I visited Michigan was for my first book tour, when I went to speak at the corporate headquarters of Borders Books in Ann Arbor. I remember telling a friend that I was going to talk to the people at Borders; my friend reacted by saying, "Will Borders even be in business when your book comes out?" I was a little shocked by her statement and that this was something she even thought could happen in the short months before my book was released. Growing up, after school I would frequent the local Borders bookstore at the Biltmore in Phoenix, to hang out, get snacks, and write papers. I loved that Borders, and the idea that such a giant chain would go under seemed impossible. I had spent so much time in the oversized bookstore, reading, writing, avoiding going home after school; the idea that it could go under just seemed unfathomable to me.

I went to visit the Borders corporate headquarters and spoke with some of their employees, followed by a question-and-answer session about my book, my time on the road with my father, and my role in politics. There were a lot of people there and they were all incredibly warm and engaging. All of them also seemed very enthusiastic about working for the company and the long legacy it had as a retailer. I remember a lot of laughs and having an unusually great time, considering it was an event where I had to "work": give a speech and schmooze with Borders employees in an attempt to get them excited about the release of my book. I also spoke at the annual dinner held for authors of books that were going to be coming out in the next few months. I just remember all of it being extremely well done, organized, and overall a really pleasurable experience. The board and representatives made me feel welcome, and the event was held in a gorgeous hotel; I left feeling like I had the support of the entire company for the upcoming release of my book, a special feeling for any author to get from a corporate book seller.

I left Michigan thinking my friend was crazy, that there was no way a company like Borders would be on its way to going under. They were obviously running a tight ship in Ann Arbor and maintained a sense of enthusiasm for the industry. Borders filed for Chapter Eleven bankruptcy and was forced to liquidate and close all of its stores about eight months later. I remember hearing the news and actually feeling really sad about it. First because, like I said, this giant Borders bookstore down the street had been a sort of parent-okayed getaway throughout my adolescence that held a lot of sentimental value—I mean, I wrote many high school essays in the coffee shop on the top floor of that Borders—and because it felt like another blow to the state of Michigan. Yet another example of another American business that, for whatever reason, had not been able to evolve with the times. As a result of its failures, both a local economy would be damaged and more Americans would be out of jobs. The fact that Borders was based in Michigan, a state that has had more than its share of bruises in this recession, made it that much more tragic.

Michael: When we're done taking turns sitting in the truck, we are led into a round room that looks like the holodeck on *Star Trek*. This is the Art of Manufacturing Theater. There're about seventy seats dotted throughout the space. Once everybody is seated, we are immersed in a multimedia film about Ford and the Rouge complex, complete with wind and water effects. It's my favorite kind of corporate propaganda: lots of shots of happy factory hands mixed with strobe lights, smoke machines, and plenty of rah-rah patriotic reverie. By the end of the spectacle, I'm ready to hug the first factory worker I see and thank them for their service.

When it's over, we've got a couple of choices. We can either head upstairs to the Observation Deck, "the world's largest living roof," or we can take the Assembly Plant Walking Tour. Environmental stuff is great, and I'm glad Ford is trying to create "a realm where environmental innovation and industrial production work together to put an entirely new face on modern manufacturing," but I just want to see some truck-making robots.

The plant tour is a third of a mile long along an elevated concrete pathway above the plant's final assembly line. I've never been inside a factory before and don't really know what to expect. In my head, I guess, it'll look like Willy Wonka's chocolate factory. I am hoping for an Inventing Room, a Great Glass Elevator, and of course, lots of Oompa-Loompas.

The reality is different. For one thing, it looks less like Willy Wonka and more like an Ikea store. The factory is spotless and brightly lit. Workers are organized into small teams of about ten people each, walking back and forth from large plastic bins where the parts for their jobs are stored. The teams work at different stations doing certain, highly specific tasks. There's a team that affixes side-view mirrors. A team that puts trim on the doors. A team that installs moonroofs.

That's all they do, day after day, fitting those components onto the endless line of truck cabs rolling along the assembly line.

During its height in the thirties, a hundred thousand people made their living at the Rouge. Now that number is down to six thousand. They've also reduced the amount of time it takes to assemble a vehicle from twelve hours to ninety-two minutes. We see them at the end of the tour, brand new F-150s just like the one we sat in at the Legacy Gallery.

It's kind of amazing to contemplate the overwhelming logistical complexity of making something like this work. All these people. All these moving parts. And this is just one factory making one product. How many factories just like this are scattered across the country? We hear all the time about manufacturing jobs being lost overseas. Well, these are the people losing those jobs, these people right here, about twenty feet below me on this factory floor. Every single one of them replaceable tomorrow. Maybe a new robot comes along that can do their job cheaper, or the president signs a new treaty that allows Ford to ship these jobs overseas, or the F-150 loses market share and they have to shut down the line.

I didn't know what to think about the automotive bailouts. From where I sat as an American consumer, Detroit was making a lot of shitty cars. One bland clunker after another. Why were my taxes going to bail out lousy companies? On the other hand, I was sympathetic to all the ancillary costs of a bankrupt American automotive industry, the devastating ripple effects it could have on an already saggy economy. To me, it seemed like a fifty-fifty proposition. Maybe the bailouts would work or maybe we'd just end up flushing another 100 billion dollars into the Detroit sewer system.

Capitalism has gotten a lot of grief lately. A lot of people with my political leanings have come to believe that the bad in capitalism outweighs the good. Michael Moore even made a whole movie whose central premise was that capitalism is inherently evil.

I disagree.

I think capitalism is an imperfect economic system, but still the best one ever devised. It alone allows the free exchange of goods, services, and ideas. It creates wealth and opportunities for more people than any other system ever attempted. I am a capitalist and proud to be one.

But I reject the idea so common on the Right now that capitalism is an unmitigated good. It's not. Capitalism is neither good nor bad. It is amoral, a tool whose purpose is the creation of wealth. But unlike other tools, capitalism has no single master, no single person in charge of its use. The master is "the corporation," which despite the Supreme Court telling us otherwise is not a person. The corporation cannot be a person because it lacks the one thing that defines humanity: a conscience. The corporation's purpose is to generate wealth, and it will do whatever it has to do to fulfill its purpose.

By itself, I don't think this is a bad thing. I love wealth. Money is one of my favorite things. I like having it, smelling it, throwing it up in the air in slow motion while lying on a hotel bed. But there are rules that govern the ways in which I make my money. I can't cheat people to make it. I can't steal it. The rules preventing me from cheating and stealing are called "laws" or "regulations." Yes, those regulations limit my ability to make money, but I'm glad they exist because they limit others from cheating and stealing from *me*.

The same principal is true for corporations. Except that, for a corporation, it's even more tempting to skirt the bounds of legality and ethics because a corporation has no soul. If it can get away with something in the service of making a few extra bucks—dumping chemicals into a river, exploiting vulnerable workers, cheating its customers—it might do so.

That's why we need laws to make sure there is a respectful balance between the needs of the corporation and the needs of the people. The two do not always go hand in hand. My personal belief is that capitalism works best when there is tension between markets and governments. American capitalism cannot work without the American government, and the American government cannot work without American capitalism. Sort of like the way airbag laws make cars safer. (Airbag legislation, by the way, was opposed by all of the automotive companies because the companies feared the bags didn't go far enough to protect drivers. Just kidding. They thought airbags would cost them too much money.)

Meghan: The factory is absolutely enormous, with a long pathway where you can look down over the entire conveyor belt. The entire place is extremely well lit, and men and women walk around putting different parts in different places. We watch as one man puts a long rubber buffer of some kind on the window of an SUV. He wears headphones, and repeats his one piece of the puzzle as each car passes by.

I know that these jobs are popular and none of the workers seem too stressed out or upset in any way, but something about it seems incredibly draining and daunting. What if one of them misses a place and doesn't add onto the car what they are supposed to? I wonder if there were ever any accidents on the line and how much it would cost to stop the production if someone got hurt. As clichéd as this might sound, it is weird to stand here looking down at "the American autoworker." Literally right beneath me are the men and women who have been the subject of discussion on the news and in articles across America for years now. These are the people pundits and politicians are talking about.

For all of the obvious reasons, I love the Ford company. It's the oldest American auto company, started in 1903 by Henry Ford, and has a long history of ingenuity. It played an integral role in both the industrial revolution and American history, starting with the introduction of the original Model A. It's a company that survived the Great Depression and has continued to be a family-controlled company for over a hundred years. It's the second-largest automaker in the United States and the fifth largest in the world. My brother drives a huge Ford F-150 truck. My father drives a Ford Fusion. My family uses another Ford F-150 in Phoenix. I don't know if there is another car that is as all-American as the Ford F-Series. Possibly a Cadillac, but for over a hundred years Ford has been a symbol of American pride with its great, solidly made automobiles and trucks.

I love a man in a Ford F-Series pickup truck, so much so that my girlfriends and I have a running joke about how all men should just do themselves a favor and buy Ford pickups, because they automatically become more attractive when driving them. Seriously, I will take a man in a Ford any day of the week over a man in a BMW.

The other thing about the Ford company is that it did not participate in the bailouts that both GM and Chrysler did in 2009. Ford did not file bankruptcy, but did take 5.9 billion dollars in low-cost government loans to overhaul its factories and bring out more fuel-efficient technology. However, compared to the 80 billion dollars that were spent bailing out the other two car companies, the amount Ford received was very small.

In September of 2011, Ford put out a television commercial critical of the Obama administration's auto bailouts. In the ad, a Ford owner says that he bought an F-Series pickup truck because Ford was the only US automaker not to have taken a bailout. The man in the ad says, "I wasn't going to buy another car that was bailed out by our government. I was going to buy from a manufacturer that's standing on their own: win, lose, or draw." The ad came under fire and was later removed from the air because of the controversy it caused and the fact that it didn't address the loan Ford had been given.

Now, I don't know if it's just me, but I have absolutely no problem with that ad and think the Ford company has every right to tout the fact that it was not bailed out by the US government. One of the cornerstones of my Republican beliefs is that I am anti-union, and do not believe in government bailouts. Not only was I against the auto bailouts when the Obama administration gave them to the automakers, it was the first time I really panicked about the extreme damage that I felt was being done by the Obama administration. I felt like I was watching a train crash and the repercussions of that crash were going to be felt, literally, in my grandchildren's lifetime.

Now, before you get ahead of yourself and start accusing me of overreacting and accusing the president of being a socialist, let me explain. One of the main, basic differences in philosophy between Republicans and Democrats is the role each party believes government should play. I believe that business and enterprise in America should be left alone as much as possible. I believe in small government. I believe in letting businesses work on their own in a free market.

The Democrats' view is that we should regulate businesses and give money to the ones they think will succeed. I do not believe that works. It didn't work under communism, it didn't work under socialism, and it doesn't work now. In regard to the auto industry, I believe we should have let automakers go bankrupt, like the thousands of other companies that have gone bankrupt and come back, either to emerge after reconstruction or fail because, well, their businesses were failures. Instead, the Obama administration put the autoworker unions in a superior position.

Why should a car company get a better deal than a small-business owner on Main Street America? What about that is fair or American?

Why do the automakers get a special deal because of the power of the unions, as opposed to all the small businesses that have gone under in Phoenix, Arizona, where I grew up? Because last time I checked, all the small family-owned businesses in America didn't get any bailouts. When small companies and businesses in America fail, they go bankrupt. Sometimes they reemerge as leaner and more capable companies. Sometimes they do not, but that's capitalism: what this country is founded on. I believe in capitalism. I believe in a free market system.

Things in America should never be too big to fail. We should not be afraid of letting bad products fail, in order to let companies come back stronger and more innovative as a result. The argument President Obama and liberal Democrats give for the bailouts is that if we had let the auto companies go bankrupt, we would have lost that industry. They don't really emphasize the fact that a large part of President Obama's Democratic base consists of labor unions, and that it is politically expedient to placate those unions. Last time I checked, companies go bankrupt every single day in America; if they're great enough companies with great enough products, they will come back and succeed. President Obama and the Democrats gave away 80 billion dollars of taxpayer money when they didn't have to. Bailing out is enabling mediocrity. It is allowing the larger problems to continue—the problems that got a company in the position where it needed to be bailed out in the first place. In my opinion, this is un-American. This country did not become the greatest country in the history of the world through bailouts.

As I gaze over the factory floor, I wonder if there is ever going to be a time when technology will completely overtake these workers' jobs, and what it will mean to the American auto industry. All I know is that I am glad this company and others like it have not been off-shored to China.

Michael: I'm so impressed with the factory tour that I do something I almost never do. I walk into the gift shop and buy myself a souvenir, a blue-and-white baseball cap with the Ford logo stitched on the front. As we board the bus for the ride back to the Henry Ford, I examine the tag sewn into the hat's lining: MADE IN CHINA.

From the factory floor to the mosque: our next stop is the Islamic Center of America. It was important to me that we spend some time hanging out with Muslims on this trip because Islam takes up such a large part of our national dialogue. Because, let's face it—Islam freaks people out.

My impression is that most Americans don't know what to think about Muslims. On the one hand, we are a nation that prides itself on accepting people of all faiths. On the other hand, Muslims scare us because of 9/11. Whether or not that's fair is a matter of opinion, but I understand the fear. If a bunch of Scientologists had blown up a couple giant buildings, we might be scared of them too.

(Actually, after seeing Tom Cruise jump on Oprah's couch, I *am* a little scared of Scientologists.)

People correctly make the argument all the time that terrorism isn't limited to Muslims. But in America, terrorism is most closely identified with Islam because most of our experience with terrorism is Islamic terrorism. There have been enough terrorist plots and terrorist acts committed against Americans by Muslims (some of them homegrown) that we have a hard time separating crazy jihadists from run-of-the-mill American Muslims just trying to go about their lives.

Part of our apprehension probably has to do with the fact that most of us do not know any Muslims. Despite all the attention it gets, Islam is still a tiny religion here, accounting for less than one percent of the population. It's easy to fear somebody when you have never met them. My best Muslim friend is a comedian with Elvis sideburns who does a videogame podcast; it's hard for me to get too worked up about Islam in general when that's the guy I most closely associate with the faith.

At the same time, Americans tend to automatically dismiss homegrown, non-Muslim terrorists like Timothy McVeigh as nut jobs because all of us know so many people who look and act like him.

Who hasn't met the paranoid, angry white guy with the buzz cut muttering about black helicopters? Most of the time, that dude is a harmless crank. When he does end up doing the unthinkable, we shrug him off as crazy. If two Muslim teenagers had gone through their high school spraying bullets like Dylan Klebold and Eric Harris did at Columbine, we would have blamed the whole religion instead of the kids. We would have said they were terrorists instead of maniacs.

Is that fair?

Even so, Muslims haven't done themselves any great service in the years since 9/11. Why don't we hear them decrying violence? Part of the problem is that they are a disparate group. There is no Muslim pope. No Muslim king. Muslims are like Jews, organized into small enclaves loosely affiliated with each other through larger umbrella organizations. They have no overall governing body. Nor is there any prominent American Muslim to stand up and speak for the faith. So, when Americans hear a collective silence from the Muslim community after an Islamic terrorist attack, they often interpret that silence as acquiescence rather than what it most likely is, a lack of leadership.

Meghan: I went to college at Columbia University with a lot of Muslim students, and I am still friends with a number of people who practice the Muslim faith. That doesn't mean I consider them my "Muslim friends." In fact, religion rarely comes up in conversation with them. I believe that, unfortunately, when it comes to stereotypes about Muslims, a few radicals have severely damaged the reputation of an entire faith. Do I think there are Muslim extremist jihadists in the Middle East who want to destroy my way of life? Yes, of course, and it scares the living hell out of me. However, Islam is the second-largest religion in the world and the vast, vast majority of Muslims reject the extremists and agree that the radicals have done damage to their faith.

I feel fortunate that I had the opportunity to go to a university that offered wonderful courses on Islamic history and faith. Not many Americans get the opportunity to advance their understanding of a religion they find mysterious and, in some cases scary. Through my different religion requirements at school, I read the Koran, studied Islamic art, and read Middle Eastern writings. I am grateful that I had the experience as a young adult to learn about the culture from educators in an environment that was safe and allowed open dialogue. I also feel lucky to have studied at a school with such a diverse student body that all races and religions are given an opportunity to share and understand each other. I had that luxury and that exposure; if you have not had that opportunity, it is easy to be scared of what you don't know.

Cousin John pulls up in our giant RV and Eide A. Alawan greets us in the parking lot of the Islamic Center of America. He is a small man with a white beard and a warm smile. He's holding a couple of head scarves and a shawl, and I suddenly realize that I'm dressed in leggings and an open-neck T-shirt. When I dressed this morning I was only thinking about this ongoing heat wave; I should have known better than to dress this way to visit a mosque. Mr. Alawan doesn't seem to mind, but asks Stephie and me to put on the head scarves, and then hands me the shawl to wrap around my shoulders and chest. I am embarrassed and feel bad for dressing in a way I would never have to visit a church. The dress code slipped my mind.

We walk in and Mr. Alawan starts giving us a tour of the mosque. There is some kind of event going on in one of the larger rooms. There are tables and balloons, teenagers everywhere. It looks like it's going to be some kind of a celebration. It reminds me of the events I used to go to at my church as a child.

Michael: The Islamic Center of America is not, as the name implies, the Islamic center of America. It's just a grandiose name for a mosque that only represents its own community, those Muslims living in Dearborn and the surrounding areas. This is one of the first things we learn from Eide.

He explains the mosque's name for us when we ask about it. Eide says it used to be Islamic Center of Detroit, but the imam thought the name should attempt to extend its reach. Personally, if that was the goal, I think they should have gone with "Islamic Center of THE UNIVERSE!!!"

Eide leads us on a tour of the mosque, which seems no different from any synagogue or church I've been to. We look in on a community room where a bunch of teenagers are hanging out getting ready for a program later in the evening.

Two young women in head scarves approach.

"Aren't you Michael Ian Black?" one of them asks.

I say I am.

"That's awesome!" the other says, and they walk away.

I did not expect to get recognized in a mosque.

"What was that all about?" asks Eide. I tell him they probably recognize me from VH1, but he seems baffled. "I thought maybe they were putting me on," he says. "I was going to apologize. I thought maybe they were drunk."

He is, of course, kidding.

We go into the prayer room, or maybe the prayer room *is* the mosque. I don't know. It's an enormous, empty round room lined with beautiful Arabic calligraphy around the perimeter of the ceiling. He asks if any of us have been in a mosque before. Stephie says she tried to enter one in Israel but was forbidden because they would not let women in. Eide seems particularly wounded by this.

"Did you have a head scarf?"

Yes.

"Were your legs covered?"

Yes, they brought clothing to cover themselves.

"I apologize," he says. "That should not have happened."

We sit in the prayer room for a long time talking. Eide tells us he's had a busy decade since September 11, doing interfaith outreach to the community. He says the day after, on September 12, a thousand Muslims gathered in Greenfield Village for a candlelight vigil. He says he was just as appalled by the attacks as everybody else. That his religion should be associated with the attacks seems to deflate him.

"I've lived here all my life, and have been practicing Islam since well before September 11," he says.

"But how do you feel about radical Islam hating what you love?" Meghan asks.

"Radicals come in every form," he answers, a response I sense he has given ten thousand times in the last decade. "I do not accept that just because somebody says he is a Muslim—and the nineteen hijackers said they were Muslim—to me, they do not represent Islam."

The subject of President Obama comes up.

"What were your feelings about the Obama Muslim controversy?" I ask.

"I believe he's a Muslim," Eide says.

Meghan seems shocked.

"You do? Really?"

Eide laughs. He's kidding. "No," he chuckles. "I keep on telling people he's a Muslim. An undercover Muslim."

He says he voted for Obama, but not because of his religion. "First time in my history I voted for a non-Republican. Don't tell your dad that," he adds as an aside to Meghan. "I voted for a Democrat because I want to see change in this country. I want to see an African American be president. I would have voted for . . . what's her name?"

"Hillary," I say.

"Hillary. I would have voted for Hillary except I have a problem with her husband. I couldn't stand the guy." He laughs again. "But the point is, I voted for Obama because he's an African American. I'm old, as you can see, and I want to see change in my lifetime."

I find his words touching. Eide is old enough to remember a time when the idea of a black or female president was unthinkable. Meghan and I are both young enough to take for granted that the realistic possibility of both of those outcomes wasn't always the case here. Of course we will have a female president, a Hispanic president, and maybe, sooner rather than later, a Mormon president. It doesn't seem possible today, but I have no doubt that one day we will also have a Muslim president. For somebody like Eide, it must seem a little amazing that such things are possible. He is relentlessly upbeat about America and his community's place here.

Stephie asks him if it troubles him that a contingent of this country is threatened by the belief that Obama *could* be a Muslim.

"To me, it doesn't represent a large percentage of the community. Like you, I love America. I wouldn't want to live anyplace else in the world. This is America, folks. I mean, Jews weren't well liked. Catholics weren't well liked by the Puritans, if you know any of your history. It's our turn in the bucket."

In a way, I find his optimism encouraging and in a way, I find it naive. My sense of what America thinks about Muslims is darker than his. He believes in America's better angels, but I am not so sure. Why does anybody need to be in the bucket?

Yes, we want to welcome all faiths, but I also know that for all of our bravado, Americans are sometimes a fearful people. Even though we welcome outsiders, they often end up scaring us once they are here. It's a strange dichotomy of the American character. I hope his vision of America wins out.

A larger concern for Eide seems to be tensions *within* the Muslim community, mainly between Sunni and Shia groups. He has a term for Muslims who can observe together: "Sushis." His own mosque is Shia, and I ask him if Sunnis would feel comfortable praying there. "Maybe two or three percent would," he answers. "But within ten or fifteen years, I think it'll be fifty-fifty."

I've met a lot of clergy. The ones I liked the most seem to radiate an inner calm. Eide is not a clergyman, but I sense a similar stillness within him. His life's passion is this work, interfaith as well as intrafaith. When I hear conservative talk radio blowhards railing against Islam, screaming about impending "Sharia law," I wonder if they have met people like Eide or the girls who recognized me from VH1, or the teenagers grilling hotdogs and hamburgers out back.

For much of our time in the mosque I've noticed a little boy about two years old running around the big, empty room. He's having a great time, just running and running, tripping over his own legs, laughing. His mother stands nearby, watching, but making no effort to stop him or silence him. Eide doesn't even seem to notice the boy. But I do, because the idea of running and laughing in a place of worship is alien to me. Every church and synagogue I have ever attended has been a place of solemnity. It never occurred to me that a prayer room could also be a place for unbridled laughter and fun. But seeing this little boy acting that way, here, makes perfect sense to me. Of course a house of prayer should be fun. It *should* be a place where there is laughter and joy. Of course.

After we say goodbye to Eide we start to exit the mosque. Before we can, a burly guy enters the room and says, *"As-salamu alaikum"* as he passes. Eide responds, *"Wa alaikum as-salaam."*

We pass. The man stops and calls to me. He's pissed.

"I say *'As-salamu alaikum'* to you!" he growls. I'm flustered and I feel my cheeks start to flush. I don't know what to say. He stares at me. "Why don't you say *'Wa alaikum as-salaam'*?"

Eide tries to interject, to explain that I didn't know, but the man's eyes remain hard and, frankly, scary. I mutter the phrase to the best of my ability, mortified. *"Wa alaikum as-salaam,"* I try to say, but it comes out more like "Wakka wakka salami."

The man glares for a few more seconds, then grumbles away.

"I'm sorry," says Eide. "He can be a little difficult."

Maybe it seems stupid, but I'm actually kind of shaken by the encounter because, after speaking with Eide for an hour, my feelings about religion, all religion, have softened. After this encounter, though, I am again reminded how strident people can be, how unyielding and prone to offense. I tell Eide it's fine. But it's not fine.

All of us thank him for his hospitality and time. Before taking our leave we somehow get onto the subject of John F. Kennedy, and the uproar caused by his Catholicism.

"You read about it now, but if you lived at the time, it was news all over the place. 'Catholics are going to rule the country now. He's going to answer to the pope.' Nothing could have been further from the truth." He pauses. "Of course, he wasn't as good a Catholic as I thought he was." He chuckles. "But the point is, Americans are always fearful. I think the fear should be in some other area . . ." he trails off.

"Somehow we survive," I say.

"Yeah, we survive," he agrees. "And we'll survive when this Muslim gets out of office."

He's kidding.

Washington, DC

America, You Sexy Bitch

Meghan: It was an obvious and natural choice to wind down our tour with a stop at our nation's capital. I used to hate Washington, DC, when I was growing up, but more recently I have come to love the city. I don't know if it is a love that has evolved with age and wisdom or my continued path toward a deeper involvement with my role in politics, but somewhere along the way I've found a great appreciation for the city. Frankly, my relatively recent fondness for Washington, DC, sometimes still surprises me.

When I was a little girl, Washington, DC, was the place that took my dad away from me and would make me cry on Sunday nights or Monday mornings when he would have to leave to fly back. I have distinct memories of watching my father on CSPAN in our big Spanish-style kitchen. My mother would be cooking dinner and something would be steaming on the stove; she would make us "watch for Daddy," and then after he left the floor of the Senate we would call him on the phone. It was a fun game we used to play and I give it up to my mother for always keeping my father's presence around even when he wasn't physically at home.

My father always looked so serious on television, sometimes visibly agitated or passionate about whatever issue he was speaking about on the Senate floor. I think he looks unnatural in a suit and tie. It's a running joke in my family that my father puts on his "uniform" nearly as soon as he gets through the door of our house in Phoenix, his uniform being really old Levi's jeans and some form of a raggedy, disgusting T-shirt, normally with a *Far Side* comic printed on the front or something else equally cheesy. Whenever he comes home and changes his clothes, our dogs start barking at him like crazy and jumping around, as if they are anticipating playing with my dad or going up to our cabin in Sedona to run around and get dirty. Every time this happens, it still makes me laugh.

Normally, my mother, brothers, sister, and I would go visit my father at his office in Washington three times a year: during Christmastime, the spring, and summer. The strongest memories I have are of the bitter-cold trips in the middle of the winter. I used to hate having to get up so early in the morning to go visit my dad at his big office, inevitably growing bored sitting and waiting around for him to go vote on a bill. The best part of visiting him was eating the navy-bean soup at the Senate dining room, and getting to eat a handful of chocolate-covered mints as we went out. I also loved riding on the train that's in the basement of the Senate building and finding it funny that the conductors knew my father by name.

Michael: After a couple of thousand miles in a stinky RV, we've finally reached the belly of the beast. I've been to DC many times before, but always as a flag-waving tourist, never as an insider. This time, escorted by Meghan, I feel like one of the elites everybody hates, somebody with access to congressmen and senators, and I have to admit, it feels pretty cool.

We knew from the beginning of this trip that we'd eventually wind up here, and would eventually sit down with politicians to get their take on the current political environment. We're not reporters and our goal is not to engage in "gotcha" journalism, or even journalism at all. We just want to hear them out as people and as citizens. One of those people will be the 2008 Republican nominee for president of the United States, John McCain.

I've been dreading meeting Meghan's father from the get-go. I don't know why. I was far less nervous meeting the fathers of *actual* girlfriends than I am about meeting this guy. I'm not usually intimidated by people in positions of power and influence, but I am this time. Probably because I've been living with his twenty-seven-year-old daughter for a month under what could be construed as dubious circumstances. Were I the father, I can certainly envision myself being (to put it mildly) suspicious of the dude in linen pants and Crocs my little girl was dropping by the office with to say hello.

Thankfully, our meeting with the senior senator from the great state of Arizona is still a day away. Before that, we'll be hanging out with another father: Dr. Charles Grob, proud papa of our very own bride-to-be, Nermal.

Meghan: I am forever grateful that my parents elected not to raise me in Washington, DC. I think if they had I would probably be an entirely different person, or at the very least have an entirely different view of politics and my unorthodox approach to fighting for my side of the Republican Party. It may be just my perspective, but many of the children of politicians that I have met over the years who were raised within the Beltway have a whiff of entitlement about them, or at least some jaded attitude about DC culture. I imagine it is probably a similar experience to growing up in Los Angeles with a famous actor as a parent.

Instead of being in that political bubble, watched and coddled, I got to have a more traditional childhood with more freedom: running around and getting dirty in the desert, falling out of trees, getting stitches, riding horses, going to Catholic school down the street, skipping Catholic school down the street, making best friends who I still cherish today, barbequing with my family, hiking, swimming, being allowed to grow and live on my own terms. There really are not too many bad things I can say about my childhood in Arizona. I was allowed to make my typical childhood mistakes without the prying eyes of reporters or other political families all around me. Most important, I truly believe there is something about growing up in the Wild West that has given me an independent perspective. One of my father's strategists once described me as "unnaturally fearless for a politician's daughter." It's one of the weirdest, yet also one of the best compliments anyone has ever given me. Something about being raised in the desert in Arizona directly contributed to that fearlessness.

I simply do not believe I would be as open with my life or as independent with my opinions if I had grown up with the kind of pressure from DC culture that I have only come to know in my twenties. On the stump, my father often quotes the line "Politicians came to Washington to change things and Washington changed us." That's the weird thing about Washington, DC: it's filled with hopeful dreamers, oftentimes new to the Hill, who come bright-eyed and bushy-tailed with the greatest of intentions, wanting to change the country and make it a better place. Sometimes they do, but a lot of times they don't. Washington, DC, is a city where you can quite literally change the world and make it a better place, or you can get your soul absolutely corrupted and end up doing irreparable damage to America and your life.

Washington, DC, is a city of ultimate power, and as Henry Kissinger infamously said, "Power is the ultimate aphrodisiac." Kissinger was right; most people, once they come into positions of absolute power, will go to absolutely any lengths to keep it. Not exactly the same, but how do you explain a person like John Edwards and his behavior? That's the thing about politics; it truly exaggerates the very best and the very worst in people. I wish there were more of a happy medium.

The other obvious points of going to Washington, DC, are to introduce Michael to my father and to tour Capitol Hill. We also planned to interview a few politicians while we were in town. Unfortunately for us, Congress is now smack-dab in the midst of budget ceiling negotiations, and many of the people we were supposed to interview have cancelled at the last minute. Nevertheless, I am confident Washington, DC, will not disappoint us.

Michael: Stephie's dad, Charlie, flew in from California to hang out with us and his boyhood best friend, Larry, with whom we're staying. Larry and his wife, Ellie, live just outside the city, and are members of the reviled Washington bureaucracy. Despite the stereotype of the lazy career civil servant, they both seem engaged, motivated, and passionate about their work. They also seem like old hippies, which they are.

Larry wears his long hair tied back into a bushy ponytail. He's got a salt-and-pepper droopy mustache and a soft, Long Island accent. Ellie wears a sleeveless tank top and a long skirt. Their home is decorated with folk art and photos from their frequent travels to Peru. Larry is also a musician. He shows us his basement music studio and his extensive music collection, which is, of course, heavy on the Grateful Dead and Bob Dylan side of things.

We arrive at their home in the early evening, and are greeted with glasses of homemade Lemon Slushy Booze Yum-Yums, a name I just made up to describe the frozen deliciousness Ellie has concocted in her blender. I think her idea is to dispel whatever awkwardness we all might have from meeting each other for the first time by getting us hammered. It works. Within half an hour we are all jabbering away like old, drunk friends. And though this is not a cookbook, I feel the urge to share this recipe right here, right now.

Once the slushy is frozen, you scrape layers off, like you would an Italian ice, mound into a glass, then drizzle with enough bourbon to get the overall consistency of a Slurpee, or to taste, depending

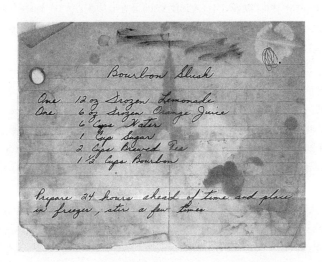

on how much you like your bourbon. It will cleanse the RV blues right out of your soul.

Meghan: It is so wonderful that Stephie has reached out to her father's best friend for a place for us to stay while we're in DC, and even more wonderful that this group of perfect strangers were willing to host us. We could really use a little home-style TLC after the days of the RV and motels. When we pull up to a pretty house surrounded by trees with an outdoor deck and a pool, I am suddenly a little embarrassed at the state of all of us: we are absolutely filthy. We walk into the house and introduce ourselves to everyone. Stephie's father is adorable; he's an older man with gray hair, a beard, a small build, glasses, a warm smile, and a genuine laugh. I like him pretty much from the second I meet him. We walk into a kitchen where our new hosts, Larry and Ellie, greet us in their open kitchen with glass doors facing out to the deck and pool.

Their house is really cute, decorated with lots of art from their trips to Peru, various guitars, sitars, and mandolins. The house feels very comfortable and lived in. Almost as soon as we walk in, Ellie hands me a glass filled with a slushy drink of some kind.

"What's in it?" I ask.

"Bourbon, you'll love it," she answers, and love it I do. From now on if anyone ever comes to visit me, I am going to hand them this slushy drink as soon as they walk in the door. It tastes like fruit punch and goes down easy.

Ellie and Larry both work for the United States government but seem more like artists than Washington bureaucrats. Larry has a long gray pony tail that he has cut off only once when he was younger, and hated his short hair so much that he grew the pony tail right back. Ellie has long, braided dirty-blond hair, and wears a flowing skirt over sandals. They are both relaxed, friendly, and curious about our adventure. Stephie, Michael, Larry, Ellie, Cousin John, Larry and Ellie's son Ian, Charlie, and I sit around their kitchen talking about everything from God and atheism to President Obama, our preferred choices in exercise classes, and love and relationships. I feel almost instantly comfortable around them and am relieved the evening feels relaxed and easy. That's not always the case, as we have learned, when I first meet new people.

Michael: The conversation centers on American drug policy, a subject upon which Charlie Grob is highly conversant. He's the chief child psychologist at the David Geffen School of Medicine at UCLA. More interestingly, he's also a renowned research scientist in the field of hallucinogens and MDMA (Ecstasy). He studies the use of hallucinogenic drugs and MDMA as therapeutic treatments for, among other things, PTSD. We had lunch once before in California, in which we discussed my own experiences with hallucinogenic drugs (which were few and far between, but *fantastic*). To my disappointment, he did not slip me any drugs after our meal.

I am going to paraphrase Dr. Grob's considered opinion of American drug policy: he thinks it's fucked. Incidentally, so do I. So does everybody in the room and, I suspect, everybody in the country. Yet we persist in our absurd "war on drugs" as if it's doing anything productive other than making a bunch of Mexican drug lords obscenely wealthy and a lot of other people dead.

The fact is this: people want to get high. They have always gotten high and will continue to get high. They do it with legal means and they do it with illegal means and it's very hard to reconcile where the line is drawn. Why is pot more dangerous than booze? Why is heroin worse than oxycodone? Why is the government in the business of telling people what they can and cannot voluntarily put into their bodies? It's a game they cannot win. Telling people not to get high doesn't work. Imprisoning them for getting high doesn't work. Nothing works. Because people want to get high.

The war on drugs as we know it commenced in 1973, under the direction of President Nixon. Since then, according to *Time* magazine, the United States has spent 2.5 *trillion* dollars fighting this "war." What gains have we made? Literally every adult I know has tried marijuana. Many, if not most, of them have tried other illegal drugs. Some have gotten addicted. But then again, many more are addicted to alcohol, to gambling, to shopping. Maybe we should declare a war on shopping.

"The issue with the drug war you have to ask is, is it effective?" Dr. Grob says. "And it seems to me that it's just not doing what it's supposed to be doing, which is containing the use of dangerous drugs. They call these drugs 'controlled drugs,' and yet they're the most out of control drugs there are."

He points out that the most common drug people are arrested for is marijuana, a drug that "is incredibly benign on its effects on people." He says the entire scientific literature on marijuana corroborates that it's safe, doesn't make people mentally ill or turn them into "bad people." Nor, he says, is it "necessarily an enabling drug." In other words, the idea that pot is a "gateway drug" is a complete myth. Probably started by tripped-out stoners.

We talk about the Mexican cartels and the Afghani poppy growers. Larry has some experience in dealing with programs designed to encourage "alternative development" in Afghanistan, whereby the US government tries to get poppy farmers to grow other crops. The programs have largely failed. Exactly what crop could replace the amount of cash a poppy field generates? Maybe rhubarb?

Both Charlie and Larry talk about the need for a "Nixon goes to China moment," a strong politician to stand up and say what everybody knows, that the drug war is a miserable and pointless failure, and that we should legalize and regulate, at the very least, marijuana. But what politician is willing to stick their neck out for drugs? None. Except maybe Ron Paul.

Dr. Grob talks about the Mexican cartels and how "with the stroke of a pen" we could eliminate their power. Also, the government could generate billions of tax dollars through legalization. I've heard that marijuana is the largest cash crop in the country, a crop that is going totally untaxed. I don't know if that's true or not, but the fact that it's believable is enough.

I don't even know what the counterarguments to this are. That if we legalize marijuana people are going to go crazy? That people are going to go around stabbing each other for weed? Was society made safer under Prohibition?

Personally, I don't smoke pot. I've tried it and it doesn't do much for me. As for harder drugs, I don't know how I feel about legalizing heroin, or meth, or whatever. My instinct tells me we should because fighting certain selected drugs is a study in futility. Let's take some of the money we would generate by regulating and taxing drugs and pour it into treatment centers. Surely that's a better alternative than prisons.

We sit around their kitchen for an hour talking about this stuff, buzzing off our totally legal alcoholic beverages. What's the difference between our legal drug and the illegal stuff? Crushed ice and lemonade.

Meghan: As we get further into the night and start eating dinner, we talk about drugs and the war on drugs in America. I am fascinated by Charlie's take on X, because for all of my adult life all I have ever heard about MDMA is that it is an extremely dangerous drug that will rot your brain matter and dry out your spinal fluid.

When I was in middle school, we were shown a video of a young woman who had done Ecstasy. In it a doctor shows her an X-ray of her brain, and a portion of it looks like it had disintegrated. The video also showed the woman playing Scrabble for "brain food"; she needed to do those exercises for her brain because of all the damage she had done by taking Ecstasy. Congratulations to whoever put that video together—it scared the crap out of me, and I have never done a drug in my life (except marijuana), let alone Ecstasy.

I have always pretty much held the conviction that all drugs are bad, and yet I have a different feeling about marijuana. I think it's because marijuana is a plant, and the times I have smoked it (a number I can count on one hand) I have felt very mellow and calm. Also, I'm sorry everyone, but marijuana is absolutely everywhere. I have been to numerous parties in my life where it was available—

and by parties I don't mean raves in the middle of the desert; I mean dinner parties where people pass around a joint like they're pouring wine.

That's the weirdest thing to me about marijuana legalization in this country; I have friends who have medical prescriptions for marijuana for "anxiety" and "insomnia" and it is easily obtained. Why is marijuana legal for doctors to write prescriptions for, if it is so dangerous?

Pretty much any other drug except marijuana, I still have a very strict opinion about. I have always been too scared to indulge in anything stronger than whiskey or marijuana, and the idea of taking Ecstasy still evokes images of people ruining their lives and melting their brains. I didn't even know that Ecstasy research was being done in the United States, so I am interested to hear Charlie's take on it. We get on the topic initially by talking about religion and God, and he says his belief in a higher power or "a feeling of connectedness with the universe" came after an experience he had on a hallucinogen in the woods when he was in his twenties.

Charlie continues to talk about his experiences with testing hallucinogens, but the first time my ears really perk up is when he says, "We actually have had really positive results using it to help soldiers combat posttraumatic stress syndrome."

"What?" I say, jerking my head in his direction. "Why is this not being talked about more?!" I had no idea that Ecstasy was being used to help soldiers combat PTSD, and I am a little annoyed that it has been effective but there hasn't been more written about it publicly.

My conversation with Stephie's dad only adds to the questions I have regarding our country's attitude towards the war on drugs in America. I mean, just the fact that there is a legal profession where someone tests hallucinogens for their effect on treating posttraumatic stress disorder is fascinating to me. Also, when it comes to marijuana, why are we ignoring the fact that many people smoke weed recreationally for different reasons and are not doing anything else illegal? Should we really consider a person caught with marijuana to be on the same level as someone who robs a bank?

I think my biggest problem is the moral ambiguity of it all. I think all of us can agree that there needs to be a change in attitude towards the legalizing and regulation of marijuana in this country, or at least the attitude we have towards "criminals" caught with small amounts of weed on them. I also believe we are painfully ignoring the prescription-drug problem that is also facing many people in this country: the overprescribing to patients and the repercussions it is having on our culture. There are many layers to the drug problem in America, and I don't pretend to have all of the answers. I know, however, that the war on drugs is one we continue to lose, and a change in perspective about the realities of the situation would be beneficial. My conversation with Stephie's father only increases my confusion about America's current approach to the war on drugs.

After dinner we all go to Larry's recording studio, where we sit on giant plush couches and cushions while he plays us some of his folky rock music. It's pretty much a perfect night. My eyes start fading; all the bourbon and steak from the evening are making me feel hazy. I hug everyone good night and whisper to Michael right before I leave to go to bed, "Let's visit Ellie and Larry again at this exact same time next summer." These people and this house feel weirdly familiar, and I feel like I am around old friends. I notice a homemade Obama poster in Ellie and Larry's son's room that someone obviously made in the last election; it kind of makes me chuckle before I drift off to sleep. I bet when they made that I was the last person they imagined would be sleeping down the hall.

Michael: In the morning, we rise late and lounge around the house before our planned afternoon at the Capitol Building. Stephie's been trying to wrangle interviews with congressmen and senators since we started our road trip, and has met with mixed success. Most disappointing to me was Senator Al Franken's response, which was a flat no. No explanation given. I am particularly galled because he is the only senatorial candidate to whom I have ever given money. Plus my wife is from Minnesota, the state he represents. Plus Al and I are both comedians. And I am the only person in the world who regularly listened to his Air America radio show, which, I can now say without the slightest remorse, sucked. The least he could do is say hello. No dice. It makes Yakov's blow-off look effusive by comparison.

A few people have agreed to meet with us, most notably Representative Dennis Kucinich, the perpetual Democratic presidential candidate. He runs every four years on his quirky platform, and every four years his candidacy is greeted with mild amusement and slight derision. He's an issues guy who knows he has no chance of actually winning the nomination; he's kind of like the Democratic version of Ron Paul.

Meghan: This might be the only day on the entire trip that all three of us are showered, clean, and dressed up nice. I didn't even know Michael had brought a suit on the trip, but he is wearing one as we head towards the Capitol, and I have on the one nice black dress that I brought with me. We pose for pictures in the living room before we leave with Ellie, Larry, and Charlie. It feels weirdly like we are heading off to the prom or something.

The entrance to the US Senate Building is one I have made hundreds, if not thousands, of times before. The outside steps felt so much bigger to me as a child, almost like they were the steps to heaven. I don't know if I will get to heaven, but if I do, I hope the steps are exactly like the white marble ones leading into Congress.

My father's press secretary meets us by the entrance, and guides us down the long corridors. The hallways that lead to his office are marble, on which high heels make distinct clicking sounds as you walk. The various wooden doors are enormous and looming. Down the long corridors, senators have offices across from each other. In case you miss which one is my father's office, there is a giant Arizona state flag standing aggressively outside it, next to two really large wooden doors. There are a few side offices connected by a hallway that leads to my father's giant room, which is filled with an enormous wooden desk, a red leather couch, chairs, and a fireplace. Staffers have to walk through my father's office, which sits in the middle of all of them, in order to make it from one side of the office area to the other. There are embarrassing pictures of my family and me everywhere.

That's the thing about coming from a political family; every awkward or ugly stage of your life is extremely well documented. There are more pictures of me than I would like hanging around my father's office, in which I am the victim of being dressed entirely in American flag clothing, have a very short 1970s gymnast haircut, or just simply am an awkward teen who hasn't yet figured out how to pose at a flattering angle for a Christmas card picture.

One of my favorite things about my father's staff is that many of them have been working for him their whole careers. His assistant, Ellen, has been with him thirty years. Joe Donoghue, my father's chief of staff, has been working for him since he was eighteen. Mark Busey, my father's communications director, has been around since what seems like the Triassic period. I think that's why Capitol Hill feels so familiar; many of the people who work for my father are like extended family.

I am relieved that Joe Donoghue is going to be around to talk to Michael and me. I don't know what to say about Joe other than he is, in every conceivable way, salt of the earth. He is truly like a big brother to me. There is something about him being in the office with my father that has always given me peace of mind. I know he has a genuine love and respect for my dad, which my father has for him in return. Joe also has a fantastic sense of humor, and miraculously, even though he has been working on Capitol Hill since he was a teenager, seems to have maintained a passion for politics.

Michael: Senator McCain's office looks just like I thought it would: spacious and comfortable, decorated with family photos, Native American mementos, and Arizona miscellanea. The room is clubby and warm, but not ostentatious, the sort of comfy retreat I imagine the captain of a successful whaling ship having. At one point, I excuse myself to take a whiz in the senator's small personal bathroom. If you are wondering whether senatorial toilets have good water flow, I can now confidently report that they do. A senatorial flush is a powerful flush indeed.

Meghan's dad is away from the office, so we hang out for a while shooting the breeze with Joe Donoghue, Senator McCain's legislative director. Joe is a handsome but rumpled guy in (I'm guessing) his mid-forties who has worked for Senator McCain his entire professional life. He's a Massachusetts Irish Catholic who grew up revering JFK, along with his own parents and twelve brothers and sisters. His older brother John got a job working for Ted Kennedy in the mid-seventies, and when Joe started college in DC a few years later, John suggested that Joe bang on some doors on Capitol Hill to get a part-time job.

"So I started going around to different offices, and this one needed someone to work part-time in the mail room," he says, referring to McCain's office. "I didn't even know if he was a Republican or a Democrat. I just knew they were paying me six thousand dollars a year, and I thought I was going to be the richest kid on the planet." He pauses. "Now they pay me twelve grand a year."

We all laugh.

After starting in the mail room of the freshman senator, he never left. Joe tells us how Meghan's dad took him under his wing, mentored him, and over the years gave him more and more responsibilities. Now he's a lifer.

Meghan asks why he stayed so long.

"Lack of ambition, that's all," he replies before turning serious. "I don't want to sound sappy or anything but I really do, honestly, love this guy. He's been like a dad to me . . . I'm still scared shit of him, like you would your grumpy old dad sometimes."

This guy's scared of him after twenty-something years together? Great. Now I'm even more nervous to meet Papa.

Joe has to go back to his office to monitor what's happening on the Senate floor. Our visit here occurs in the middle of a huge debate about raising the debt ceiling. Everybody in Washington is talking about whether or not the president and Congress will reach a deal to allow the government to borrow yet more money to keep the government operational. It's been a partisan, contentious debate, more so even than every other partisan, contentious debate they've had since Obama took office. Before he goes, I ask Joe if the tenor in Washington has actually gotten worse, or is that a misperception?

He considers this and says, "It used to be really fun . . . You came to work every day knowing you were going to do something cool. The perception and the reality is that we're so polarized that we're not getting anything done, but there are still instances where there's still a ray of hope."

Knowing what he knows now, would he recommend going into politics to his younger self? Joe answers that he would certainly recommend to any young person who has the opportunity to spend some time working on Capitol Hill to see how democracy actually works, but "would I recommend somebody go into it as a career?" He pauses for a second. "I don't think so."

He excuses himself and goes.

In the anteroom, there is bustle and commotion. I recognize the familiar gravelly voice before I see the man; Senator McCain is definitely in da house. He bustles into the office followed by a small retinue of assistants and staffers. I stand out of instinct and deference, but the senator doesn't register my presence at all.

I've been around a lot of famous people before, but it's still a slight shock to see somebody so well known right in front of me. John McCain is not a large man, but he's stocky, and he fills the space around him. I watch him trundle through the office, glancing at papers on his desk, turning an eye to the TV monitor, answering staff questions, his voice loud enough to be heard but no louder. When he moves, he gives the impression of somebody leaning into wind, or charging a hill, as if the world with all of its troubles can be tamed if only enough force and energy are brought to bear.

Finally, his staff retires with their marching orders and he turns his attention to his daughter. She greets him with a hug, and introduces me. We shake hands and settle onto his couches for a couple of minutes of chitchat. I know Meghan has explained the book to him before, but he still seems at a slight loss as to who I am and what I am doing with his daughter. I try explaining the book to him but his mind is obviously elsewhere, and after confirming that we will be having dinner later that evening, he grumbles something like "see ya later" to me, gives Meghan a quick kiss goodbye and heads back out, his secretary confirming appointments and handing him stacks of phone messages as he goes, taking all the air with him.

Meghan: I don't think it takes a rocket scientist to understand that things in Washington have changed within my lifetime. There was a time when Tip O'Neill and Ronald Reagan were good friends and would socialize after the business of politics had ended for the day. There is even a famous story of Tip O'Neill visiting Reagan in the hospital after he was shot. Can you possibly imagine John Boehner and Nancy Pelosi doing absolutely anything together after hearings close for the day? The "you are either with us or against us" attitude completely permeates politics and the political narrative today, and I think anyone with half a brain can see the damage it has inflicted on this country.

The thing that makes me so sad during our discussion is when Joe says that "it used to be fun" working on Capitol Hill and now it isn't. When Joe was younger and worked in my father's office, I remember he also worked at night at a BBQ restaurant called Red Hot and Blue and had a reputation for being a lady's man around the office. I remember it looked like he was having such a great time in a young-kid-takes-on-Capitol-Hill type of way. Michael asks if Joe would recommend anyone going into this business and he pauses, takes a breath, looks at me, and says, "I don't think so." My heart breaks a little bit hearing that. Granted Joe has been on the

Hill, well, forever, but it still makes me sad. I just hope things haven't changed so much that at some point it can't return to being fun again.

Joe leaves to go back to his desk; he has votes to watch and work to do. I can hear my father coming in from the side of the office. There's always a sort of rustling-of-papers noise when he walks into his office and people start going on alert. "Hang on," I tell Michael and Stephie. I get up and rush to the other side of the office.

"Hey, Meggie!" He gives me a quick kiss.

"Hi, Dad. Remember that comedian is here with me for that book I'm working on, and he is in the other room waiting. Please just be nice and don't freak him out." My father sort of half chuckles and says, "Whatever you say." For the life of me, ever since this project began I have had an extremely difficult time explaining to my father *exactly* who Michael Ian Black is. Do you know how difficult it is to explain what an alternative comedian is to a man who is seventy-five, and basically unless you are David Petraeus or Henry Kissinger he doesn't have time for you?

We walk in together and I introduce my father to everyone. Michael is standing off to the side and looks . . . well, Michael looks petrified. I don't blame Michael; most people are petrified of my father. His physical presence is intimidating, his reputation is intimidating, and he doesn't suffer fools lightly. My father seems really frustrated and preoccupied with everything that is going on with the debt ceiling crisis. I can tell he is stressed out and, quite frankly, I don't want to bother him. A quick chat and he's out of there, back to the business of governing.

Before our afternoon meeting with Congressman Kucinich, we go on a tour of the Senate and House of Representatives with a young, flirty, Irish intern named Jack. I could have given this tour, but Jack is charming and starts gossiping with us about what life as an intern is really like. I have always thought a fantastic idea for a reality show would be following Capitol Hill interns around during the day—and night. Sex! Parties! Legislature! The opportunities for drama are endless!

We eat lunch in a Senate cafeteria and a few people recognize both me and Michael; they seem excited about the concept for the book, which makes me happy, especially because no one on my father's staff nor my father seem to have any real understanding of what exactly Michael and I are doing there.

Toward the end of our tour we go to the Capitol rotunda and look at the statues that occupy the bottom lobby area. Jack points out to us a giant statue of a woman draped in fabric, holding a sword and a shield. She is wearing a feathered helmet and her eyes are looking off into the distance. It's my favorite statue and I recognize it instantly. She's Lady Freedom.

"If you notice, her eyes are facing off into the east because the sun never sets on freedom," he says. We all look up at her and I sort of say under my breath, "That's because America is one sexy bitch." It's a ridiculous thing to say, but it makes everyone laugh. I feel patriotic and nostalgic looking at her. Despite all the things that make me sad about Washington, DC, and the Capitol, it's too easy to forget that for all of our problems and issues, America is the greatest goddamn country in the history of the world. There never was a country greater and there never will be. Something about Lady Freedom puts a grin on my face and makes me smile, and my spirits are lifted, which is good because our next stop is visiting Dennis Kucinich.

Michael: I'm just going to lay this out there and readers can take from it what they will: Dennis Kucinich is my new hero. I certainly didn't expect that to be the case when we went to meet with him, but I emerged from his office a convert to the Kucinich Way.

The first thing I notice as we walk towards his office is how out of the way it is. We walk and walk and walk. We take elevators and wander hallways and finally arrive at a small suite of offices tucked into a distant corner of the Capitol. I have to wonder if the house leadership put him here on purpose. Is he too kooky to get the good offices? Instead of a staff of dozens like at Senator McCain's, Representative Kucinich's office seems like it is comprised entirely of college interns on break from Oberlin. If the average age is much above twenty-two, I'd be surprised. We tell the teenager at the reception area we have an appointment. She refers us to some twelve-year-old who tells us to take a seat. We chitchat with them about Justin Bieber and training bras until Representative Kucinich emerges from his office and ushers us inside.

The desk is oriented around a single round, wooden table placed in the middle of the room. We take seats around it and I ask if I can record the conversation. "Of course," he says, which is atypical among politicians.

Meghan begins by thanking him for taking time to meet with us. He pshaws. "I admire your dad, and I feel that we have a congressional family here and you're entitled to meet with anybody you want to meet with."

You hear that, Senator Franken? A congressional family!

Before meeting with him, I wasn't that familiar with Dennis Kucinich, having really only seen him sporadically during the Democratic debates when he ran for president in 2004 and 2008, but I just accepted what people said about him: too left wing, too loony, without having spent any time examining his record or beliefs.

He spends forty-five minutes with us, and within the first of those minutes it is clear that he may be left wing, but he's not loony. Instead I find a thoughtful, insightful, deeply empathetic man who belies every stereotype about politicians. Instead of Machiavelli, I find Deepak Chopra.

"As a kid, I had Crohn's very bad," he tells us. "It almost killed me. I was twenty years old, had radical surgery. Wasn't until years later in life that I changed my life and became a vegan. Started to use alternative medicine like Chinese medicine. I don't have that problem anymore. I had to take some personal responsibility."

He's speaking about health care, but he's also speaking about education and the way our nation engages with others: "We can't be all over the world telling people how to live and what to do. It doesn't work in interpersonal relationships and it doesn't in relationships between nations."

In terms of personal responsibility for the United States as a whole, I take from him that he believes we need to get our own house in order before trying to police the world. He walks over to a small pedestal, upon which is some sort of jagged metal object.

"I took that shell there from an apartment complex in Qana, in South Lebanon, where that was part of a thousand-pound American-made bomb that was dropped on an apartment house and killed fifty women and children who sought shelter in the basement."

The bomb was dropped in 2006 as part of the Israel-Lebanon war, a war I hadn't paid that much attention to. The shell fragment is a dull-black color, heavy. I've seen bombs before, but never an exploded one, nor have I ever considered what a bomb looks like once detonated. Never thought about the pieces left behind. He tells us he was given the shrapnel from the people of Qana as a reminder of what they'd been through. He points out that the dog tags of three captured Israeli soldiers were found along with the bomb fragment.

"It goes beyond matters of who's right because that can always shift from different points of view. In fact, the reason I have the table like this is to remind me that every point needs to be listened to."

He walks to a bookcase and retrieves a battered copy of a book from 1932 published by the Agni Yoga Society called *Heart*. He says it's one of the most important books he's ever read, telling us he's been studying it for thirty years, describing himself as being on a "spiritual journey," telling us "there's not one path, there are many paths." Exactly! Preach, Brother Kucinich, preach! He's not my new hero, he's my new god.

Meghan: Going into our meeting with Congressman Kucinich, my impression of him is pretty much what most Republicans' impressions are of this man. I think he is a radical liberal pacifist. Yes, that pretty much covers it. His views on the wars in Iraq and Afghanistan go completely against everything I believe, he claims to have seen a UFO, he sometimes comes off silly to me in debates and in-terviews, and he ran for president several times for seemingly no reason other than publicity.

I did not think I was going to like him, but I was grateful and surprised that he agreed to meet with us. We walk into his office and sort of awkwardly stand around and wait in the entrance, while all of Dennis Kucinich's staffers start telling me how much they like my work and my appearances on television. Apparently talking about not being a virgin on Chelsea Handler's show is still a favorite for some people. They could not be friendlier and more welcoming. For whatever reason, I was expecting a little aversion from Kucinich's staff because, well, I am a Republican and they are Democrats, but his staff is really warm and friendly. Just as we all start really talking, Senator Kucinich opens the door and beckons to us.

His office is quite different from my father's. In the center of the room is a large round table and the desk and other chairs reside in the corner. There is a large painting of Kucinich and his absolutely gorgeous wife, framed inspirational quotes about life and leader-ship, and different framed pictures from his travels and time as a congressman.

We sit down, and I thank him for taking the time out of his schedule to talk to me.

"I admire your dad," he says with a smile. "And I feel that we have a congressional family here and you're entitled to meet with anybody you want to meet with."

I swear my jaw drops to the floor, like some animated character in a cartoon. What is he talking about "congressional family"?! We hate each other—what about partisanship?! We sit at the table and proceed to have a *forty-five minute* conversation about politics, the media, the wars in Iraq and Afghanistan, religion, life, love, what's wrong with America, and how we can fix it. When I say this man is open and engaging, let me put it to you this way: I am as jaded as it comes to meeting politicians, and this man proceeds to move me with the way he speaks about being a congressman and his love for the country. His perspective on the direction America should take is almost the polar opposite of mine, but he seems genuine and passionate in his convictions.

During the course of this conversation, Congressman Kucinich almost makes me cry. He talks about how much he loves this country, how much he loves his wife and how grateful he is to have her in his life, how sick he is of the partisanship and toxic climate in Washington, DC, and how he worries about this country and takes the worries of the American people to bed with him at night. I would describe hearing Dennis Kucinich speak to us in this context as infectious. I don't agree with what he is saying, but I feel an appreciation for his genuineness.

"Do you know that Katy Perry song 'Firework,' Meghan?" he leans over and asks me.

"Yes, of course, sir, I love that song."

"Well, that's what I'm like when I wake up in the morning. I'm a firework! I get up and I can't contain myself from all the things I want to do and change."

I want to start singing "Firework" with the congressman, but think that might be inappropriate. I just find our conversation unbelievably refreshing. I start wondering why the hell Kucinich has not been able to catch on nationally in a more significant way. Even if his policies are too liberal for me, which of course they are, his attitude and zest for life and politics are engaging. I cannot help but love him.

The congressman continues to go into great detail about how much he respects my father and the time he toured my father's prison cell in North Vietnam. He talks about how he got emotional when he was there and that he "actually walked away understanding why Senator McCain could become president of the United States." I am not an overly emotional person, but I feel incredibly endeared towards Congressman Kucinich when he says that.

Congressman Kucinich wakes up every day with a positive attitude about his life, his wife, politics, this country, and wanting to bridge the divide in Washington, DC. I have been preaching that we have to close this divide in our country right now, and it's amazing and fantastically serendipitous to meet someone who is actually holding office that preaches a message of even more inclusion than I have been. Not only does Congressman Kucinich say this, but he seems to be living it.

We wind down the conversation and shake hands goodbye. No one will ever hear me say a negative word about this man. Politics aside, I believe that Dennis Kucinich is a good man who genuinely wants what he believes to be the best things for America. He is a living example of an antidote to the problems in politics right now.

After we leave his office, both Stephie and Michael look equally stunned.

"Okay, how fantastic was he?" I ask.

"I know! I almost started crying!" Stephie says. "I mean, he preaches my language anyway because I am liberal, but how inspiring."

Even Michael looks moved. It didn't really matter that we didn't get to meet with ten congressmen, because that meeting with Dennis Kucinich was plenty.

Michael: When we return to Senator McCain's office to head out for dinner, we tell him that we've just been to see Representative Kucinich. A slight smile plays on his face and he says, "Good man."

McCain's office has made reservations at a fancy steak house, the kind of place I always imagined that politicos go to eat. He grouses about the restaurant as we drive there in his (American made) car, but when we arrive, his countenance changes and I see him step into his public self.

When pundits describe certain politicians as "rock stars," I always think they're exaggerating, but here in Washington, DC, with Senator John McCain I honestly feel as if I am with rock 'n' roll royalty. People fall over themselves when he approaches. "After you, Senator." "Right this way, Senator." "Can I get a picture, Senator?"

He's gracious with everybody, shaking hands, patting backs, taking photos. People love this guy. Seeing him like this, I do too.

The maître d' leads us to a private room at the back of the restaurant and deposits us at a table. Meghan apologizes to her dad for having to come to this restaurant. She knows he hates it, but it seemed like the best choice given the timing and location. She doesn't realize the manager is standing right there.

When she looks up, her cheeks turn scarlet. Senator McCain chokes back a smile. The manager pretends he didn't hear anything. I want to hide under the table. But that would be weird because the senator's feet are right there.

"Is Lindsey coming?" Meghan asks.

"Yeah. He should be here," responds the senator.

"Lindsey" is Lindsey Graham, Republican senator from South Carolina. He, Senator McCain, and Senator Joe Lieberman are senatorial BFFs, often hanging out together. Senator Graham is supposed to be joining us for dinner, which I think will be good because Senator McCain and I have nothing to talk about.

We study the menus for a while and listen as he describes some of the senatorial machinations occurring regarding the debt ceiling. To my ears, it sounds like a big clusterfuck. He doesn't use that word, although in retrospect it would have been awesome if he had.

Senator Graham arrives a few minutes later, with apologies. I remember him chiefly from his time as Grand Inquisitor during the Clinton impeachment trial. (I'm not sure "Grand Inquisitor" is the correct title, but it was something like that.) As such I am predisposed towards thinking of him as a supercilious right-wing blowhard. I am not prepared, however, for my actual reaction, which is to absolutely love the guy. He is, and I can think of no better way to describe him, a hoot. The guy is just funny: deadpan and sarcastic. Within moments of his arrival, all of us are laughing. Whatever tension existed before evaporates as the senior senator from South Carolina cracks wise about the debt ceiling and Social Security and various political arcana. He asks about the book, about me, and promises to watch my upcoming stand-up special on Comedy Central.

"You're not going to watch," I say.

"Nah, I won't," he agrees.

The meal turns out to be pretty fun. I just kind of sit back and watch the two senators talk shop. The deeper I get into politics, and the closer I get to politicians, the more I learn something surprising and a little bit startling. I had always assumed that politicians, especially elite politicians like these guys, are operating off different information from everybody else, that the news that we get is only the tip of the iceberg in terms of what is actually happening out there, and that guys like this are making their decisions based not on what is reported in the news, but what *isn't* reported in the news. This is, yes, conspiracy minded on my part, but I am a guy who is still undecided about Bigfoot, so I am susceptible to conspiracies.

But what I am learning is that, for the most part, politicians operate off the same imperfect information everybody has. The first inkling I got of this was when talking to Meghan's mom back in Arizona. Her arguments to me in private were the same as the ones I hear in public. The same as I hear on Fox and MSNBC. This is also true when I hear Senators McCain and Graham gossiping. Yes, there's a little inside baseball going on, but for the most part, the stuff they're talking about is no different from anything you could read in any major newspaper. Even Representative Kucinich threw me for a loop when we asked him about Iraq.

Why did he think we went there, I asked.

"Oil," he said like a true lib.

"That's it?"

"That's it."

Right out of the pages of *Mother Jones*.

In a way, I am heartened to learn that the information I have as a citizen is largely similar to the information our representatives are using to determine policy, but in a way it's also scary because it implies that there is no fundamental truth out there, that oftentimes both sides have equal claims to their positions, that people are making the best judgment calls they can, and that nobody knows what the hell is actually going on.

A young man sticks his head into the doorway of our dining room.

"Senator McCain?" he says.

Meghan's dad looks up at him.

Our waiter tries to usher the young man out, but the senator tells him to let him enter. The young man says he's a soldier, back from Iraq, and he wanted to say hello and thank the senator for supporting the military. Senator McCain rises and thanks the young man in turn for his service. They shake hands. The waiter takes their picture and the young soldier departs. Before he does, though, Senator McCain wishes him well and thanks him again. It's not platitudes with him. He means it. One look at him is all you need to know that he means it. I am reminded once again of Meghan's passion for the military, for military culture, for her family's long history of service to the country. Cynicism is not possible in moments like these.

Meghan: For most of the dinner, we talk politics, or really, Dad and Lindsey start talking heavy politics about the debt ceiling. The most entertaining part of the entire thing is the look on Michael's face: he is absolutely mesmerized. It makes me happy to see that Michael is interested and seems to be enjoying himself. It's easy for me to sometimes forget how fascinating politicians are—I mean the debt ceiling crisis is going on and Lindsey and my father are discussing the future of what is going to happen and their roles in it. It doesn't get much more inside baseball than this moment, right here. It feels strange to be having dinner with my father, Lindsey, Michael, and Stephie, and a part of me just wants to get it over with since . . . well, my father and Michael don't seem to be exactly bonding. I have a moment where I think, *This is it, Michael, this is a lot of what my life has been like.*

When we finish dinner, my father is absolutely mobbed on our way out of the restaurant. We say our goodbyes, my father gives me a big hug, and says goodbye to Michael and Stephie.

Right as we are leaving, Stephie says, "It's an honor having dinner with you, Senator, and thank you for your daughter. I love her."

Michael immediately interjects with, "Yes, me too."

Michael: Meghan gives her dad a big hug. It's clear she idolizes him, and his affection for her is obvious too, never more so than when she blurted out her faux pas about the restaurant. He looked so mischievous in that moment, like a kid with his hand in the cookie jar. As they say goodbye I am filled with affection for them both, father and daughter bidding each other good night. The car comes and he shakes my hand, wishing us well with our project. As he drives away, I am positive he still has no idea who I am.

We've got one more meeting tonight, an after-dinner get-together with the Log Cabin Republicans. If there is one group in Washington who gets zero respect from anybody, it's them. The Democrats can't understand why any group of homosexuals would align themselves with the Republican Party, the party of (among others) Rick "If the Supreme Court says that you have the right to consensual [gay] sex within your home, then you have the right to bigamy, you have the right to polygamy, you have the right to incest" Santorum and Michele "If you're involved in the gay and lesbian lifestyle, it's bondage; it is personal bondage, personal despair and personal enslavement" Bachmann. As for Republicans, many of them won't even accept campaign contributions from the Log Cabin Republicans, which is the equivalent of Bill Clinton refusing a blow job.

And yet they persist. Meghan, of course, has connections to them because she is one of the few outspoken prominent Republicans advocating for gay marriage. In fact, she might be the only one. As I've mentioned, I grew up in a lesbian household, so this issue is personal for me.

We assemble at some out-of-the-way restaurant-bar, and it doesn't occur to me until much later that perhaps the reason we met at this dead spot is because they do not want to be seen together. I really hope I am wrong about this, but DC is filled with hip and happening nightspots where people come to see and be seen, and this empty, backwater bar is not one of them.

There are maybe a dozen people there, ten men and a woman. We take a private room in the back and assemble chairs into a circle. Every member here is successful, young, Republican, and gay. One person works on the House Energy and Commerce Committee, another works for Citizens Against Government Waste, several are congressional staffers. These are serious people. It seems like such a shame to me that I even have to make the point that they are serious people, but to outsiders like me, it's difficult to imagine how they reconcile their sexuality with their political affiliation. It's a question they're used to, the "self-loathing question," as Meghan puts it.

One guy says people who think they must be self-loathing because they are Republican gays have it exactly backwards. "My Republican friends are a lot better with me being gay than my gay friends are with me being a Republican."

Many of the others agree. They say that their Republican colleagues don't care about their sexuality, that it's other gays and Democrats who give them the most grief. Another guy acknowledges that DC may be an aberration. He says he was basically "driven out" of his hometown in Florida because of his sexuality, that nobody in politics "on either side of the aisle" would hire him after he came out. He's wearing tight white denim pants, and when talking about the difficulties he had finding a job and says, "There are certain offices you walk in where you can just feel the flames coming off of people" I respond that, to be honest, I can feel the flames coming off him. It gets a laugh.

As liberal as I like to think my own industry is, one guy mentions that he was dating somebody in the media, a reporter for one of the networks, who could not come out because "in the media world it's not an asset." This troubles me because he's right. Hollywood has an image as the most socially liberal city in the world, but it's true that when their money is threatened, as they fear it might be if big stars start coming out of the closet, they get a lot more conservative. Who are the huge gay movie stars? There are none. Everybody knows that the arts attract homosexuals in greater numbers than other professions, and yet when it comes to actors and actresses, the image is almost uniformly that of beautiful straight people. This just isn't reality. In every other aspect of society, we have a word for beautiful men with perfect skin, amazing clothes, and an incredible figure. That word is "gay."

The Log Cabin Republicans make their case to us: that they are conservatives first and gays second, that they are more interested in tax policy than marriage equality, that they can do more good working from the inside than the out. Their earnestness is compelling, but it also bums me out.

I'm sure it's true when they tell me that, behind closed doors, the various congresspeople they work for support gay rights. I'm sure it's true that they catch no grief about their sexuality in Washington, DC. But it's also true that their party is known for being almost stridently anti-gay, a party in which nearly all of its presidential candidates favor *amending the Constitution* to prohibit gays and lesbians from marrying. This is a party that routinely equates homosexuality with deviant sexual behavior such as bestiality and incest. The party of small government and freedom wants to leave everybody alone until they decide who to love. Then they want to legislate.

Why?

Money. Like all things, it comes back to money. The Republican Party has so closely aligned itself with the religious Right and has become so dependent on their money and support that most Republican candidates cannot stray from evangelical orthodoxy if they want to get elected and stay in office. Perhaps they think, like all these sincere people sitting in front of me, that they can do more good by being inside than out, but I don't believe it. The way they can do the most good is by speaking up, even if it costs them votes. Even if it costs them their jobs. The status quo is definitely changing regarding gay-rights issues. Eventually gays will be able to marry in every state. Eventually we will wonder why there was ever a fuss about this to begin with. But the change is not occurring because of brave Republicans like these guys; it is happening *in spite* of Republicans.

So when I hear Ann Coulter (who once called John Edwards "a faggot") telling GOProud, a conservative gay group that is rival to the Log Cabin Republicans, that "marriage isn't a civil right—you're not black," I get angry. Because the issue of gay marriage, or gay rights in general, *is* a question of civil rights. In fact, it is the definition of civil rights: "the rights of citizens to political and social freedom and equality." Incidentally, Ann Coulter is now serving on GOProud's advisory council as "Honorary Chair."

Self-loathing, anyone?

Back at Larry and Ellie's, I keep thinking about the Log Cabin Republicans and the seeming futility of their organization. But the more I think about them, the more I realize something: yes, they are a small, largely ineffective group who spend their days running around trying to change an entrenched majority to their point of view, but isn't that Washington as a whole? Isn't that exactly the way our entire country works? A few people decide something's a good idea, get together, and make it so. That's America, from the Revolution on out. I'm not comparing the guy tonight in tight white denim pants to Sam Adams, but I do find myself feeling moderately better.

Every issue has its own Log Cabin Republicans, from our misguided "war on drugs" to American military intervention. There's a group in Washington who spend all their time trying to move Election Day from Tuesday to the weekend. Everybody here has their own little passion. Even Meghan and me. After all, what have we been doing out on the road for the last month, if not that? Here we are, driving around in our own smelly log cabin, and we know we're not going to change anything by doing this. Yet here we are, trying. We're our own tiny special-interest group.

One of the surprising things I discover about Washingtonians is their optimism. Everywhere else in the country, people we've met have berated Washington lethargy and partisanship. Here, though, people seem curiously upbeat. Even Joe Donoghue, despite his slumped shoulders, spoke to us about moments of possibility that still exist, moments when actual change occurs.

Change comes too slowly for most of us, but it comes. Depending on your point of view, it doesn't always come for the better, but it comes. The fallacy of American thinking, I'm starting to suspect, is when people look to Washington to effect that change. Washington is a reactive city. The people here aren't the ones banging pots and pans in the streets; when there's a march here, it's because people from outside came in.

The weird thing about Washington is how cynical it makes me feel about our government as a whole and yet how optimistic it makes me feel about the individuals within it. Dennis Kucinich and John McCain could not be more different, yet they both work here, doing the same job, both of them, I think, trying to make the best decisions for the people they were elected to represent. That's not to say they don't both also make political calculations for their own lesser good as opposed to the greater good, but isn't that true of all of us? Don't we all do that? The people here in Washington are no better or worse than Americans as a whole. And, as a whole, I've spent the past month interviewing Americans and finding them to be pretty good.

Yeah, our country's screwed up. Yeah, we're probably more divided than we've been in a long time. Yeah, there's a lot to be worried about and a lot of reasons to be pessimistic. But we're also resilient, and the people I've met here and everywhere else have surprised me with their knowledge and energy. People are engaged. That's the main thing. If our government is ever going to get its shit together, we've got to have that above all else.

And we've got that.

It's late when I finally get to sleep, my back rebelling against the loose springs on the pull-out couch. I'm tired and I can't bear the thought of slipping into my filthy linen pants one last time. But in the morning, I will put them on and don my Crocs and get into the RV with my special-interest group. Tomorrow, finally, I'm going home.

Redding, Connecticut

Lost and Found

Michael: There might not be a worse drive in the United States than the I-95 Northeastern Corridor. Traffic is always horrible and the view sucks, particularly after you cross the Delaware Water Gap and inch your way up the New Jersey Turnpike. If I have anything positive to say about my home state it's this: New Jersey has the most consistently excellent pizza of any state in the union. Here's a startling, totally made-up fact: New Jersey has three pizzerias for every one resident!

Meghan has a political crush on Chris Christie, New Jersey's blustery Republican governor. He's a guy who prides himself on speaking his mind without hesitation, a guy unafraid to call bullshit, a guy whose demeanor would fit right in on *The Sopranos.* Honestly, I like Governor Christie too, and could see myself voting for him if I was still a New Jersey resident. But I am not because New Jersey is a sucky state.

(Governor Christie, if you are reading this, please don't hit me.)

Over the years, I have probably eaten at every rest stop along the New Jersey Turnpike during various excursions to Atlantic City where I sometimes do charity work donating money to local casinos. New Jersey Turnpike rest stops are the only places in the world where Roy Rogers restaurants still exist, as if the highway is caught in some fast food time warp where Roy Rogers fried chicken and Mrs. Fields cookies are still considered *au courant.*

I would love to stop and eat some of that warmed-over chicken, but I've got to get home. I told Martha I'd be arriving sometime in the early afternoon, but we got a late start and now the sun is beginning to set as we pass Newark airport, where United Airlines flight 93 took off from on September 11. Out our right window, at the mouth of the Hudson River, is the Statue of Liberty. Nestled into the tip of lower Manhattan, we can see the spiraling Freedom Tower growing from where the World Trade Center used to stand. Beyond that, Connecticut and home.

Meghan: The final RV ride from Washington, DC, to Michael's house in Redding, Connecticut, is an absolutely miserable experience. The RV has reached an utterly disgusting state: cluttered with dust, food crumbs, old magazines, trash, stained pillows, and Cousin John's ass sweat. The toilet is almost completely broken, and the stench from inside its little cubicle has murked into the rest of the space. The air-conditioning has never worked properly, but on this final ride to Connecticut I think it's completely dead. The pump from the generator makes an incredibly loud, annoying, buzzing noise and only serves to circulate the stagnant air to the back half of the RV.

I hate that stupid RV air-conditioning. Advertising that the RV came with working air-conditioning was a total lie and, as per usual, all of us are in a constant state of sweating through our clothes. Yeah, real glamorous and sexy. We have eaten our last few lunches on the road at gas stations and fast food restaurants, at a Subway if we were lucky. Pretzels and diet Dr Pepper if it was a longer day. I think it was finally really starting to wear on all of us. On the trek to Connecticut I feel bloated, sweaty, tired, and in desperate need of a healthy meal.

The only thing that hasn't changed is the simple fact that I am still having a great time with Michael, Stephie, and Cousin John. By the time we left DC on our way to Connecticut, I knew so much about Stephie and Michael, and them about me, that they felt like old family members. It's nice. It's also a little weird because I've only known them for three weeks.

Michael: We cross the George Washington Bridge and head up the I-95 into Connecticut. I scoot up to the front seat beside Cousin John for the final sixty miles or so. We chitchat as I give him directions. He's going to hang out with us in Redding for a day, then take a few days to drive the RV all the way back to Austin. From there, he'll fly home to Aspen, where he does not know what he's going to do. Maybe go back to work at the hotel. Maybe drive tow trucks again.

Meghan has decided to move back to New York after a miserable year in Los Angeles. The city, and its men, didn't suit her. She went to school in New York so she knows what she's in for. Over the years so many of my friends have made the opposite journey: New York to LA. I'll be glad to have a friend make the reverse migration.

The big New York apartment houses slowly shrink behind us, until they disappear altogether, replaced by single-family homes and trees. The road is wet; a big, quick storm has just blown through, and now it's dark as we cross into Connecticut. I don't know whether it's because I've seen so much road over the past few weeks, but as we make our way north, nothing looks familiar, and it is occurring to me, as embarrassing as this is to admit, that I'm not actually sure how to get to my house.

Normally when I drive home from New York City I take a different route because, as I said, I-95 is the worst road in America. I try to play it cool as the exits feel increasingly foreign. Eventually I just pick one and direct John to make various rights and lefts in the hope that the road will eventually lead me someplace I recognize. It does not. After about forty minutes of aimless wandering, it's pretty apparent to everyone that I am completely lost.

Meghan: I wake up from a nap sometime in the early evening to the sound of Michael and Cousin John bickering. I have no idea where we were, but it doesn't look like New Jersey or Connecticut, which it should have been by now. We seem to be swerving around and driving in circles. I sit up from my bench and see the concerned look on Stephie's face, which causes me to surmise that we are probably lost and the two Magellans in the front seat probably couldn't find their way out of a theme park, let alone to Connecticut.

"You're lost, aren't you?" I ask, not at all surprised that Michael would not be able to find his own house with both hands. He looks back at me from the front seat, clearly embarrassed and annoyed.

"No!" he snaps.

I am already nervous about going to Michael's house, and now I am stressed out that we are not going to make it at a reasonable hour and will proceed to piss off his entire family. I met Michael's statuesque wife, Martha, before we went on our trip but have not actually spent any significant amount of time with her. I'm not really in the mood to make a bad second impression.

I am also worried that Michael's kids will not like me. I have found from experience that I have very little in common with most children and don't always interact well with them. I also know how much I used to hate it when random people would come home with my father. I equated them with taking his attention away from me. Home time was home time and I did not appreciate strangers invading it. I pretty much figure Michael's children will have the same reaction to me.

I really want Michael's wife, Martha, to like me. One of the most intriguing things about Michael is what an extremely devoted family man he is. He got married in his mid-twenties, had kids by the time he was thirty, and has been happily married ever since. We have had numerous conversations about love, marriage, and relationships, because really, what else are you going to talk about in an RV for hours on end, and intimate conversations always have a way of circling back to love. It is clear Michael is proud of his wife and the life they have built together. It was the first thing that made me warm up to him: the incredibly endearing way he speaks about his family. In fact, I told him early on he reminded me of a snarky Dick Van Dyke.

For all of Michael's liberal beliefs and politics, when it comes right down to it, Michael is a pretty conservative family man. He is living the happy 1950s nuclear family ideal that so seldom exists in 2012—one he did not have growing up.

I am in a constant struggle with what love, marriage, relationships, and children mean to me. I have never been the best at maintaining long-term relationships with men. I value my freedom above most other things in my life. I do love children and find them adorable. That being said, I worry about reconciling my world and my crazy life with someday having a family. I had such an incredible childhood and wonderful experiences growing up that I feel more certain as I get older that I do one day want to have a family. I just can't really figure out what that would look like or how it would all fit together in my world. As much as I feel like I have found a clear path in my work and the world of politics, and that I am certain of my convictions and the future I want when it comes to love, marriage, and children, my sentiments are alternately murky and complex.

Right now in America, marriage is not something that every citizen has an equal right to. How meaningful can marriage be if only straight people can do it? I do find the idea of marriage romantic, but in the same way that I find great poetry romantic but not necessarily realistic. I cry at weddings and always want the marriages to last forever. In reality, however, more than 50 percent of marriages end in divorce, people still get married strictly for business or social purposes, and, like I said, gay people are denied this right.

I'm conflicted about what marriage means for me and the rest of my generation. We do not have the same pressures generations before us had "to settle down." Sometimes family and marriage are something I can see happening and really want; at other times I think it could never work with my personality and lifestyle, and I fantasize about spending the rest of my life on the road *Easy Rider* style, riding motorcycles, drinking beer, and wreaking havoc within the Republican Party. I do think about the kind of love and support I derive from my family and the insurmountable role my family plays in my life. My parents and my brothers and sister are a huge, bright light in my life. They all bring so much joy and comfort to me that I also feel like it would be a shame not to some-day have a family myself. Who knows, maybe I can do both and have an *Easy Rider* family or something. I know my feelings are ever evolving, but I also know that Michael had clearer ideas about marriage and family at my age than I do. I mean, Michael met Martha, he knew she was the one, and soon after got married and had two lovely children. Love and relationships just have never been as simple for me as they were for Michael. For me marriage, love, and having a family continue to raise unanswered questions about the kind of future I see myself having.

We continue on the windy roads to Michael's house; apparently, according to Cousin John, we have in fact found Connecticut. The evening has turned into night. Night has turned into very late night. I am getting really carsick from just absolutely everything. Michael might get to experience me puking all over him during the eleventh hour of our trip. I'm nauseous, hot, and worried that we have entered the Bermuda Triangle and we will all just be stuck in this RV for the rest of eternity. For the record, if I die and end up in purgatory, I am completely certain that the waiting area between heaven and hell is getting lost in this RV with Michael, Stephie, and Cousin John. Yes, I am convinced of that.

"Gumdrop, get me to Redding, please!" I yell towards Cousin John as I lie on my back trying to ebb off nausea.

"Workin' on it, Gumdrop!" Cousin John knows how to talk to a woman.

Michael: "You're lost, aren't you?" Meghan asks. She's being kind of bitchy because we've been in the RV for six hours and she's hot and probably needs to throw up.

"No!" I lie.

"If you're lost, just say you're lost!"

"I'm not lost!" I tell Cousin John to make a right. I have no idea where I am.

Stephie has grown silent, the way Stephie does when she is try-ing to contain her anger. The only other time I've seen her this angry is when we went to a Pittsburgh Pirates baseball game. After five or six innings, Meghan and I were both bored, but neither of us was willing to call it. Stephie wanted to get back on the road to beat the crowds and kept imploring us to stop being babies and leave. When neither of us was willing to surrender to the other, Stephie finally stormed out of the stadium, leaving us alone.

"Should we call it?" Meghan asked after Stephie's heated exit.

"You can call it if you want," I said.

"Fuck you, Black. I'm not calling it."

We sat there through a drizzle and all nine innings, only leaving when security made us go. Stephie was waiting for us, fuming. We were both kind of ashamed of our behavior, but that's the price of victory. Freedom doesn't come free, baby.

Back in the RV, everybody knows I have no idea where I am. "Do you want me to take out the GPS?" Cousin John asks. The GPS has been banished to the glove box for the duration of the trip because Cousin John does not trust it. To have him ask if we should take it out is like George Washington asking if he should surrender to the British. Hell no, we don't need to take out the goddamned GPS! Damn the torpedoes and full steam ahead!

"Take a left," I bark.

He turns left, and in a few minutes I recognize a landmark. I don't know how I did it but I somehow steered us true. I know where we are! We're at the corner of the Road with That House and Some Other Road with That Other House. I act nonchalant, of course, as if there was never any doubt in my mind. We're maybe ten minutes away from home. A mile or so later, a police car blocks the road. We slow. The policeman tells us a tree is down.

"Road's out," he informs us.

He gives us complicated directions for a detour. Cousin John looks at me.

"You got that?"

"Yep," I answer.

Three minutes later, we're lost again. I steer us in circles for miles until we come to another familiar landmark. We are now farther away than we were at the roadblock, but at least I know where we are.

"Just go straight," I tell Cousin John.

He does. As we approach the turn-off for my road, there is another police car. Another tree is down. This is insane.

"Road's out," the second cop tells us. Again, he gives us directions for the detour. I think Meghan might start screaming. Stephie has grown even more silent, which shouldn't be possible because earlier she was totally silent. She might actually be *absorbing* sound at this point.

This is going to sound like a lie, but I swear to you: as we get close, we reach a *third* downed tree and a *third* closed road. It's actually getting kind of funny. I mean, come on, three trees down? That's funny! Except nobody's laughing. Even I'm not laughing. It's not funny.

I could call my wife and ask her for directions from our current location, but that is not going to happen. She already mocks me for never knowing where I am. I would rather perish out here in the wilds of Connecticut with my friends than ask her for help. Not going to happen.

Finally, hours after I said we'd be there, we pull into my driveway. I'm carsick, sweaty, and filthy, but I'm home. We unfold ourselves from the RV and head inside.

"Daddy!" my daughter, Ruthie, yells, running at me from the kitchen. I hug her. She smells like bathwater and shampoo. My son, Elijah, is ten, too cool for long hugs, but he lets me put my arms around him anyway. "Hey, Dad," he says.

I kiss Martha and usher the rest of our vagabonds into the house. There is much kerfuffle as suitcases are brought upstairs and downstairs, drinks are poured, chitchat made. The kids show me the tarantula and scorpion I sent them from Arizona. Ruthie tells me she was terrified and had to run out of the room when she opened the package. Elijah says the tarantula was no big deal, but I suspect it freaked him out too, which pleases me to no end.

They lead us down into the basement, where they've made a giant hand-colored banner that reads WELCOME HOME DADDY, MEGHAN, AND STEPHIE!!!" Cousin John is not included on the banner. Martha says they spent all day working on it and did not want to add another name when they learned Cousin John was spending the night; he says it's okay.

Meghan seems a little shell-shocked. I think maybe it's the whole "I just spent a month living with your husband" thing. Which is understandable, I guess, except that Martha doesn't give a shit. We've been married thirteen years. She trusts me. She knows I would never, ever cheat on her with a hot blonde with big boobs. Never. And, despite my "methinks the lady doth protest too much" act, she's right.

Once we get the kids to bed, the four of us sit in the living room and trade stories from the road: the strippers in Vegas, Branson, Graceland, the heat, dinner with Meghan's dad.

"How was it overall?" Martha asks.

Good question. Now that it's just about done, it's hard to process what we've just been through other than in the broadest generalities.

"It was amazing," I say.

It's an easy answer, but incomplete. Yes, the trip was amazing, but what I actually discovered about America was more of a mixed bag. I am, by nature, a cynic. My cynical view on our nation is simple: we're fucked. Before leaving for the trip. I thought our current fuckedness was a temporary aberration, a cyclical pothole along America's long and continued prosperous march towards life, liberty, and the pursuit of happiness. But after diving deeper into our problems, I started to realize that America has some serious, perhaps fundamental, troubles.

If you start to talk about healthcare, for example, you have to talk about the poor. If you talk about the poor, you have to talk about jobs. If you talk about jobs, you have to talk about globalization. If you talk about globalization, you have to talk about China and India and Brazil and overpopulation and income inequity and currency valuation and energy and pretty soon you're not talking about anything because you're talking about everything. Each issue is so hopelessly entwined with every other one that they're like a ball of yarn the cat's gotten into.

Republicans criticize Obama for his "lack of leadership." As much as I prefer Obama to them, I think they have a point. America is lacking a coherent mission statement. Who are we right now? What are our aspirations? What are trying to achieve as a nation? Politicians keep talking about a romantic notion of "the American dream." But what is that dream? Can the American dream be applied, not just to its people, but to America?

We're at our best when we have common purpose. Usually it takes a tragedy or a war for us to find this common purpose, but it doesn't need to be that way. Our president, and *all* presidents, should lay out some national purpose that people can rally behind. Public service. Infrastructure. Lowering the deficit. Something, anything.

So many of us voted for President Obama because he promised to unite the country, to move us past a nation of petty bickering. All presidential candidates make similar promises, but millions of people like me thought maybe this guy really could move us beyond the acidic rancor of the W. and Clinton years. He didn't do that, and in retrospect, it was naïve to hope he could. I don't fault Obama for not succeeding, but I do fault him for failing to give us a reason to try. Platitudes aren't enough. We need more than that. And we're not getting it. From anybody.

As goofy as the idea was, when Newt Gingrich proposed building a moon colony, I found myself thinking, *You know something? That's a pretty awesome idea.* Not because we need a moon colony but because we need something—anything—to make us feel as if we're utilizing the best of who and what we are to achieve something great. And also because, let's face it, we need a moon colony.

When we agreed to write this book, Meghan and I had a simple premise: that Americans have more in common than they don't, and that even two near strangers with almost nothing in common could spend a month together talking about politics and still have a great time. We did that, which leads me to my optimism.

One of the great, unresolved philosophical debates in this country is the notion of "American Exceptionalism," the grandiose idea that the United States holds a special place, not only in the present world, but in all of world history. Generally, Republicans take the concept of American Exceptionalism as a truth, as indelible as the Declaration of Independence. Democrats are a little more wary because they are wary, not of greatness, but of hubris. It's easy to conflate "exceptional" with "correct," and I refuse to accept that America is always correct. The "my country right or wrong" crowd always leaves me leery.

But I do believe that America has exceptional qualities, primarily an endless capacity for self-invention and rejuvenation. We are the Lady Gaga of nations. There is something rooted in the American character that lends itself to relentless striving towards betterment, as in "to create a more perfect union." We are a nation of problem solvers, and it is our capacity for applying creative thinking to seemingly intractable problems that preserves my optimism about my country.

Time after time since its inception, Americans have figured out a way to move forward, sometimes in sprints and sometimes in ugly lurches, but always, relentlessly, forward. I do believe that America, on balance, has made the world a better place, and I'm grateful to be an American citizen.

While I love my country, I am never going to be one of those chest-pounding guys chanting "U-S-A!" I think of America as the high school kid who has everything: good looks, rich parents, the best car. Kids like that are always better received when they are humble, modest, and share with others. Sometimes we act like that and sometimes we act the way those kids more commonly act: like douchebags. If I had three wishes for my country, they would be these: keep fighting, keep moving forward, and don't act like a douchebag.

Meghan: Stephie and I sit on the couch next to Martha and look at old photo albums. Martha shows me pictures from when she and Michael were younger, when they got married, when they lived in New York City. They both have '90s haircuts and big smiles in all the pictures. Martha quips that she wished she had not worn long white satin gloves with her wedding dress, and comments on pictures of the guests at the wedding.

Michael and Martha are an adorable couple and have built an impressive life together. I don't know Martha very well but I like her energy. She has a sarcastic sense of humor and seems confident in herself. We talk a little politics and I end up in a fit of laughter because apparently her brother knows Frank Luntz, the Republican pollster, and she shares some personal stories about him, which are pretty funny. We have a beer, look at more photos, and all get a little tired.

I'm exhausted, we say good night, I go to bed. I unpack in Michael's basement, put my pajamas on, and call my mother to let her know I got to Michael's house safely.

"Now, be respectful in Michael's home. Remember you're a guest," she says. Pretty much the same advice she used to give me in middle school about visiting people's houses. For the first time on the entire trip, I feel a hell of a lot younger than Michael and weirdly out of place. As much as I do not want it to, it feels awkward. Michael and Martha's house feels very real and lived in; it is also huge and picturesque, which goes along quite well with the picture-perfect-family-man image I already have of Michael. His house, wife, and children could be cast in any movie or television show about a "happy American family." Ironically or not, it is also the first time I really see Michael as a full-grown adult and family man. This house is no joke. His wife is no joke. His kids are no joke. I can see how it must be difficult for him to leave it to travel so often. I'm just hoping I can make it through the next day without offending Martha and Michael's children.

In the morning I wake up around nine o'clock when I hear people walking around upstairs. I make my way up the stairs from the basement to the kitchen, still bleary-eyed, and say hello to everyone, still in my pajamas . . . and I feel like I'm doing the walk of shame. Martha is chipper standing in the kitchen in a baseball T-shirt and jeans, and asks me if I want breakfast. Once again I feel like I am at a sleepover in middle school and I got up before my friends, to end up having a somewhat awkward conversation with my friend's mom.

We all spend the morning going on a hike through "the wilds of Connecticut," as Michael calls it, with Martha, Michael, Stephie, and Cousin John, after which we take everyone for a ride down the street in the RV and pick up his daughter from summer camp. The kids have a great time in the RV. Michael's son, Elijah, climbs to the perch area above the front seat, where Michael has been known to nap, to explore the view from the top of the RV. Ruthie bounces around on the back bed. I can't believe these kids are having such a great time just jumping around in this extremely disgusting RV, but it's sweet to see just the same.

Michael: Tonight Martha is throwing us a welcome home party with our local friends. These are all people we've met since moving to Connecticut almost nine years ago. They're pretty much like us: couples in their thirties and forties with kids, mostly Democrats (the parents, not the kids). Also, some friends of ours from England happen to be in the area and will be stopping by too. I've been looking forward to the party as a way to officially wind up the trip and also as a counterpoint to the Fourth of July celebration in Prescott that kicked us off. Sadly, at my party there will be no semi-automatic assault rifles. Maybe we'll watch some PBS instead.

Martha pulls me aside as she's making guacamole to warn me that some of our guests have been saying they can't wait to corner Meghan about various Republican policies with which they disagree. Martha has told them to back off, that this is a party, not a policy discussion, but she's still worried that people are going to get some Bud Lights in their systems and it's going to become a yuppie throw-down.

"Don't worry," I tell her. "I'm sure nobody's going to be mean."

I am not sure of that at all.

My friends are all lovely people, but I worry that the Republican stereotype of Democrats might be true. Maybe we *are* all strident, holier-than-thou elitists. Maybe we *do* look down at our noses at our less urbane Republican compatriots out there in the hinterlands. I *know* some of us do. But hasn't it always been like this? Even in Revolutionary times, didn't the Boston urbanites look askance at Ethan Allen and his Green Mountain Boys from the backwoods of Vermont?

This is part of the problem with our country, though. It's so big, and we have so little exposure to each other beyond what we see on television, that it's easy to start pigeonholing our fellow Americans as somehow different than we are. For whatever reason, people are always seeking to differentiate themselves from each other. There is no group too small for us to do this with: Mets fans vs. Yankees fans, "tastes great" vs. "less filling." It never ends. Much of it is good-hearted, yes, but when it comes to Republican vs. Democrat, it feels increasingly less so. That's why we did this trip in the first place, and if my friends are going to show up at my house and be dicks to Meghan, I feel like the whole trip will have been for naught.

Our friends Matthew and Jessica arrive first. They're the Brits. Well, technically, she's American, but she married Matthew ten years ago and has been living abroad ever since. She's even developed that Madonna thing where she has a British lilt to her voice, so I will consider her a Brit. We've known them for years, and I love them both. Matthew is a tattooed television director, Jessica a stay-at-home mom with a graduate degree in American studies. They live in a comfortable but creaky townhouse on the south side of London, and every summer they come to the States to summer at an old beach house her family has had since the thirties.

I'm curious to hear about the British National Health Service, a single-payer system, which has become a bogeyman here in the United States. The Republicans routinely point to Canada and England as examples of the path on which Obamacare is leading us, and never in a complimentary fashion. They never say, for example, "Obamacare will make our health care system like England's! And it will be great! Cucumber sandwiches for everybody!"

Whether or not we are ultimately headed for a single-payer system I have no idea, but I am curious to hear what Jessica's experience with it is like, since she's dealt with both the American and British systems.

To the disappointment of my liberal heart, Jessica is quite critical of the NHS. She says, "The advantage of always having health care available is balanced with the frustration that if you need something taken care of that isn't life threatening, doctors and surgeons are happy to let you wait months and months, maybe even a few years to have it taken care of."

Damn it! This is exactly the argument that Republicans make all the time. She's my friend: she's supposed to automatically agree with my opinion. Isn't that what friends do? I'm very disappointed in her, very disappointed indeed, the damned Tory!

On the other hand, I've done some acting work in Canada and often ask people about their experience with a single-payer system. Although they complain about certain aspects, it seems like, for the most part, they are satisfied with their system. Consider this: no Canadian ever goes bankrupt when they get sick. If a Canadian requires chemotherapy or a heart operation, they never have to mortgage their home or deplete their entire life savings to pay for it. They never have to beg their church congregations for help. Here's what they do: they go to the doctor and get their treatment.

Canadians pay higher taxes for this privilege but that seems like a fair trade-off to me. I would much rather pay an additional few percentage points in taxes for the peace of mind that comes from knowing my health care is not linked to my job, and that my kids will be covered if they're ever injured or ill. Despite the hysteria waged by a certain, nameless Republican woman whose name rhymes with Tara Malin, Canada has no death panels, although if you hang around enough screaming Canucks fans during hockey season, you may wish they did.

I am not going to tell Meghan about Jessica's criticism of the British National Health Service because I do not want her to feel vindicated.

Meghan: I walk outside with Stephie to the back lawn where the BBQ is. We help Martha hang up a string of outdoor lights. Martha hands me a "baby Bud Light," which is literally a small half-can of Bud Light. I laugh and tell her, "It will probably take about eight of these to feel anything." She doesn't really laugh and I feel like a jerk for making fun of baby beers. I mean, the woman went out and especially got me Bud Light because Michael clearly told her I like them.

Slowly people filter into Michael's backyard, which sits on top of a sprawling grassy hill. His house has a large white deck wrapped around it, and there is a significantly large grill, and flags strewn everywhere. It looks like Martha decorated for the Fourth of July, which I think is really sweet. Stephie and I sort of huddle together and I flirt with Cousin John because he is the only single man at the party and probably within a radius of thirty miles, and of course because he is my Gumdrop. Michael keeps coming around and asking us "if we're doing okay" and to "seriously go over to the table and try the food." It's comical. I am reverted right back to my childhood when my parents would throw giant parties in Sedona and there was a kid's table and a kid's area that we were always quarantined to. I cannot help it, everyone is nice and pleasant, but a great deal older than I am. There is a weird film of tension permeating the entire party, and Stephie, Cousin John, and I look like a trio whose car broke down near Michael's house and ended up getting invited for dinner. We stick out like a sore thumb. That being said, Michael's friends seem pretty curious about the book and me.

"So, how did you guys *actually* meet and come up with the idea for the book?" asks one woman. "I mean, I've known Michael and

Martha for a *long* time, and I'm sorry, I just don't get the concept for this . . . project? Book?"

I try to explain to her the concept for the project and Stephie helps by interjecting here and there. Basically the woman looks at me like I am some girl who has taken her good friend's husband out for a joy ride in America, complete with strippers and guns. Which is pretty much exactly what I am. Another guy approaches us and is a lot warmer.

"Listen, I'm a Democrat, okay," he says. "But I wish we would all find more common ground in politics." I tell him that was the point of this project, a social experiment to see if two different people, from two completely different walks of life and perspectives, can find common ground. I am pleased to report back that we did and that means anyone can.

Before too long, the alcohol starts flowing and everyone seems to loosen up a little bit. A fire pit is lit and eventually s'mores are burned at the ends of long sticks. The only "incident" happens when one random lady who had too much wine approaches me and insists that she used to be a fan of my father's, but "he sold his soul to Washington, DC." I love it when people say crap like that to me, to my face. Like they've been waiting their entire life for me to walk into it so they can tell John McCain's offspring what they really think of him. I answer it as best I can. By which I mean I give her a bitchy response and she walks off. I look over at Stephie and she rolls her eyes in absolute horror at the woman. Nermal has turned into a fantastic wingman.

Unfortunately, people say things like that to me more often than not. I have no idea where people's manners go, but I would never go up to anyone, even if I hated the air that a member of their family breathed, and say anything nasty about their father, brother, whatever. There's something about coming from such a public family that people feel like nothing's private and every opinion deserves to be heard. There is a weird sense of entitlement people sometimes feel, and they somehow use that situation to get off their chest the things they think in their living room while watching cable news. It does not bother me as much as it once did, but it is not a pleasant experience.

This same woman joins a group I am talking to later and goes on to say that what America really needs is a dictatorship to rule over everything. My only answer is, "Are you actually kidding me with this right now?" I am a few baby beers in and I cannot even pretend to feign interest in talking with a stranger about why she believes America needs a giant dictator. It's comical. It's pretty much the typical thing I would imagine an out-of-touch liberal to wax poetic about at a party. Stephie once again looks confused and horrified, and as soon as the woman walks away Stephie whispers, "Ohh, no, no, no. I wanted to stop and tell her, 'If you know one thing about Meghan McCain, you will know Meghan McCain will not respond well to being told America needs a dictator to control the country.'" I love Stephie.

Michael's friends are pleasant otherwise, but they are not really my people. I do not mean that to come off in a mean way; they are just much older than me and in completely different spaces in their lives. It's just a little difficult, for whatever reason, to find a spark with another person at the party that would lead to a mind-blowing conversation. It is all very pleasant, but uneventful. I am of the mind-set that in order for people to truly bond at a party there needs to be some combination of whiskey shots, fireworks, or fire arms, and none of those things were happening. But nonetheless it is a nice evening and nice of Martha to go out of her way to throw a party for the end of our trip.

I start to fade toward the end of the night. I'm feeling a little woozy and sweaty and am certain I can no longer drink any more baby Bud Lights or talk about why America is such a polarizing place right now. Right before I head off to bed, truly exhausted, Michael yells towards me, "You called it!"

"Ughh," I sort of yell-grunt back, but he's right. On the final night, I did call it.

Michael: Meghan says good night and I wonder if she's had a nice time. One advantage of being a politician's daughter, I guess, is that you learn to adapt to new social situations with ease. Even so, these are not her people; they are mostly white, heterosexual, married suburbanites with children. They are, in other words, what the world thinks of when it thinks of Republicans.

Stereotypes have a funny way of falling apart when you actually talk to people. This was one of the great lessons of the trip. I am as guilty of indulging in stereotypes as anybody, and I definitely had my preconceived notions of what I would find on the road. Yet the only generality I would apply to the people we met is that all of them care about their country and want it to succeed. Almost none of them thought of themselves primarily as "Republicans" or "Democrats," none of them embodied the media caricatures we see shown to us on various cable news outlets. As far as I could tell, every single person wanted the same things: the opportunity to succeed and to make a productive life for themselves and their children. No more, no less.

The funny thing about Meghan's life and my own is that, judging only by lifestyle, we represent the stereotypes of the opposing political party. She's the young, free-spirited wild child who lives in big cities. I'm the buttoned-up family guy with the wife, two kids, and house with the (literal, in my case) white picket fence. But people aren't stereotypes, they're just people.

(Actually Omar the Anarchist was a stereotype, but he's the exception that proves the rule.)

Not long after Meghan calls it (and I would like to note for the record that on our final night, she *did* call it, the wuss), Stephie's giving me the "see you later" wave from across the yard. She'd been sticking close to Meghan all night. Whether she was feeling shy or just protective, I don't know, but it's amazing to me how close these two have grown. They could not be more different. Stephie: the yoga-practicing vegetarian who artfully origamied her month's worth of clothing into a fanny pack is totally BFFs with the gun-toting, high-heel-wearing Meghan McCain. Again, stereotypes are a poor predictor of actual human interactions.

Most people are gone by midnight. Matthew and Jessica are spending the night with their two kids, so they're still here, and the house is pretty full. Cousin John, graciously, has agreed to sleep in the RV again to make room for everybody. He's already there as those of us still awake lean against each other on the patio comparing notes on the evening.

For the most part, I think my liberal friends behaved themselves. Yes, there was the unfortunate comment about Meghan's dad selling his soul and another one along the lines of "what this country needs is a benevolent dictator," but considering the amount of alcohol and s'mores consumed, I would say we did okay.

We're just standing around the fire pit, watching the small flames burn themselves down, and I'm thrilled to be home, but also a little sad that our cross-country tour is at an end. My brain goes to that scene in *The Breakfast Club,* a favorite movie from my teenage years, released the year Meghan was born. Towards the end, there's a scene in which the various characters—each of them a high school stereotype—have bonded and are talking about how they'll all be going back to their regular lives when school resumes in a couple of days. Anthony Michael Hall's character, the nerd, says something like, "We'll still be friends Monday, right?"

That's sort of how it feels here tonight with Meghan. After tonight we go back to our regular lives, and I like to think we'll still be friends on Monday, but I don't know if we will. It's a big country and we're just two people in it.

When I wake up in the morning, I go outside to see if Cousin John wants some coffee. But when I get out there, the big RV is already gone. I'm not sure why he didn't say goodbye to us. Maybe because goodbyes are tough, or maybe because he just wanted to be an Aspen cowboy and ride off into the sunrise. Adios, Gumdrop, adios.

As for Meghan, she'll be taking a car to the airport for her long flight back to the West Coast. I'm sure she's just as anxious to get back to her home as I was to mine, even though it won't be her home for long. She's already got a realtor in New York scouting apartments for her to look at. I was getting married when I was her age, and she's still trying to figure out where she's going to sleep from month to month. I envy her freedom and her spirit, but I don't envy her suitcase, which is probably at least thirty pounds over any airline's weight limit.

I help her lug the thing up from the basement bedroom where she slept. She is in her pajamas but fully made up. The rest of us are not nearly so well put together. Martha looks like she slept in a Dyson vacuum cleaner. Frankly, we're a mess.

Even so, the mood around the kitchen table is pretty good as we eat a greasy breakfast designed to blot up whatever alcohol still soaks our brains. There's some lazy talk about how to fill the day after Meghan heads for the airport and Stephie takes the train back to New York City to reunite with her fiancé. Her wedding is in three months. Meghan and I will see each other there, if not sooner.

After spending pretty much every waking moment for the past month together, we're both a little sad to say goodbye. One thing that makes it easier for her, I'm sure, is the presence of screaming children. Once hyperactive kids are introduced to the mix, farewells become much, much simpler. By the time her car shows up, I think she is more than ready to go.

We drag her beastly suitcase out to the car and exchange our goodbyes. I am not a huggy person by nature, and I have been particularly untouchy during this trip lest she think, even for a second, that my intentions are anything less than honorable. Even so, I give her a big hug in our driveway and tell her I will miss her.

"I'll miss you too, Black."

And with that, she disappears into the Lincoln Town Car, bound for sunny California all the way back across this big and beautiful screwed up country. We are, as a nation, a hot mess. I stand and wave as Meghan's car drives away, then head back inside to enjoy in America with my family and friends.

Meghan: I wake up very early the next morning and hug everyone goodbye. I thank Martha for her hospitality. Michael, well I just hug Michael and tell him I will miss him, which is true. I will miss him.

As I stand outside of Michael's gorgeous home, I gaze across his well-kept yard at his perfect matched set of kids, beautiful wife, and BMW X-something or other, and fight back an ironic laugh. Michael may be a liberal, Obama Kool-Aid-drinking Democrat, but underneath it all, at his core, he is a conservative family man, with family values, who lives the life of Ward Cleaver. I may be a conservative, Jesus-loving Republican, who'd rather shoot a gun, throw back some whiskey, and split hairs over health care, but at my core, I am a real free spirit who never really wants to live in the suburbs, and finds the idea of having sex with one person for the rest of my life akin to some kind of punishment. Here we are, assigned our roles, and playing them with all the heart we can muster.

How about them apples? I think that ended up being the funniest part about our assumed divide. That our roles completely reverse when we step away from how we want our government run and look closer at how we live our own personal lives. Labels are stupid. The world is incredibly gray and people who want to turn it into something strictly black and white have either never experienced the other side or are lying to themselves about something.

On the car ride to the airport I still have a weird feeling that I have been doing the walk of shame after a late night out, or hanging out at someone's house who I don't know very well. As much as I think Michael and I have grown close and come to find a meeting place and common ground with many things, I wonder if we really will stay in touch and remain friends.

The ugly truth is that we are entirely different species and in entirely different places in our lives. I have no regrets about taking on this crazy idea and road trip. I know Michael believes in nothing and I believe in everything, but I do believe that we came into each other's lives for a reason. I am surprised to think back at how initially judgmental I was of Michael and Stephie—to a degree—and how much I have wound up loving both of them, and of course

Cousin John. I hope Michael feels the same way, but I cannot be certain.

Will Michael and I actually end up remaining friends? Who knows? His life is so different, his world is so different, he still has a way of getting on my last possible nerve. Regardless, I leave his house that morning at the crack of dawn with no regrets. More than anything it was fun to be part of a social experiment and, dare I say, it felt important. I believe in what we just went through together and am hopeful that in some small way it might offer a different perspective about two completely opposite people attempting in every way they can to have a common ground.

As I sit in the backseat of the car that's driving me to the airport, I am also frankly a bit relieved that I made it out of the situation relatively unscathed. I wonder if Michael and I will continue to play a significant role in each other's lives. For the moment, however, I am happy to say goodbye. I am happy to go back to the world I love and the people who understand me. I have had fun on this journey but am relieved to be returning to a place and a life where I do not have to explain who I am, why I do what I do, or believe what I believe to anyone.

As soon as I get back to LA, I email Michael thanking him for everything and for going on the trip with me, half expecting this to be one of the last times we are in touch on a personal level. I hope I'm wrong.

A week later I get a package. I do not remember ordering anything. I tear open the package to find a pair of black-and-pink Crocs. In my size. I can't help but break out into a fit of laughter and produce a huge smile. I press Michael's number on my phone.

"Nice try, Black," I say as I hug them to me. "They are going in the garbage."

Acknowledgments

Thank you to everybody who helped us plan our trip and spoke to us along the way: Senator John McCain, Cindy McCain, Jack McCain, James McCain, Bridget McCain, Martha Hagen-Black, Ruthie Black, Elijah Black, Jill Schwartz, Sandy Sherman, Betsy, David, and Eli Schneider, Laurye Blackford, Robert Guinsler, Barry Goldblatt, Flip Brophy, Jill Ehrenreich, Jackie White, Paul Carr, Jennifer and Michael Cornthwaite, Daisy Delfina, Jessica Janson, G-Cup Bitch, Larry Fink, Carl Arky, Deb Lindner, Patrice and Dave Arent, Christopher, Robert, and Jessica Cargill, Jonah Evans, Glen from New Orleans, Jacques Morial, Milton Walker, Nina Zapala, Cathy and Ken Plante, Nancy and Burt Walker, John Richardson, Alicia Dean, Darlene Bieber, Rick Rzepka, Bradley Morrow, Erin Stattel, Tom and Anita Metzger, Frank and Lauren LaRose, Eide Alawan, Joyce and Jimmy Schenck, Charlie Grob, Rep. Andrew Schock, Rep. Dennis Kucinich, Rep. Richard Hanna, Phil Elliott, Christian Berle, Casey Pick, David Black, Matt Simeon, Andrew Brady, Andrew Powaleny, Ben Grove, Ashton Randle, and Joe Donoghue.

We would also like to thank our agents Max Stubblefield, Geoff Suddleson, Jay Gassner, Ted Schachter and Mike Berkowitz, and everyone at United Talent Agency without which our road trip and this book never would have happened.

Special thanks to "Cousin" John Harvey.

And extra special thanks to Mrs. Stephie "Nermal" Grob Plante, without whom we would not have survived.

And finally, thank you to the all the men and women in our armed forces who have served and continue to serve this country and make sacrifices for us every day.